FORD 351 Cleveland Engines

How to Build for Max Performance

George Reid

CarTech®

CarTech®

CarTech®, Inc.
6118 Main Street
North Branch, MN 55056
Phone: 651-277-1200 or 800-551-4754
Fax: 651-277-1203
www.cartechbooks.com

Edit by Bob Wilson
Layout by Monica Seiberlich

ISBN 978-1-61325-048-8
Item No. SA252

Library of Congress Cataloging-in-Publication Data

Reid, George.
Ford 351 Cleveland engines : how to build for max performance / by George Reid.
p. cm.
ISBN 978-1-61325-048-8
1. Ford automobile–Motors. 2. Ford automobile–Motors–Performance. I. Title.

TL215.F7R388 2013
629.25'040288–dc23

2012050276

Written, edited, and designed in the U.S.A.
Printed in China
10 9 8 7

Front Cover: *Engine builder Mark McKeown of MME Racing in Waldorf, Maryland, is the first engine builder to build an all-new aftermarket Cleveland. Known as the Titus Ultimate Street Engine with CHI induction and heads with F.A.S.T. fuel injection, this engine makes 640 hp. The Titus has a 4340 steel crank with 4340 steel H-beam rods, Ross forged pistons, and an MME Racing custom hydraulic roller camshaft. (Photo Courtesy MME, Inc.)*

Title Page: *This is what Jeff Huneycutt of www.horsepower.com did with a 400 Ford: 565 ft-lbs of real stump-pulling torque and 504.8 hp. Although the Ford 400 has long been the performance pig no one wants, this is what you can do with this engine for around $7,000.*

Back Cover Photos

Top Left: *The 335-series 351-ci engine introduced for 1970 quickly became known as the "Cleveland" for identification purposes because there was also the raised-deck 289/302 engine displacing 351 ci known as the "Windsor" introduced a year earlier in 1969, which made things confusing for Ford dealer service technicians and shop mechanics everywhere. The visual differences between Cleveland and Windsor versions are obvious with huge, broad-shouldered valve covers on the Cleveland and traditional, narrow small-block Ford valve covers on the Windsor.*

Top Right: *Compression is also affected by stroke. What you do with stroke is also determined by rod length (rod ratio). You want the longest dwell time possible by having the highest rod ratio possible. Dwell time enables you to glean the greatest bore charge possible.*

Middle Left: *Here's the Titus block in rough cast before machine work. Two deck heights are available: 9.200 and 9.500 inches. The Titus is also available in custom deck heights by special order.*

Middle Right: *All pump rotor clearances must be checked. Rotor endplay should be .001 to .004 inch. Radial clearance should be .006 to .013 inch. Shaft to housing bore clearance should be .0015 to .0029 inch. If clearances are not within Ford specifications, reject the pump.*

Bottom Left: *Look at the port and bowl work on this Scott Cook head; minimal or no valve shrouding and buttery-smooth CNC bowl work for improved flow. These ports flow well right out of the box. You can net even more improvement with finish work in the bowls.*

Bottom Right: *It is one thing to choose the right carburetor and another to pick the right carb and manifold combination. Manifold selection depends on what type of driving you intend to do. Basic rule of thumb is dual-plane for driving and low-end torque and single-plane for high-RPM use. This is a single-plane Edelbrock Torker 351, which is not a good street manifold, but good for drag racing and high RPM. This manifold lives at 3,000 to 7,000 rpm and was born for racing. It does not fit the 351C with 2-barrel heads.*

DISTRIBUTION BY:

Europe
PGUK
63 Hatton Garden
London EC1N 8LE, England
Phone: 020 7061 1980 • Fax: 020 7242 3725
www.pguk.co.uk

Australia
Renniks Publications Ltd.
3/37-39 Green Street
Banksmeadow, NSW 2109, Australia
Phone: 2 9695 7055 • Fax: 2 9695 7355
www.renniks.com

Canada
Login Canada
300 Saulteaux Crescent
Winnipeg, MB, R3J 3T2 Canada
Phone: 800 665 1148 • Fax: 800 665 0103
www.lb.ca

CONTENTS

ACKNOWLEDGMENTS

What keeps me interested in writing books like this for CarTech is my thirst for knowledge and the opportunity to share it. CarTech asked me to write a book on how to get more performance from Ford's 351C, 351M, and 400 engines. The more I thought about it, the more curious I became about Ford's 335-series Cleveland engines because I've always held great respect for these short-lived powerhouses. The 351C's reputation for performance has spoken for itself in racing and on the street. It's larger sibling, the 400 and destroked 351M, has always been pegged a choked-out smog mill.

As performance enthusiasts, we tend to take for granted what we are told without giving it enough thought—and that's what gets us into trouble. We wind up knowing just enough to be dangerous instead of probing further to see what else we can learn. This book is an opportunity for you to learn more about what's possible from one of Ford's most legendary engines.

There are a number of great websites out there dedicated to Ford's 335-series "Cleveland" engine. Great engine builders such as Tim Meyer of TMeyer, Inc; Mark McKeown of MME Motorsports; Marvin McAfee of MCE Engines; Mark Jeffrey of Trans Am Racing; and Jim Grubbs and Jeff Latimer of JGM Performance Engineering have shown me the way it is done. I couldn't have accomplished my work effectively through the years without them.

Particularly helpful with this book have been Alan Rebescher of Summit Racing Equipment and Mike Downs of Trick Flow Specialties (TFS) who have gone above and beyond the call of duty. Alan Davis of Eagle Specialties came to my rescue with displacement-increasing stroker kits. More help came from Trent Goodwin of Comp Cams; Scott Cook of Australia; Denny Knepper of Denny's Auto Machine in Williamport, Maryland; Randy Millard; Mark Capps of The Mustang Ranch in Fresno, California; David H. Lehr of Classic Junk Yard; Jeff Huneycutt of www.horsepowermonster.com; Andrew Keys of www.twperformanceparts.com; Sean Holloway; Eric Blakely of Edelbrock; and Bill Faull and Ron Bramlett of Mustangs Plus.

A book of this caliber doesn't happen without a lot of help and the great gift of knowledge from all who helped make it possible, which adds up to a great team to which I will be forever grateful. Thank you one and all for your help.

George Reid

INTRODUCTION

We will probably never know the entire story behind the origins of Ford's 335-series middle-block 351C and its tall-deck brethren, the 400 and 351M. What we do know is what these engines did for Ford during their brief North American production lives in the 1970s and even longer production periods in Australia. These engines didn't live long enough in production nor did they realize their great potential as factory high-performance engines due mostly to the unfortunate timing of tougher federal emission standards and higher auto insurance rates. It arrived during a period of changing attitudes about high-performance automobiles.

The 335-series 351-ci engine introduced for 1970 quickly became known as the "Cleveland" for identification purposes because there was also the raised-deck 289/302 engine displacing 351 ci known as the "Windsor" introduced a year earlier in 1969, which made things confusing for Ford dealer service technicians and shop mechanics everywhere. The visual differences between Cleveland and Windsor are obvious with huge, broad-shouldered valve covers on the Cleveland and traditional, narrow small-block Ford valve covers on the Windsor. Ford issued a technical service bulletin shortly after the 351C's introduction differentiating the two types of 351-ci engines and how to identify them. Ford came up with the words "Windsor" and "Cleveland" to describe the two 351-ci-based engine families and so they have been used for decades.

The broad-shouldered 351C with its wide valve covers and poly-angle valves got the "Cleveland" name for the plant and foundry of its manufacture. The 289/302-based 351-ci engine became known as the "Windsor" for its Canadian birthplace across the river from Detroit. If you have a 351, you have either a Windsor or a Cleveland. And "Cleveland" has always denoted muscle and power. In fact, based on what I've learned from Ford insiders who were there at the time, the original game plan was to ultimately drop the 351W and keep the 351C, which in theory had better block architecture and growth potential. The 351W was a stopgap, mid-displacement, V-8 Ford hurried into production to compete with middle-inch Detroit V-8s such as GM's 350s, Chrysler's 318 and 340, and AMC's 343 and 360.

This book is all about the 351 Cleveland, or 351C, which was produced in North America from 1970 to 1974 and in Australia from 1972 to 1982. It is also about the raised-deck version of this engine known as the 400 and the 351M. It has never been confirmed with any certainty what the "M" means, from anyone including Ford Motor Company. Some say "Midland" and others say "Modified," including Ford. The 400 has often been called the 400M in the years since 1975 but when the 400 was destroked to become the 351M, Ford didn't call the 400 "400M" in factory publications.

The 400 was produced from 1971 to 1979 as a replacement for the 390-ci FE big-block. In 1975, the 351C was dropped and the 400 was destroked to displace 351 ci and became known as the 351M, which was produced through 1982. This was an obvious effort to consolidate both displacements into one block. The 351C, as well as a lower-displacement 302C, was produced in Australia from 1972 to 1982.

There are so many unanswered questions about how the 335 engine came to be, especially considering it copped a number of General Motors engineering nuances (wide cylinder heads with poly-angle valves and huge ports like a big-block Chevy, and block architecture on a par with Oldsmobile with a 12/6 fuel pump and steel timing cover plate). However, the engineering that went into Ford's all-new 351C for 1970 was remarkable for its time. What made the new 351C extraordinary was its cylinder head with a near-perfect wedge combustion chamber with just the right amount of quench with early 4V heads. What hurt the Cleveland was an ill-timed debut; Ford got out of racing in 1970 right after the Cleveland's introduction.

Though the 351C has a reputation for power and performance, most were garden-variety vanilla mills with 2-barrel carburetion and open-chamber heads fitted to intermediate and full-size Fords and Mercurys. They delivered snap, but not the kind of screaming, high-RPM horsepower the Cleveland was developed for.

The Cleveland shares the same bore spacing as the 289/302/351 engines; however, it in no way has the same block architecture. The 335 block is heavier and thicker than its Windsor counterparts—a casting conceived for durability with a completely different oiling and cooling system, smaller (yet wider) main journals, and a dry induction completely bypassed by the cooling system.

From a performance enthusiast's standpoint, the Cleveland was a disappointing mill because, as enthusiasts, we could see great potential in this engine, yet there were not enough factory performance pieces available at the time. This continues to be true even today because the Cleveland's production life in the United States was all too brief and parts all too scarce. For those of us in North America, this has long meant looking to Australia for desirable Cleveland pieces, such as cylinder heads never available north of the Equator. For Ford North America, the Cleveland's focus became more federal emissions than performance, which is why the Boss and High Output Clevelands lived such a short time here. In fact, the 351C High Output was dropped well before the end of the 1972 model year.

Based on what buff books had to say at the time, the 351C fell short of expectations. *Hot Rod* magazine had this to say about the new 351C in August 1970: "While the Cleveland is inherently better in design and potential than the Windsor pattern, it is released for production with a good many compromises." *Hot Rod* went on to say, "The stock hydraulic cam has .430-inch intake lift and .450-inch exhaust lift. Intake valve duration is 268 degrees, exhaust is 280 degrees, and overlap is a scant 37 degrees. The canted valve arrangement is a good idea, but for reasons of production and ease of assembly, a cylindrical fulcrum is used to hold the individual stamped steel rockers in place."

Hot Rod sung the Cleveland's praises as a good production engine, but concluded the engine fell considerably short of the mark when it came to performance. Ford's Ak Miller teased *Hot Rod* readers with a dynamometer test-cell

This is the 351C-4V most know, with its broad-shouldered attitude and wide valve covers. Although the 351C is known for its power potential, most were the vanilla 2-barrel version with open-chamber cylinder heads.

Here's the more common 351C-2V engine, easily identified by its smaller air cleaner and Autolite/Motorcraft 2100 or 2150 2-barrel carburetor.

The 351C-2V Ram-Air of 1973–1974 leaves most of us scratching our heads because the 4V engine was not available with ram air that year due to tougher federal emissions standards. The 2V passed federal emissions; the 4V did not.

experience in Long Beach, California, with an Autolite in-line carbureted 351C to demonstrate the engine's potential. *Hot Rod* speculated what it would take to reach the 351C's potential, including Boss 302 cylinder head and valvetrain modifications to accommodate adjustable rocker arms, screw-in studs, guide plates, and the rest of it.

Ultimately, Ford presented hot rodders with the Boss 351C engine with a hot mechanical cam, adjustable rocker arms, screw-in studs, guide plates, and one heck of a middle-block powerhouse. In *Hot Rod*'s 1970 351C dyno testing with Ak Miller, it was able to get nearly 400 hp with no attention being paid to torque. Of course 400 hp is laughable by today's standards because the 351C stroked to 408 ci with the right heads can produce more than 600 hp courting 8,000 rpm.

I suppose you could call it ironic we call this engine the Cleveland considering Cleveland castings were also produced at the Windsor, Ontario, foundry. All you have to do is look for "WF" on Boss 302 and 351C heads to discover this irony. There are also Michigan casting pieces, which appear to have no foundry markings. However, all 351C engines were assembled at Ford's Cleveland Engine Plant #2. Australian Cleveland engines were cast and assembled at the Geelong engine plant just outside of Melbourne from 1974 to 1982.

You don't need to rub your eyes. Ford Australia did a 302-ci Cleveland with a 3-inch stroke and 4-inch bore. The Aussie 302C is a destroked 351C. According to one Australian source, the 302C head was similar to the 351C wedge head except for smaller 58-cc chambers to keep compression where it belongs. If you're thinking about 302C heads for your 351C, forget it. Compression would be too high at 11.0:1 with today's pump gas.

To understand the Cleveland's performance image, you have to know a little bit about how this engine came to be. Although there's a lot we still don't know about its development, here's what we do know. The 351C was developed to be a high-performance street and racing engine from the start, according to George Pence of the popular "Clevelands Forever" website (www.351c.net). "I have found the best way for me to understand the Cleveland is to first respect the knowledge and experience of the engineers who designed it. I am convinced every aspect of the design of the 351C 4V was deliberate," Pence comments in the website, "If some design aspect seems fudged to me I have learned it's because I don't understand WHY they designed it that way. In other words, I'm the one who is ignorant, not the engineers who designed the 351C 4V."

Pence further comments, "The engineers who designed the 351C-4V were heavy hitters in the world of race engine design. These guys weren't novices. Bill Gay's group represented an amazing depth of experience in the design of state-of-the-art race engines. With all due respect to anyone out there that disagrees with me, I believe anyone among us who critiques the engineering of the 351C 4V is like one of the Catholic clerics who opposed the heliocentric science of Galileo. None of us have the knowledge and experience those guys were privileged to have. We are not in the same league. When it comes to engine design we are fumbling in the dark compared to the 351C 4V engineers." Pence is accurate in his observations regarding the Cleveland's development. What he has to say is enlightening.

Pence goes on to say, "The Cleveland was a racing engine from the get-go; heavy duty and designed to get out there and race. It was designed by the same people who brought us the legendary FE-series 427 big-block with its cross-bolted main caps, heavy main bearing webs, and side-oiler design—all features intended to help an engine live, and win.

"These same engineers designed the 351C for the same type of racing yet they included none of those features. Had they forgotten everything they learned? Had they gone daft? Were they idiots? You can't straddle the fence on this issue. They were either idiots and decided their new engine didn't need those features, or they were up to something new with the 351C 4V—something very deliberate. Engineers knew they would have to contend with the same forces which required cross bolted mains, thick bulkheads, steel cranks and side oiling when they had previously designed the 427 FE, " Pence observes. "The 351C 4V benefited from the new ways of doing things the engineers had learned while designing racing engines such as the Indy racing engines of 1963–1965. Design of the Cosworth DFV Formula One engine was also wrapping up in England in 1966. The 427-powered Ford GT40 was dominating LeMans and the World Endurance Racing series in 1966."

Ford's engineers took what they learned from the 427 FE and applied it to the Cleveland's development. Ford termed the Cleveland "an engine that reflects the racing heritage of Ford products on the world's toughest race courses." The objective was to mass-produce a high-performance engine as inexpensively as possible employing new technology and manufacturing methods. The 351C had wider main bearing caps, which eliminated the need for cross bolting. Ironically, Ford has since gone back to skirted blocks and cross-bolted main caps in its series of overhead cam modular V-8s, which has proven very successful.

Pence further reflects, "When the 351C 4V entered the scene in 1970, NASCAR was dominated by 7-liter endurance racing engines that cruised around the ovals at about 7,000 rpm making about 500 bhp. Endurance camshafts of the day had about .600-inch lift. It was no accident that when equipped with a .600-inch lift endurance racing camshaft the 351C 4V makes about 500 bhp at about 7,000 rpm. From 5.75 liters! 7-liter hemi engine torque and horsepower from 5.75 liters at the same RPM. Engineers hit their mark dead on. No mistakes. No getting lucky. It was all very deliberate. The Cleveland is an amazing racing engine. It just lacks the curb appeal of the hemi engines with their big aluminum heads and centrally located spark plugs."

How Clevelands Stack Up

Ford engine codes can be confusing, especially considering the same engine codes often applied to two different engine families. The 351C, for example, had the same engine codes as the 351W, which means it isn't always easy to tell which engine your Ford originally had.

Engine Code	Type	Model Years	Engine Code	Type	Model Years
H	351C-2V	1970–1974	R	Boss 351C	1971 only
M	351C-4V	1970–1974		High Output 351C	1972 only
Q	351C-4V Cobra Jet	1971–1972	S	400	1971–1979
	(high compression)		H	351M	1975–1982
	351C-4V Cobra Jet	1973–1974			
	(low compression)				

The high-performance 1971 Boss 351C and 1972 351C High Output are the same except for compression ratio and horsepower ratings (SAE net for 1972). Both are ram-air engines. The 1972 351C High Output is extremely rare. Very few were produced, and even fewer have survived to today.

The 351C-4V engine for 1973–1974 was never available with ram air though enthusiasts like to upgrade. This one has its original large air cleaner with vacuum-operated, auxiliary air door for wide-open-throttle operation.

Here's the 351W V-8, a raised-deck version of the 289/302 with 4.000-inch bores, 3.500-inch stroke, and much smaller cylinder heads. It is easily identified by its smaller valve covers and cylinder heads, which aren't as wide as the Cleveland's.

The 351C block has the same decks and bore spacing as the 351W, which is the only thing these engines have in common. This makes head swaps possible from 351C to 351W to create a "Clevor" engine. What makes the 351C block different is its oiling system, steel-plate timing cover, 12/6 o'clock fuel pump, and smaller 2.7500-inch main bearing journals. The front of the block closely resembles Oldsmobile's Rocket V-8 with cast iron wrapped around the timing set. Coolant bypasses the intake manifold and is contained in the block and heads.

What Pence so eloquently says is the 351C was ahead of its time with its poly-angle valves, generous ports, near-perfect combustion chambers, and meaty bottom end. The Cleveland's 4V cylinder heads were designed for a hefty .600-inch-lift cam and 7,000-rpm performance making a solid 500 hp in 1970. These are performance numbers quite at home in the twenty-first century with its alloy heads and super flow numbers.

"As the 351C-4V-powered Fords thundered around the banked ovals at 7,200 rpm for 500 miles, they did so with complete reliability. They were reliable in spite of their nodular iron cranks instead of steel cranks, in spite of their thin wall block instead of thick bulkheads, in spite of their lack of cross bolting AND in spite of their lack of side oiling. The engineers achieved the 351C 4V's reliability with all those short cuts because they weren't short cuts. Like the wide main bearing caps, the engineers deliberately chose engineered solutions instead of brute force to make the engine reliable. The 351C did not have a reputation for problems in the early years," Pence observes.

Pence punctuates the 351C's performance message informing us what went into the development of Ford's out-of-the-blue middle-block V-8. The 351C and its fans were victims of unfortunate timing when it entered the marketplace. In North America, the Cleveland went vanilla and went away in just four short years. In Australia, bold "no worries" Aussies took the Cleveland to its potential and stayed with it for more than a decade. Some forty years later, the Aussies continue to bring us great Cleveland performance parts including alloy heads as well as an anticipated supply of aftermarket blocks.

As you cruise this book, keep in mind the Cleveland aftermarket continues to evolve, with exciting performance parts yet to come for Ford's venerable Cleveland powerhouse.

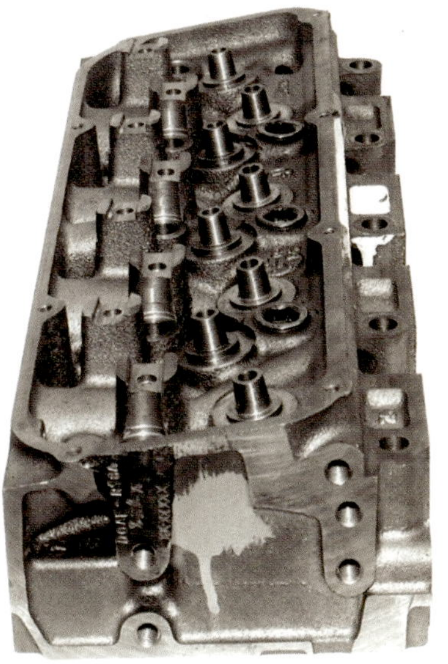

The 351C's wide cylinder heads offer canted (poly-angle) valves for improved cross flow. Four basic types of cylinder heads were cast to the best of my knowledge—large port/wedge (closed) chamber, small-port/open chamber, large port/open chamber, and small port/wedge chamber. The small port/wedge chamber is a Ford Australia head, which offers the optimum combination of 2V size ports for better torque coupled with wedge chambers for improved quench and more desirable compression.

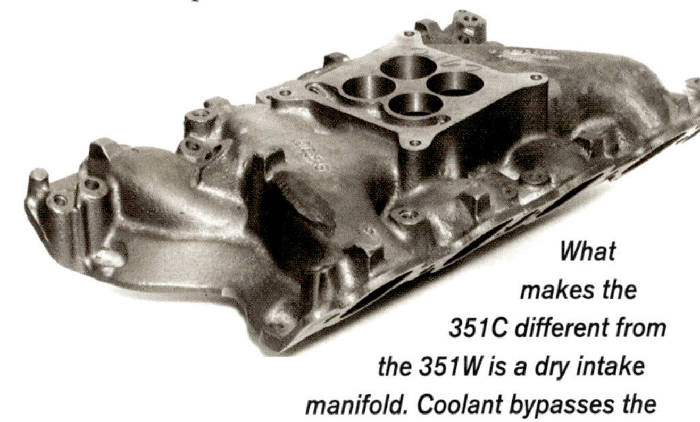

What makes the 351C different from the 351W is a dry intake manifold. Coolant bypasses the intake manifold, an unusual step for Ford, with the thermostat located in the block along with a brass restrictor.

Building Basics

Engine-building technology has made huge advances over the past thirty years and the 335 Cleveland engine family is no exception. Cylinder head and cam technology have come a long way just to name two areas. Small details can make or break an engine build regardless of technology. The biggest two I can think of are checking clearances and workmanship, again and again. Far too many of us learn the hard way because we're not attentive enough to detail. We get in a hurry to finish and hear it run missing important detail in the process. We learn when an overlooked rod bolt fails halfway down the track. And we learn when a carelessly seated valve keeper escapes at high revs.

Once you understand what you want your Cleveland to do, you can plan the engine's basic architecture beginning with good bones. You've got to know what works well together and what doesn't. The right block and head combination. A solid bottom end (crank, rods, and pistons). A cam that works well with all of these components and for your driving agenda.

Even if you're building a warmed-up stock Cleveland with a factory crank and rods along with hypereutectic or forged pistons, you need to know your engine's physics. Again, I am going to presume you've got no larger than a 4.040-inch bore. There are sticky issues such as compression height, swept volume, piston dimensions, and chamber size to think of. You can wind up with too much or too little compression. Knowing these issues going in, you can know almost exactly what your Cleveland is going to do when it's fired.

Planning is the most effective engine-building tool you can have. Far too many engine projects fail because there isn't proper planning. At the least, these projects produce disappointing results because you don't amass the right combination of parts and technique. Time and money are wasted when you don't think about what you want the engine to do. A big part of building an engine is knowing exactly what you can afford, then not giving in to ego and temptation. In other words, be truthful and realistic with yourself. That's the mistake a lot of us

This is what most of us start with—a core engine—with little idea of what's inside. It's easy to tell if an engine has been apart by studying gaskets and bolt heads. Ideally, you have a standard-bore block that has never been apart. If your core engine has been apart, it is probably a 4.030-inch bore. Normal practice is not to go past 4.040 inches with your overbore. However, if you decide to go to 4.060 inches, sonic check the block prior to boring to ascertain cylinder wall thickness.

make along the way. We want to impress our peers. But this isn't the right reason to build an engine. Don't build an engine to impress anyone besides yourself.

Every engine-building project should begin with a realistic plan. You wouldn't build a house or landscape your backyard without a plan would you? What do you want your engine to do? Forget the notion you can build a radical racing engine for the street and use it for the daily commute because, no matter what the buff magazines tell you with "800 Streetable Horsepower On Pump Gas" claims, it is a long shot mixing street and race experiences without conflict. There are strictly street engines, weekend bracket racing engines, and all-out racing engines. Street and weekend bracket racing mix as long as you achieve a nice balance of the two.

Daily driver/weekend race engines need a civilized street attitude to where your teeth aren't being jarred at a traffic light yet you can crack a 13-second quarter-mile on Saturday night. And yes, this is doable using a large amount of common sense. Street engines need to be designed and built for torque, not horsepower. Horsepower is a high-RPM wide-open throttle, maximum power on a racetrack event. Torque is the real street power that gets you going out of a traffic light and onto the freeway. Weekend horsepower should be realistic with the peak coming somewhere around 6,000 rpm and torque at 4,500 rpm. In the real world, you want a broad power band on the street where torque begins to come on strong around 3,000 and peaks at 4,000 to 4,500 rpm. This enables you to snuff out upstarts at traffic lights and achieve good quarter-mile elapsed times, yet have something you can live with daily. Of course common-sense gearing and your driving ability are the rest of it.

Because most Cleveland engines have been around the block a time or two, you never know what you will find inside. This four-bolt main 351C has Comp Cams roller-tip, stamped-steel, rocker arms and a flat-tappet hydraulic cam. Poor rocker arm geometry has caused excessive wear rendering these precision rockers scrap metal. The roller tips have seized from stress and have to be replaced.

Marvin McAfee of MCE Engines in Los Angeles approaches every engine teardown with detailed forensics. Every part is closely inspected for normal and abnormal wear patterns.

A plan begins with a foundation on which to build expectations. First, what horsepower and torque numbers do you expect and what can you afford? No use in dreamy-eyed bench racing where you're expecting 600 hp and 550 ft-lbs of torque with a modest budget and a daily commuter street plan. On the street, 400 to 450 hp is plenty along with more than 400 ft-lbs of torque. It is also affordable if you plan and execute properly. And no matter what big-talking bench racers say, you don't need any more than 450 hp/400 ft-lbs on the street.

Organization

I cannot stress enough the importance of keeping a clean, organized shop. Do your engine teardown work where you can catalog everything and keep it in its place. Keep engine parts and fasteners in jars or plastic containers labeled with a marker. Haul the block, heads, crankshaft, and connecting rods to a machine shop immediately upon disassembly. This avoids any confusion and keeps the project moving. If you cannot afford a machine shop at this time, leave the engine assembled until you can. (I speak from experience on this one because too much is lost both mentally and physically once the engine is disassembled.) Keep disassembly, cleaning, machine work, and assembly as cohesive as possible. Know what you're going to do and when you're going to do it. Then get busy and see your engine project through to completion. Nothing's more discouraging than a disassembled engine that's going nowhere because you didn't have a plan, or money.

Avoid Dust

When it is time to assemble the engine, you must have a hospital-clean shop. Even simple house dust (which is actually dead human skin cells and

Expect to replace your Cleveland's harmonic balancer, which consists of at least two pieces: a hub and outer ring separated with a layer of rubber. The harmonic balancer's job is to absorb shock as the crank twists with each combustion pulse. When the rubber ring deteriorates, shock-absorbing qualities go away along with timing-mark accuracy. Choose a reputable aftermarket balancer and include it with your external dynamic balancing.

Crank journal scoring caused by oil contamination; metal trash in the oil caused by bad rocker arm geometry.

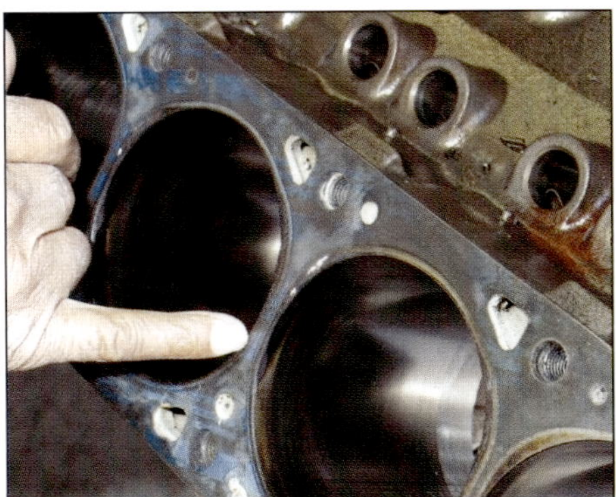

Marvin discovers a blown head gasket between two bores indicated by a voided head gasket and damaged deck. Block and head irregularity is likely the reason because the decks weren't milled during the rebuild.

decaying matter) damages an engine's mating surfaces. House dust scores bearings, journals, and cylinder walls. Whenever you're not working on the engine, keep it covered inside a plastic trash bag. When you are assembling parts, clean them first with brake cleaner or compressed air to remove any dust. Avoid engine assembly on a windy day, which generates its share of dust. Automotive bodywork and sheet-metal repair create harmful dust that damages engine parts. Keep this kind of work away from your engine. Make sure engine assembly lube and oil are pure and clean. Any kind of stray matter, no matter how small, damages your engine.

First order of business is to pull spark plugs, which are a barometer of engine health. Snow white indicates extremely lean conditions. Oily means oil is getting into the chamber via rings or bad valve seals/guides. Sooty black is a filthy, rich fuel mixture. Tan is the normal color. This is an oily firing tip indicating oil consumption.

Mark and Clean Parts

When it is time for engine assembly, everything should be in proper order. Pistons should be matched to each bore. This means each bore should have been miked and honed to the piston. Each piston should be numbered to the bore that was honed for that match, not to mention dynamic balance. All piston rings should have been custom gapped for each bore. All of your engine's critical parts should be laid out on the workbench in order for error-free assembly.

Take organization to the extreme. Number each cylinder with a felt-tip

Bore wear is also a barometer of engine health because it indicates how the engine has been treated. Excessively worn lifter bores adversely affect oil pressure and also indicate valvetrain geometry problems. Cylinder bores are checked with a dial bore indicator. These check out at 4.030 inches and have to be taken to 4.040. This is the maximum you should bore a Cleveland. Some believe you can go to 4.060 inches; however, sonic check the block first if you do.

This is a salvageable 351C four-bolt main block. Even if the bores were worn beyond salvage, it would be worth sleeving for a street application. If you're going racing, you need a standard-bore block that doesn't require sleeving. Sleeving typically costs around $100 per cylinder.

marker at the block deck. Lay pistons and rods out on the bench in cylinder number order. Get acquainted with piston domes prior to assembly, especially with a Cleveland. (You would be amazed how many engine builds I've witnessed where the pistons were installed upside down. One of them actually made a magazine cover that way.)

Keep spray cans of brake cleaner on your workbench to give a last-minute clean to parts during assembly. This eliminates any chance of dust particles and stray matter where it doesn't belong. Use lint-free tack rags (static cloths) for your last-minute clean-up work. Do not use those cheap and linty shop towels, terry cloth, or paper towels for engine assembly. Keep plenty of engine oil and assembly lube close by. Keep these items covered to keep dust and debris out.

Inspect Parts

Begin your Cleveland project with healthy parts. Because Cleveland engines have a reputation for flawed castings, you must be very cautious when selecting yours. If you're buying a junkyard core, get a written money-back guarantee. First thing to do is inspect a potential core for obvious issues—leaks, cracks, overheating, voids in castings, and poor workmanship.

Rarely is poor workmanship found in original factory-assembled engines (though it has happened). You do, however, find plenty of it in rebuilt or remanufactured engines. Incorrect parts, reused defective pieces, poor machining and assembly techniques, and the absence of maintenance all play into why an engine fails. Disassembly is a forensics experience where you get to learn all about the engine's recent past. Sometimes, you have a salvageable core. Other times, you have junk. You never really know what you have until you measure cylinder bores, clean castings, and do magnetic particle inspection to check for cracks.

Of course you need to inspect the crank, measuring journals and checking for runout. Also check for irregular wear patterns. Ditto for connecting rods, checking them for abnormal wear, trueness, and journal dimensions.

Compression Ratio

What is compression ratio and how do you calculate it? One popular misconception is that pistons alone determine compression ratio; however, this isn't true. Compression ratio comes from not only piston dome or dish features, but also stroke, bore, and combustion chamber size. Compression comes from piston travel from bottom dead center (BDC) to top dead center (TDC) with both valves closed. Cylinder volume (displacement) is squeezed into the area above the piston. Compression ratio is cylinder volume at BDC versus cylinder volume with the piston at TDC. For example, if cylinder volume with the piston at BDC is 10 times more than it is with the piston at TDC, then the compression ratio is 10.0:1, or simply 10:1.

Five basic factors affect compression ratio: swept volume, piston dome,clearance volume, head gasket volume, and combustion chamber size.

Swept Volume

Swept volume is the amount of air (or volume) the piston displaces during its journey to the top of the bore; hence the word "swept." If you enlarge swept volume by boring the cylinder oversize (or increasing stroke), you increase compression ratio.

Piston Dome

You may also increase or decrease compression ratio by changing the piston dome. If you "dish" the piston (giving it a concave shape), you lose compression. This is common with stock pistons, which are often dished to reduce compression. A good example is the 351C-2V with its dished pistons and open chambers. To raise compression ratio, the piston is "domed" (giving it a convex shape, similar to that of the combustion chamber). This reduces clearance volume at the top of the bore. When you reduce clearance volume, you increase compression ratio. Whenever you go to an aftermarket head, keep combustion chamber size in mind. The new combustion chambers can wind up larger than your stock chambers. If you desire greater compression, you can make adjustments with proper piston selection.

Cylinder Volume

Cylinder volume is calculated using a simple formula. For example, using a standard 351C bore and stroke (4.000 x 3.500 inches), the numbers work out like this:

Displacement Calculations Made Easy

Bore (inches)	*Stroke (inches)*	*Actual Displacement (ci)*	*Common Designation (ci)*
4.000	3.500	351.85	352
4.030	3.500	357.15	357
4.040	3.500	358.93	359
4.060	3.500	362.49	362
4.000	3.750	376.99	377
4.030	3.750	382.66	383
4.040	3.750	384.56	385
4.060	3.750	388.38	388
4.000	3.800	382.01	382
4.030	3.800	387.76	388
4.040	3.800	389.69	390
4.060	3.800	393.56	394
4.000	4.000	402.12	402
4.030	4.000	408.17	408
4.040	4.000	410.20	410
4.060	4.000	414.27	414
4.000	4.200	422.23	422
4.030	4.200	428.58	429
4.040	4.200	430.71	431
4.060	4.200	434.99	435

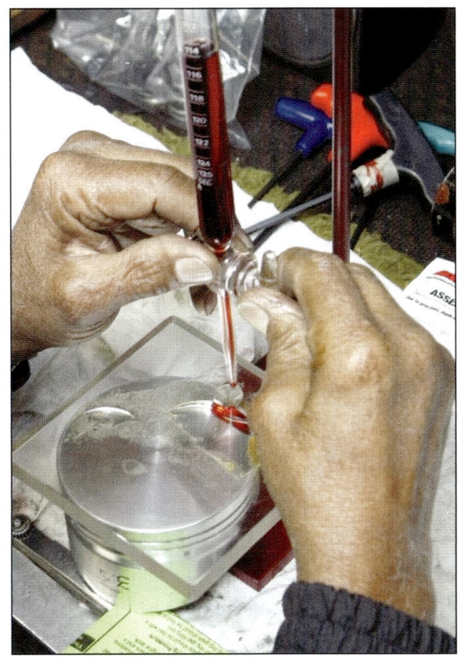

Even valve reliefs are considered part of swept volume; checked with a graduated cylinder and fluid. The larger the valve reliefs, the lower the compression ratio.

Cylinder Volume = .7853982 x bore^2 x stroke

When you apply this formula, you come up with 43.982 ci per cylinder. Multiply this number by eight and you have 351 ci. Truth is, you have 351.858, which is closer to 352 ci.

If you bore the same cylinder to 4.030 inches, you have 44.644 ci per cylinder, which comes out to 357 ci.

If you take a standard 4.000-inch bore and overbore it by .030 to 4.030 inches, compression increases by a fraction of a point. If you have a compression ratio of 10.0:1, compression increases by less than a point with a .030-inch overbore.

Clearance Volume

You compute compression increase (or decrease) by calculating the clearance volume, which is the area above the piston when it reaches TDC. It is important to understand that the piston doesn't always reach TDC flush with the block deck. In most applications, the piston comes within .005 to .020 inch below the deck surface. This is called piston deck height, which affects compression because it determines clearance volume at the top. If you have a lot of clearance volume, you have less compression. The greater the piston deck height, the lower the compression ratio.

You might be inclined to ask why you should dish a piston with an increase in stroke. The answer is pistons are dished to keep compression conservative.

The following is a formula for calculating clearance volume.

Clearance Volume = .7853982 x bore^2 x deck height

Again, let's look at our example 351C engine with a 4.000-inch bore and 3.500-inch stroke. Let's say it has a piston deck height of .015 inch below the block deck. Using the formula works out to a clearance volume of .188 ci, or just a fraction of the cylinder's 43.98 ci. If the deck height increased any amount, compression would drop. If deck height decreased any amount, compression would increase.

Next is to figure in the piston's role in all of this. Remember that if you dish the piston, you lose compression. If you dome the piston, you increase compression. Most piston manufacturers give the specifications for a piston. If it is dished, the manufacturer tells you how much. Likewise for a domed piston, you learn how much—in cubic centimeters.

You reduce swept volume with a domed piston to raise compression because you're reducing volume above the piston when it reaches TDC.

You can use the following formula to convert cubic centimeters into cubic inches.

Cubic Inches = cubic centimeters x .0610237

Back to our 351C engine. Let's say our 351 has dished pistons with a volume of 4.00 cc (or .244 ci). This lowers the compression ratio because you have more clearance volume above the piston. If you dome the piston by the same amount, you increase compression accordingly.

Cylinder Head Gasket Volume

The next factor in compression ratio is cylinder head gasket volume, which contributes to clearance volume above the piston. The thickness of the head gasket affects compression ratio. The thicker the head gasket, the greater the clearance volume. This lowers compression. The thinner the head gasket, the lower the clearance volume, which increases compression. To figure the head gasket volume (displacement), use the following formula.

Cylinder Head Gasket Volume = .7853982 x bore^2 x compressed thickness

Again our 351-ci engine with a 4.000-inch bore. You have a cylinder head gasket that is .040 inch thick. You take .7853982 x 4.000 inches to the second power x .040 inch to arrive at .502 ci of clearance.

Combustion Chamber Size

Combustion chamber volume is the actual size of the chamber in cubic centimeters. Chamber size for closed-chamber 351C-4V heads runs approximately 62 to 64 cc. Chamber size for open-chamber 351C heads runs 72 to 77 cc.

Combustion chamber volume is figured with a graduated scale using fluid. You meter fluid into the chamber and figure how much fluid is used. You get this figure in cubic centimeters. Our sample cylinder head has 64-cc chambers.

Here's how to turn cubic centimeters into cubic inches:

Combustion Chamber Volume in Cubic Inches = cubic centimeters x .0610237

Based on the formula, at 64 cc, you have 3.90 ci of volume in the chamber alone.

Compression Ratio Calculation

Now, you have all of the information needed to compute compression ratio in your 351C engine. Use the following formula.

Compression Ratio = (cylinder volume + clearance volume + piston volume + chamber volume + head gasket volume) ÷ (clearance volume + piston volume + head gasket volume + chamber volume)

The math for our 351C engine, with its 4.00-inch bores and 3.50-inch stroke, .020-inch deck height, .040-inch head gasket thickness, 64-cc chamber heads, and 4.000-cc dished pistons works out like this:

(43.982 ci + .188 cc + .244 cc + 3.90 ci + .502 ci) ÷ (.188 ci + .244 ci + .502 ci + 3.90 ci)

48.816 ÷ 4.83 = 10.10:1

These figures are added as you measure space between piston dome and block deck with the piston at BDC. You can even take this to the extreme by measuring the volume above the top ring around the piston's circumference because that also counts.

Power Physics

We've long been led to believe horsepower is what "power" is all about. But horsepower is rooted more in Madison Avenue advertising rhetoric than fact. In the power picture, horsepower doesn't count for much, especially on the street. What counts is torque and when you have the most of it. Engines make torque when you feed fuel and air into combustion chambers and squeeze the mix. Torque is what gets us going, and horsepower is the force that keeps us moving at speed.

Engines do their best work when they reach peak torque where they are making the most low- and mid-range twist. When an engine is below the torque peak, it has more than enough time to completely fill the cylinder with air and fuel. When engine RPM rises above the torque peak, there isn't enough time to completely fill the cylinders with air and fuel.

The power you feel from an engine is torque multiplied by engine speed (RPM) to produce a number that tells us something about the engine's output. This theory dates back to steam engines and James Watt who invented the steam engine in the 1800s. Watt's theory was a simple one. It compared the work his steam engine could do with the same work an equal number of horses could do. Watt determined a single horse could pull a 180-pound load 181 feet in one minute. This formula figured out to 32,580 pounds per foot per minute. Watt rounded it off to 33,000 pounds per foot per minute. He divided this figure by 60 seconds, which worked out to 550 pounds per foot per second. And this became the standard definition for 1 hp.

As a result of Watt's calculations, horsepower has become a measure of force in pounds against a distance in feet for the brief period of one minute. You can take this formula and apply it to an engine's crankshaft at each journal throw to arrive at horsepower. This is based on the number 5,252, which comes from Watt's calculations. 5,252 rpm is normally

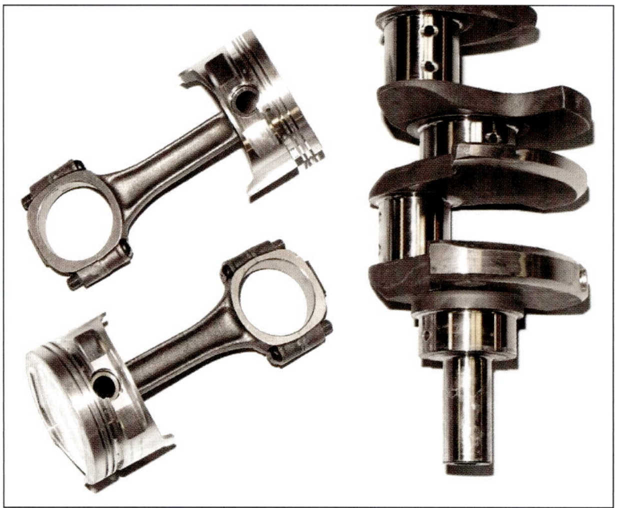

Compression is also affected by stroke. What you do with stroke is also determined by rod length (rod ratio). You want the longest dwell time possible by having the highest rod ratio possible. Dwell time enables you to glean the greatest bore charge possible.

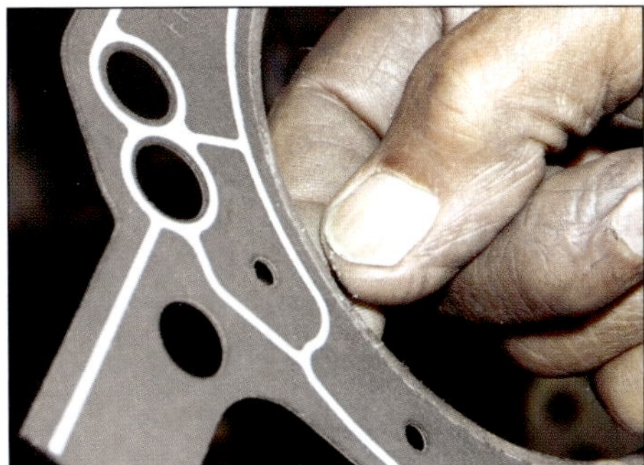

Cylinder head gasket thickness adds volume above the piston, which also affects compression ratio because you are increasing chamber size when the piston reaches TDC.

The smaller 351C wedge chamber offers better quench and higher compression. Be careful because not all 351C-4V heads have this chamber. Large ports do not always mean this wedge chamber.

This is the larger open 351C-2V/351M/400 74- to 77-cc chamber that coincides with the smaller 2V ports. You gain torque via smaller ports. However, you also lose power due to reduced compression and poor quench. Detonation is quite common with this head. Keep in mind the 351C-4V engine also got this chamber in 1973–1974 to reduce compression. This is likely the worst possible scenario—large ports (poor low end torque) and open chambers (lower compression and poor quench).

where horsepower and torque pass each other in a dyno pull.

Torque is the measure of an engine's work. Horsepower is a measure of how quickly the engine does the work. Torque comes from displacement and stroke mostly. This means the real power you derive from an engine is expressed in a torque curve. A broad torque curve comes from making the most of the fuel/air mixture across a broad RPM range. The broader the torque curve, the better the power package.

A broader torque curve is best accomplished with a longer stroke and a larger bore. And this is what strokers are all about: making the most torque across the broadest range. Truth is, you're never going to get the best of everything, even with fuel-injected engines. Your engine needs to be planned and built based on the way you're going to use it. What you choose in terms of a camshaft, cylinder heads, and induction system determines how your engine performs.

Giving Power Away

When you're planning for power, you rarely stop to consider how power gets wasted in an engine's design and construction. Friction is the power pickpocket hiding in all sorts of places inside your engines. Most of the friction occurs at the pistons and rings. Some of it gets lost at the bearings and journals. Yet more of it gets consumed at piston wrist pins, lifters and bores, camlobes and lifters, rocker arm fulcrums and valvestems.

Your objective needs to be compromise between having tolerances that are too loose or too tight. Piston to cylinder wall clearances are critical in order to have good cylinder sealing, yet not too much friction so you consume power. The same is true for rod and main bearing clearances. You want liberal clearances for good oil flow and heat transfer—yet less friction.

Another power-loss potential is engine breathing. You want an induction system that helps your engine breathe well at the RPM range it is designed and built for. This means using the appropriate intake manifold and carburetor. Go too small on carburetor sizing and you restrict breathing. If port sizes don't match, you restrict breathing. Opt for cylinder heads where port sizing is too limited for your displacement and you restrict breathing.

The exhaust needs a scavenging system that makes sense. You don't need long-tube headers for great breathing. Shorty headers do the job just as well, and without the shortcomings of long-tube headers. Go too large on header tube size and you hurt torque. Go too small and you hurt power on the high end. This is where your exhaust system has to work hand-in-hand with the heads, camshaft, and induction system.

Building a Cleveland Stroker

Just what is a stroker anyway? It is an engine with increased or decreased stroke, which is the distance the piston

Piston to cylinder wall clearances and ring end gaps may also be run closer to maximums for reduced friction. Also keep in mind the greater operating temperatures. Expect to sacrifice some durability in the process.

Connecting rods are reconditioned and fitted with new ARP 3/8-inch bolts for durability. Side clearances should be on the wide side of maximum due to high journal temperatures and reduced friction.

Check crankshaft rotation when you torque each rod. Reason being, if you check for freedom of movement with each rod, you immediately confirm if clearances are too tight.

Connecting rod side clearances should be on the wide side of maximum due to high journal temperatures and reduced friction. When you go with wider side clearance, you improve oil flow across the bearing and journal and allow for thermal expansion.

travels in the cylinder bore. Changing the stroke changes when and how the engine makes power. By increasing an engine's stroke, you gain displacement. By the same token, when you decrease an engine's stroke, you lose displacement. Short-stroke engines like high RPM, where they make the most torque. Our focus is about increasing stroke in order to achieve greater amounts of torque and horsepower.

"Stroking" an engine does more than just increase displacement. It increases torque by giving the engine more of an internal mechanical advantage. When you increase stroke, you increase the length of the engine's crankshaft arm (or lever), which makes the most of a combustion cycle. The longer the stroke, the greater the torque or twist.

The stroke number is the length of the crankshaft's rod journal arm, doubled. You double the length of the crankshaft arm because that arm moves in two directions: to TDC then to BDC. For example, if the arm is 1.5 inches (measured from the crankshaft centerline to the end), you have a 3-inch stroke.

So how do you get more power from a stroker? Power comes from the greater mechanical advantage of a longer crankshaft arm. You are also filling the cylinder with a greater volume of air and fuel, which gives more power all by itself. From stroke (and cylinder swept volume), you get torque. Torque is the truest measure of an engine's power output.

So what exactly is torque? Think of the crankshaft's arm as a simple lever. Torque equals the downward force of the stroke times the length of the lever (or arm). At a 351C engine's 370 ft-lbs of peak torque, each cylinder bore is producing 740 pounds of pressure on each power stroke. Remember, you increase torque when you increase the length of the arm. And when you increase the length of the arm, you increase stroke.

A stock 351C engine's arm is 1.75 inches long, which means the 351C engine has a 3.50-inch stroke. If you add 1/4 inch to the arm, you increase the arm length to 1.875 inches. That means you have 3.750 inches to achieve 377 ci with the standard 4.000-inch bore. This gives you 40 additional foot-pounds of torque. Overbore the cylinders .030 inch and you have 383 ci. Push the bore to 4.060 inches and have 388 ci. You also have more torque.

In addition to the advantages of a stroker, there are disadvantages, especially if you're bent on pumping the most displacement possible into a 351C or 400 engine. When you stroke a 351C or 400 to its limits, you lose piston skirt, which hurts stability. You also push the piston pin into the piston ring land area, which weakens piston design. It also puts the pin close to the piston dome, which exerts too much heat on the pin and boss. These are disadvantages that shorten engine life.

Another factor with stroking is rod length. When you haul that piston deep into the cylinder bore, you are also

I cannot stress enough the importance of degreeing a camshaft. Never trust what's on the cam card. Cams get mispackaged and people make mistakes in mass production. Always know what's going into your block. Not knowing can be costly, meaning piston to valve contact.

Deck surfaces must be hospital clean. Use a tack rag, never a shop towel or paper towel. Even tiny pieces of lint can cause unseen head gasket distortion.

Free Power

Free Power? You might think there's no such thing. However, you can find hidden power in friction-reduction efforts such as roller cams and rocker arms, Torrington bearings, and more liberal clearances.

Without question, roller cams, dual-roller timing sets, and roller rocker arms are expensive. This is why so many go with flat-tappet cams, conventional timing sets, and stamped-steel rocker arms. However, when you consider the cost differential and the power gained for your hard-earned dollars, gain outweighs the financial losses.

This is how a flat tappet sits on a conventional cam lobe. As the lobe revolves, it spins the tappet for uniform wear and smooth function. Always remember to use moly coat on lobes and engine assembly lube on journals. Never use moly coat on journals.

Power is found with a complete roller cam package consisting of roller tappets, one-piece pushrods for durability, and needle-bearing aluminum rockers. Aluminum gets unnecessary weight out of the valvetrain. Roller tips and fulcrums greatly reduce valvetrain friction.

bringing it closer to the crankshaft counterweights, which creates conflict. This means you need a longer connecting rod to get the piston down there without interference with the counterweights. Sometimes you can find off-the-shelf connecting rods to complete your stroker. Other times you are forced to custom make connecting rods that work. More expensive stroker kits have custom parts such as rods and pistons. More affordable kits have off-the-shelf parts.

Stroker kits often mandate custom pistons to keep things friendly at the top of the bore. A 408 or 427-ci stroker, for example, has custom pistons with pin bosses pushed way up into the ring lands. This drives the cost up. It also shortens engine life.

Stroker Power Facts

There are plenty of myths about making power, especially in the Ford camp. Folklore tells us it's easier to make power with a Chevrolet than a Ford. But this is pure nonsense. You can make just as much power with a Ford for the same amount of money you can with a Chevrolet. What gives the Chevrolet an advantage is numbers—shear volume. Chevys are simply more commonplace than Fords. But even this is changing because Ford's popularity has grown dramatically in recent years. When it comes to seat-of-the-pants performance, there's no black magic here, just the simple physics of taking thermal expansion and turning it into rotary motion that makes you feel good about your engine.

To learn how to make power, you first have to understand how power is made inside an engine. The amount of power an engine makes depends on how much air and fuel you can pump through the engine, plus what you do with that fuel/air mixture during the split second it lives and dies in the combustion chambers.

You have to think of an internal combustion engine as an air pump. The more air and fuel you can "pump" through the cylinders, the more power you're going to make. This is why racers use big carburetors, manifolds, heads, superchargers, turbochargers, and nitrous oxide. Racers understand this air pump theory and practice it with reckless abandon; sometimes with catastrophic results. But good racers also understand the "too much of a good thing" theory. Sometimes it can cost you a race. It can sometimes cost you an engine.

Getting power from the "air pump" takes getting liberal amounts of air and fuel into the chambers, then squeezing the mixture as hard as you can without damaging the engine. When you raise compression, you increase the power the mixture yields. It is the intense heat of compression coupled with the ignition system that sparks the yield of energy from a mixture. The more compression you have, the greater the heat you have to ignite the mixture.

Problem is, when there's too much compression, and the resulting heat, the air/fuel mixture can ignite prematurely resulting in preignition and detonation. So you have to achieve the right compression ratio to get the most from the fuel you have. Today's street fuels don't tolerate much more than 10.5:1 compression. This means you have to look elsewhere for answers in the power equation, such as more aggressive camshaft profiles, better heads, better port work, hotter ignition systems, exhaust headers that breathe better, state-of-the-art intake manifolds and carburetors, even

Head gasket cooling passages always go at the back of the block. No exceptions. "FRONT" on the gasket means front. Use The Right Stuff around crossover passages at the front of the block and heads.

Though there are plenty of 351C-2V heads lying around, the best overall head is the 4V head with smaller 62- to 64-cc wedge chambers. Although these heads lack in low-end torque, the smaller wedge chamber offers greater compression and quench.

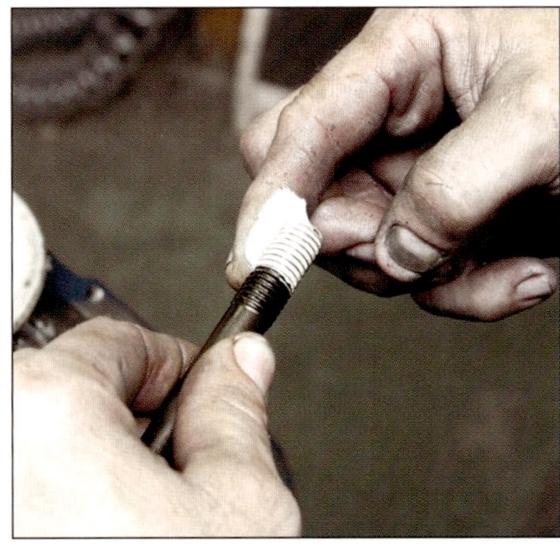

Use commercial-grade Teflon sealer on wet-deck bolt or stud threads. Without it, you will have coolant leaks.

electronic fuel injection where you never thought of using it before.

The thing to remember about gasoline engines is this: The air/fuel mixture does not explode in the combustion chambers; it "lights off" just like a gas furnace or water heater. Because the mixture is compressed and ignited, it lights off more rapidly. Combustion in a piston engine is a "quick fire" that sends a flame front across the top of the piston. Under ideal circumstances, the flame front travels smoothly across the piston dome, yielding heat and pressure that act on the piston and rod uniformly to create rotary motion at the crankshaft.

A bad light-off that originates at two opposing points in the chamber is the pre-ignition or detonation factor. The opposing light-offs collide creating a shock that hammers the piston dome,

Find More Power

Power is found anywhere you can reduce or eliminate internal friction. Anything you can do to make the going smooth frees up power. Keep in mind finding power costs money, but look at the dividends. When you set your clearances more liberally, the initial cost is free. What you tend to sacrifice is longevity. Some engine life is lost in the long term, especially when it comes to bearing and piston to cylinder wall clearances. Friction-reducing parts such as timing set Torrington bearings cost money, but free up power.

A timing set with Torrington bearings reduces friction at the timing sprocket. These pieces don't come cheap; however, they free up precious power.

Marvin McAfee of MCE Engines is an efficiency expert always searching for ways to eliminate unnecessary internal friction right down to valvestem to guide clearances. He wants valvestems slip-slide smooth with Teflon seals.

There's always debate over the use of one- or two-piece fuel pump eccentrics. The one-piece eccentric offers durability. The two-piece reduces friction, but not in a measurable amount.

Always torque cylinder heads in three stages from the center outward. This allows bolts a proper stretch along with uniform head and gasket seating. At 500 to 1,000 miles, retorque your heads even if the manufacturer says you don't have to.

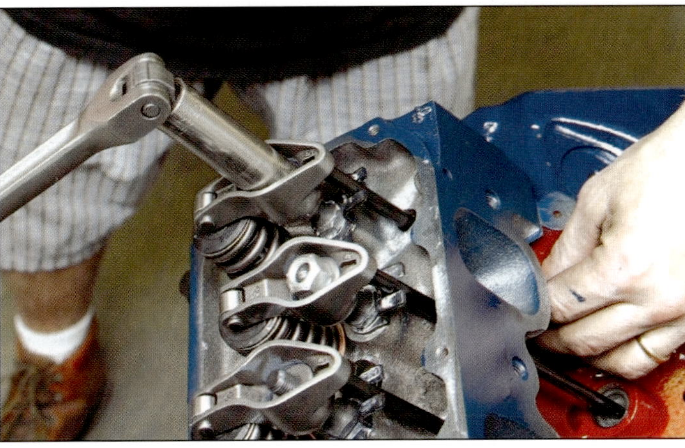

Hydraulic-lifter valve adjustment doesn't have to be baffling. Following your engine's firing order, hand crank the engine until each bore is at TDC compression stroke, as each valve has just closed. Twirl the pushrod while running the rocker arm nut down. When the pushrod becomes resistant to turning, tighten the nut 1/4 to 1/2 turn. This should move the lifter plunger 50 percent of its total travel.

which is the pinging or spark knock you hear under acceleration. The objective is to get a smooth, quick fire, with the flame front traveling in one, smooth direction for maximum power. An abnormal light-off can also happen prematurely from advanced ignition timing or red-hot carbon in the chamber.

Power management is having the right balance of ignition timing, fuel mixture, compression ratio, valve timing events, and even external forces such as blower boost or nitrous input. All of these elements have to work together if you're to make productive power. Let's talk about some of the elements you need to make power.

For one thing, the science of making power must tie in with how you intend to use the engine. And that's where most of us get it wrong all too often. In our quest for stroker torque, we sometimes forget how the vehicle is going to be driven and used. If you are building a stroker to go drag racing, the way you build your engine is going to be different than the guy who builds one for trailer towing. By the same token, road racing engines should be executed differently than drag racing powerplants.

So how do you approach each engine's game plan? Street engines for the daily commute need to be approached for good low- and mid-range torque. Drag racing engines need to make power at high-RPM ranges. Road racing engines need to be able to do it all; down low, in the middle, and at high RPM because they're going to live in all of these ranges while racing. Engines scheduled for trailer towing need plenty of low-end torque. They also need to be able to live comfortably at mid range when you're going to be pulling a grade.

Proper Assembly Technique

When it comes to assembly practices, engine professionals stress two main areas: cleanliness and double-checking your work. Never assemble an engine in the same area where it is torn down. Even minute amounts of dirt, dust, or grit can stop an engine cold.

I stress double-checking your work because this approach actually saves time. If you think it's inconvenient to check your work two and three times, consider the inconvenience involved in a nuisance tear down because there's high oil consumption or having to collect the pieces of a scattered engine because something critical was missed during the assembly process. Even check it thrice and sleep better.

Engine building is an exacting exercise in physics where every detail must be covered to ensure success. Power comes from taking all of that thermal energy and harnessing it above the piston during light-off. Fuel and air don't explode in a combustion chamber as you have been led to believe. Combustion is a quick-fire and the smooth application of heat energy. In theory, it should be a smooth quick-fire with a nice flame front across the tops of the pistons converted to rotary motion with an attitude. You want to make the most of a brief moment of heat energy times eight.

The easiest way to make power is to raise compression. However, you don't want too much compression. Compression ratio depends upon the plan and the fuel available. The other quickest way to unleash power is less internal friction. Internal friction is reduced with obvious means such as roller tappets, double-roller timing set, and lightweight, full roller rocker arms. However, there are other ways, such as more liberal clearances and lightweight components, which is a balancing act in itself because you also want durability, good oil pressure, and low oil consumption.

Even with all details covered, it is no guarantee an engine will stay together or make the power expected. It is those troublesome areas you cannot foresee, material weaknesses and defects, which can fail when least expected. This means you must be attentive to everything you have control over in the build process. When in doubt, check it out.

The most savvy engine builders begin assembly with a mock-up phase where the bottom end is assembled and lubed up without piston rings and checked for proper clearancing, especially if they're building a stroker. A mock-up allows you to check critical clearances all around. This means rods and journals have to be checked to make sure they're going to clear the bottoms of the bores. You must have .060-inch minimum clearance between rod and block. Be careful how much iron is ground away because you risk going all the way through. The most you're going to be able to get into a 351C is 408 ci with a 4.040-inch bore. Again, a 4.060-inch bore is discouraged unless you are very confident of a sonic check.

You need to dimple any surface where gaskets can slip out.

Magnetic particle inspection should be performed on all castings. This is one way to determine casting integrity before spending money on machine work. Sonic checking is yet another means.

Never Take it for Granted

We often fall into the mistaken belief that because a part is new and right out of the box it is a good part. Every part should be inspected for flaws. Though this doesn't guarantee a perfect part, it enables you to sleep better.

Oil pumps must never be installed right out of the box. Always disassemble and check all clearances before installation. Check pressure-relief valve for function. During reassembly, fill the pump cavity with engine assembly lube for a good, well-lubed startup.

Block machine work should consist of decks, cylinder bores, and cam and main journal honing. Main bearing saddles need to be honed for bearing crush and security. Deck thickness should be sonic checked where possible before any millwork.

If you're building a Cleveland stroker, you must first do a mock-up assembly to determine rod to block clearances. You must also check counterweight to oil pump/pick-up clearances as well.

Always use brass freeze plugs, never steel, for durability. Go with the widest freeze plug you can find. Marvin McAfee of MCE Engines suggests using JBWeld to secure your freeze plugs.

Oil galley plugs should be screwed in using Teflon sealer, which is normally performed during the machining process.

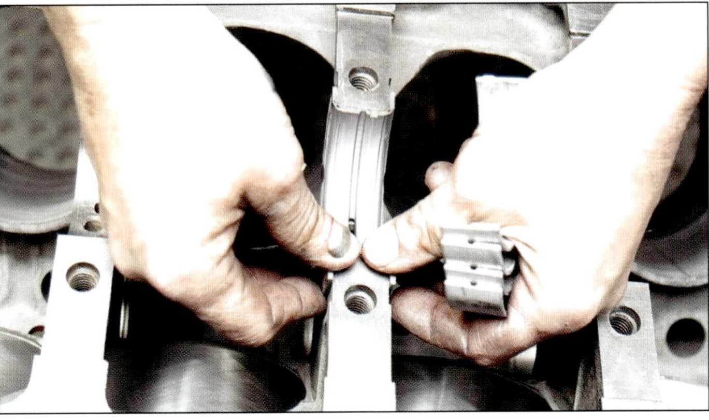

All bearings must be installed dry, meaning no oil between the bearing and saddle. You want good bearing crush and security. Check the oil galley hole to bearing groove alignment.

Rear main bearing cap (number 5) gets Permatex's The Right Stuff between cap and block as shown, which minimizes the risk of oil leakage.

Clevelands were originally fitted with rope rear main seals secured by a pin in this location. Check your main cap and remove this pin if it's still there. If you forget the pin it distorts the new neoprene half-seal.

Main bearings and journals should get generous amounts of engine assembly lube to ensure a wet startup. Main caps should be torqued in three stages beginning with #3 cap, then #2, then #4, then #1, and finally #5. Crank rotation should be checked each time a cap is torqued.

A mock-up should always include valve to piston clearances, which can actually be performed when you are degreeing the cam. This step gives you solid mechanical confirmation. You want at least .060-inch clearance between valve and piston.

Run a high-flow water pump along with a Cleveland-specific 180-degree F thermostat with the thermostat to bypass plate adaptor hat. In other words, do not use a conventional thermostat on your Cleveland, but instead use one designed specifically for the Cleveland's unique bypass cooling system. I suggest you stay away from a 160-degree F thermostat. Never run your Cleveland without a thermostat. If you are running an engine-driven fan, go with a Flex-A-Lite flex fan or a factory thermostatic fan clutch for efficient cooling. The fan must be halfway into a shroud for best results.

Does your machine shop use a torque plate during cylinder honing? If not, find another machine shop. The torque plate simulates cylinder head installation by getting the block where it would be with heads installed and bolts torqued. You want cylinder walls dimensionally where they would be with heads installed.

CHAPTER 2

The Block

When Ford introduced the 351C engine for 1970, it carefully detailed for car buyers and performance enthusiasts what this all-new engine was about. Ford was thinking about future displacement growth when it conceived the Cleveland block. It was also thinking about strength—a rugged, well-thought-out casting that could take a lot of punishment and have room for growth. The plan was to create a mid-size V-8 that would ultimately replace the FE big-block. And to some degree, it would also replace the 302/351W engines as well because it offered growth potential these small-blocks did not. When Ford introduced the Cleveland, it was known as the "new 351-4V engine."

Here's what Ford said, "Ford has designed and developed a brand new 351-ci for its 1970 product line. The new engine—identified as the 351-4V—will be produced on the most modern equipment in the industry at Ford's Cleveland, Ohio manufacturing complex. A new addition to the Cleveland Engine Plant #2 encompassing over 510,000 square feet was recently completed to handle the anticipated production volume of this engine. The new facility contains computer-controlled machines, along with television communications, to assure maximum quality."

Ford's original game plan was to ultimately drop the 351W engine, which was actually a short-term answer to middle-inch competition from Chevrolet (327 and 350), Pontiac, Oldsmobile and Buick (350), Chrysler (318 and 340), and American Motors (343 and 360). In fact, Ford's plan was to grow the new Cleveland engine to greater displacements so it would become a mainstream engine, which led to the 400 a year later and the 351M in 1975. What made the 335 block desirable was growth potential, which doesn't stop at 400 ci. You can cram as much as 460 ci into this block without being concerned about block and cam clearances. McKeown Motorsport Engineering (MME) is developing a new 335-series "Titus" Cleveland block with a pinch more deck height making it

Shown here is a completely machined 351C block ready for assembly.

possible to build a bulletproof Cleveland with a lot of displacement—big-block displacement from a mid-size block.

Ford's original goal was an engine with fewer potential leak points, more perfect mating surfaces, wider main bearing journals, and better gasket/seal technology. Ford's belief was the Cleveland had fewer potential leakage points thanks to a steel-plate timing cover, a better relationship between oil pan and block, and a cooling system that bypassed the intake manifold. Coolant flowed across the block instead of the induction system, which reduced or eliminated leaks. This approach also reduced induction temperatures.

One Ford insider closely involved with the development of the Cleveland said the 335 engine family was originally going to be 335 ci, which explains the "335" designation. The same is true for the 385 big-block at 385 ci—which ultimately became the 429 and 460 ci. The 335 became 351 ci with the same bore and stroke as the 351W along with the same bore spacing.

Cleveland blocks were designed to provide for four-bolt main bearing caps. Ford engineers wanted more beefcake down under for added strength without a skirted block and cross-bolted main caps. Though Ford produced 302 and 351C engines in Australia, none were fitted with four-bolt main caps. Australian Cleveland blocks did not have traditional North American Ford casting numbers, though it is believed North American casting molds were shipped there when 351C production ended in 1974. If you find a Cleveland block void of a Ford North American casting number and a "GF" foundry designation, you've found an Aussie block.

The orifice plate below the thermostat on a 351C engine block is there to control coolant flow to the thermostat and should never be removed. Remove this insert and you will have thermostat malfunction and resulting overheating issues. Ford called this the Controlled Bypass System. The new coolant control system provided improved cooling without frequent thermostat cycling. It also provided for improved warmup. When Ford introduced the 400 a year later and the 351M in 1975, it eliminated the orifice plate, instead molding the controlled bypass system right into the block.

Although the 400 and 351M engines get a lot of criticism and very little respect, there's more to these overlooked engines than meets the eye. The 400 and castrated 351M get criticism because they were never developed to their potential by the factory. Had things gone differently in the 1970s, the 400 would have easily been factory grown to 430 to 450 ci—a mid-size block with a big-block personality without the weight penalty. The 400 could have easily been what the 351C became. And with good cylinder heads and induction on top, the 400 block can be grown in terms of displacement and power. I am talking more than 600 hp thanks to an intuitive aftermarket and building talent.

Cleveland Block Identification

There has always been some confusion when it comes to Cleveland block identification. The 351C block castings, despite different casting numbers, are all basically the same casting and can all be converted to four-bolt main caps with help from a qualified machine shop. All have the same main webs and pan rails. And if you take away the casting

Ford's objective with the 335 block was strength with thicker decks and main webs. The oiling system, which gets a lot of criticism, was a cost issue more than anything to reduce the number of machining steps. For the street and weekend drag racing, the 335's oiling system is adequate.

This is the four-bolt main 351C block with a D2AE-CA casting number. Thing is, not all D2AE-CA blocks have four-bolt main caps. Never believe what you see until the pan is pulled and the caps are inspected.

numbers and date codes, these blocks tend to defy detection except for minor casting changes. Any Cleveland two-bolt main block can be converted to a four-bolt main if you have the stock iron or aftermarket steel billet caps.

Where Cleveland blocks and terminology get confusing is 351C versus 400 and 351M. Though the 400 is called the "400M" by a lot of people, it has never been called this by Ford Motor Company. The raised-deck 400 Cleveland, first introduced for model year 1971, was always known as the "400." When Ford destroked the 400 to 351 ci and called it the 351M in 1975, people started calling the largest Cleveland the 400M. No matter how you look at the 400 or the 351M (for Modified or Midland), both use the same block casting that was in production from 1971 to 1982 though there are different part numbers. The "M" designation was

When you're building a 351C, 351M, or 400, keep in mind these blocks differ significantly from other Ford V-8s of the era including this Cleveland-specific 12 and 6 o'clock fuel pump configuration. The Cleveland was engineered to have fewer leak points and improved gasket technology.

Here's a 351C two-bolt D0AE-L main block. However, D0AE-L doesn't always mean a two-bolt main block. I've seen D0AE-L blocks with four-bolt main caps out of Boss 351 Mustangs. I've also seen D2AE-CA blocks with two-bolt main caps. The 351C block is basically the same casting, drilled or not drilled for four-bolt main caps. And, it is simple for a machine shop to make a four-bolt main block out of a two-bolt.

This 351C block at MCE Engines being built for Mustang Monthly *magazine has been decked and honed. Aside from customary honing, MCE Engines puts on a nice fine finish hone for good ring seating. Block deck should be sonic checked and checked for warpage before any milling is performed. And when you mill, mill only the bare minimum necessary.*

This brass bypass orifice plug (D0AZ-8K217-A) must never be removed and is exclusive to the 351C engine family. It can be removed for block cleaning, but must always be replaced. You can find reproductions of this orifice plug on eBay.

The 351C block is very similar to the Oldsmobile block with a steel timing cover plate and 12/6 o'clock fuel pump. The goal was to have fewer potential leak points.

The Cleveland's lubrication system preparation is something to consider during block prep. The 289/302/351W oiling system has three main oil galleys, whereas the 351C has two. There are two lifter galleys that feed cam bearings. The right-hand galley also feeds main and rod bearings. The savvy Cleveland builder knows how to get around oiling system shortcomings (see Chapter 6 for more detail).

Foundry identification comes from this "CF" logo, which stands for Cleveland Foundry. 351C blocks cast in Australia have a "GF" for Geelong, Australia, foundry. When the 302C and 351C were introduced in Australia, North American blocks from the Cleveland foundry were shipped to Geelong for assembly.

The 351C block casting number and date code are located just above the starter. This D2AE-CA casting number indicates a four-bolt main block according to the Ford Master Parts Catalog, but not all are. This casting date code "2F30" means June 30, 1972.

conceived to differentiate the 351C from the raised-deck 351M, which replaced the 351C in 1975.

One thing that stumps Cleveland enthusiasts more than anything else are the nuances not explained in the Ford parts books. For example, did you know Ford produced 400 blocks in 1971 with small-block bellhousing bolt patterns and undrilled big-block bolt patterns (which can be drilled and tapped)? And did you also know Australian Cleveland blocks are different than their North American counterparts? Though the Cleveland V-8 is as popular in Australia as the small-block Chevy or 5.0L Ford is here, Ford never produced the 400 or 351M in Australia. The 302C and 351C were produced in Australia from 1972 to 1982.

At least two things make the Australian Cleveland block different than its North American cousin. As a rule, Aussie Cleveland castings don't have Ford North America casting numbers (as mentioned earlier), though it is believed some of the North American molds were shipped to Ford's Geelong, Australia, foundry for those first Aussie castings, which means

This is a head-on view of the 400 Cleveland block, which has a 10.987-inch deck height. At a glance, it can be tricky to tell the difference between the 400 and 351C. Look for the taller deck and valley walls coupled with a raised boss in front. Also look for the cast-in orifice below the thermostat. (Photo Courtesy Denny's Auto Machine)

This 1971 400 block (D1AE-A2C) has a small-block bellhousing bolt pattern, which is quite rare. Notice the undrilled 385 series big-block pattern in the casting. A good machine shop can drill this block to go either way. There are a lot of theories about the small-block/big-block pattern, but so far all I've ever seen is the D1AE-A2C casting number with both patterns. The rest are 385 series big-block bellhousing patterns. (Photo Courtesy Denny's Auto Machine)

there are some with North American Ford casting numbers cast in Australia. Another belief is Ford North America shipped discontinued Cleveland casting molds to Australia in 1974 when production ended here.

The terms "D" block and "square" block refer to the boss that rises from the left-hand block deck near the distributor above the fuel pump. D blocks have a D-shaped boss and square blocks have a male or female boss. Early 351C blocks have the D boss primarily, which may have been a provision for a water temperature sending unit on some early-production blocks (but I haven't seen enough of a production pattern to confirm this theory). I've also learned Ford Australia never produced a four-bolt main Cleveland block though they're as easy to convert as their US counterparts. So, don't be surprised if you find an Aussie Cleveland street block with four-bolt mains.

Another point to be mindful of is obscure block castings hidden away in race shops, garages, and barns. These rare blocks can be very limited production pieces to factory experimental "XE" and "SK" castings. I've seen factory aluminum Cleveland blocks, unusual iron blocks with heavier webbing and pan rails, you name it, most with the XE factory experimental casting identification.

There isn't a consistent pattern of XE and SK numbers. These blocks followed convoluted paths all over the world from North America and Australia, leaving us with more questions than answers. You may find these block castings at estate auctions, garage sales, eBay, Craigslist, classified ads, old dusty race shops, and other places. You find them completely machined and partially machined. Sometimes, you find raw castings. Expect to also see rough-cut Cleveland blocks with 3.990-inch unfinished bores. And, expect to see some that have never been hot with standard-size bores.

According to various sources online, some XE blocks found their way into regular production because they weren't acceptable for racing (bad core shift and thin cylinder walls), but worked well in passenger vehicles. That makes your Cleveland block search a crapshoot because it is unknown what you will find out there. Another find known as the "pillow" blocks are race blocks that have bulges or "pillows" in the external block walls.

On top, you can see the 400's differences: the raised boss just to the right of the distributor. Look for this with the 400 and 351M blocks only. (Photo Courtesy Denny's Auto Machine)

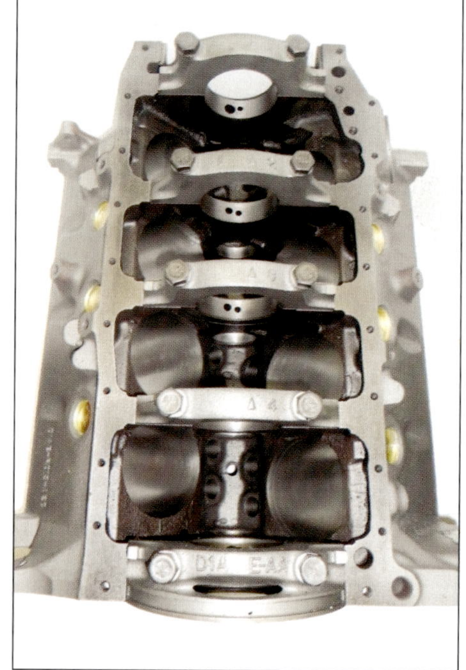

The 400 and 351M blocks have larger 3.000-inch main journals and two-bolt mains. TMeyer offers steel billet four-bolt main caps for the 400/351M block. (Photo Courtesy Tim Meyer, TMeyer, Inc.)

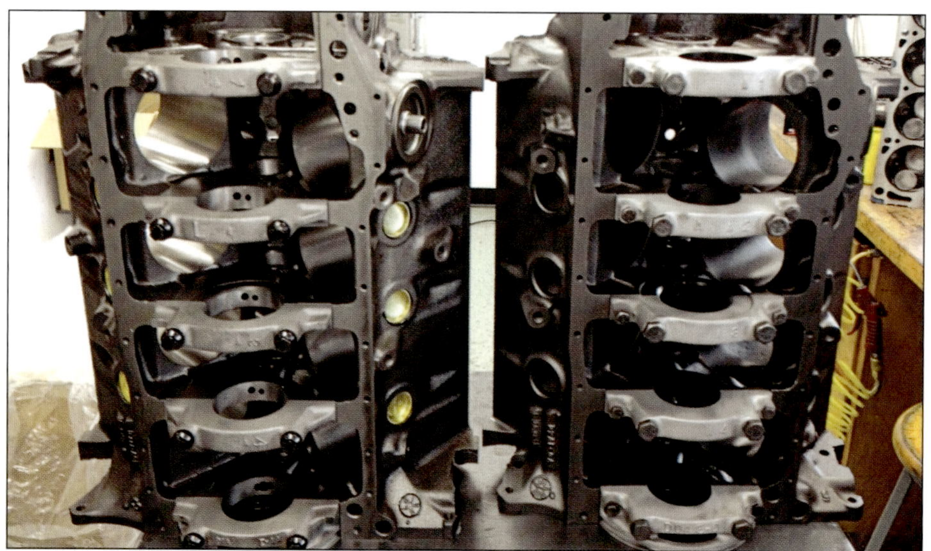

On the left is a two-bolt main 400 block. On the right is a 351C with four-bolt mains. (Photo Courtesy Tim Meyer, TMeyer, Inc.)

It has been often theorized in Internet forums that the Xs and Ys in the lifter valley of most Cleveland blocks means a higher nickel content, but Ford has never confirmed this. It's like that old story of Mexican blocks being of higher nickel content than their US counterparts, which has never been proven beyond hearsay and bench racing. Mexican blocks and US blocks weigh within a pound of one another, which means there's no difference in nickel content. It is believe the Xs and Ys were cast in to prevent cracking, a running production change in Cleveland blocks.

Although I try to touch on just about everything you might find, there are going to be unusual, limited-production castings that surface breaking all the rules and posing new questions. There has been factory Cleveland development documentation dating back to 1965 that tells us this engine was in development for a long time before it debuted late in 1969.

The most obvious difference between the 351C (left) and 400 (right) is the bellhousing bolt pattern. The 351C has a six-bolt, small-block bolt pattern. The 400/351M block has the 385-series big-block six-bolt bellhousing pattern. (Photo Courtesy Tim Meyer, TMeyer, Inc.)

On the left here is the 400/351M block with its raised 10.987-inch deck alongside the shorter 9.206-inch deck 351C block. (Photo Courtesy Tim Meyer, TMeyer, Inc.)

Here are the 351C and 400 blocks side by side for a deck comparison. The 351C is in front; the 400 is behind it. Do you see the height difference? (Photo Courtesy Tim Meyer, TMeyer, Inc.)

This is a four-bolt steel billet main caps on a 400 Cleveland. You don't need to look all over the place for a four-bolt main Cleveland block because conversion is quite simple in the hands of a competent machinist. I suggest you stud your main caps, even with stockers. It only improves security. Four-bolt main conversions call for line boring and honing.

Block prep should include thread chasing—and I mean every single bolthole. All bolt holes should be clean and free of burrs for accurate torque readings.

Factory race shops knew about the Cleveland long before it entered production making it Ford's own mystery engine, not unlike the big-block Chevy.

Early Cleveland blocks seem to have been plagued with cracking issues in the lifter valley. And when they cracked, coolant found its way into the oil. It appears the best Cleveland block to use is the D2AE-CA casting. Though the Ford Master Parts Catalog indicates the D2AE-CA block is a four-bolt main casting, not all of them were drilled for four-bolt mains. Always pull the pan to confirm before committing to a D2AE-CA block casting.

Block Specifications

Note that not all block castings are shown here.

Displacement/Years	Casting Number (6015)	Part Number (6015)	Bore Size (inches)	Deck Height (inches)	Other Information
351C 1970–1971	DOAE-A	DOAZ-D	4.000	9.2060	2-bolt main
351C 1970–1971	DOAE-C	DOAZ-D	4.000	9.2060	2-bolt main
351C 1970–1971	DOAE-E	DOAZ-D	4.000	9.2060	2-bolt main
351C 1970–1971	DOAE-G	DOAZ-D	4.000	9.2060	2-bolt main
351C 1970–1971	DOAE-J	DOAZ-D	4.000	9.2060	2-bolt main
351C 1970–1971	DOAE-L	DOAZ-D	4.000	9.2060	2-bolt main
351C 1970–1971	D2AE-DA	DOAZ-D	4.000	9.2060	2-bolt main
351C Australian	XE 192540	D6HM-L	3.990	N/A	4-bolt main; NASCAR block cast at Geelong, circa 1975-1976
351C Australian	XE 192540	D6HM-1	3.990	N/A	4-bolt main; NASCAR block cast at Geelong, circa 1975-1976
351C Australian	XE 192540	D1ZZ-T	3.990	N/A	4-bolt main; NASCAR block cast at Geelong, circa 1975-1976
351C Australian, Marketed in US by Ford SVO	XE 192540, M-6015-A3	N/A	3.990	N/A	4-bolt main; NASCAR block cast at Geelong, circa 1982-1983
351C Australian	XE 195820	N/A	N/A	N/A	4-bolt main; Siamesed Bores
351C Australian	XE 182540	N/A	N/A	N/A	4-bolt main
351C 1971	DOAE-B	N/A	4.000	9.2060	4-bolt main
351C 1971	DOAE-D	N/A	4.000	9.2060	4-bolt main
351C 1971	DOAE-F	N/A	4.000	9.2060	4-bolt main
351C 1971	DOAE-H	N/A	4.000	9.2060	4-bolt main
351C 1971 Boss 351	D1ZE-A	D1ZZ-D	4.000	9.2060	4-bolt main
351C 1971	D1ZE-B	D1ZZ-D	4.000	9.2060	4-bolt main
351C 1971, 351 High Output	D2AE-CA	D1ZZ-A, D3ZZ-A	4.000	9.2060	4-bolt main
351C 1972	D2AE-EA	D1ZZ-D	4.000	9.2060	4-bolt main
400 1971–1982	D1AE-A	D1AZ-A	4.000	10.297	2-bolt main; 385-series bell bolt pattern
400 1971–1982	D1AE-AC	D1AZ-A	4.000	10.297	2-bolt main; 385-series bell bolt pattern
351M 1975–1982	D1AE-A2C	D1AZ-A	4.000	10.297	2-bolt main; small-block and 385-series
351M 1975–1982	D4AE-B2A	D1AZ-A	4.000	10.297	2-bolt main; 385-series bell bolt pattern
351M 1975–1982	D5AZ	D1AZ-A	4.000	10.297	2-bolt main; 385-series bell bolt pattern
351M 1975–1982	D7TE-A2B	D1AZ-A	4.000	10.297	2-bolt main; 385-series bell bolt pattern
351M 1975–1982	D8TE	D1AZ-A	4.000	10.297	2-bolt main; 385-series bell bolt pattern

Stud the mains for solid integrity, even if you're building a stock Cleveland. Never run studs all the way down. Leave 1/4 inch between stud and bottom. Use engine oil sparingly on stud threads; however, never fill the bolt hole with oil, which can crack the block.

Before a 351C block can be line-honed, torque the main studs. Apply moly coat to provide lubrication and an accurate torque reading. Torque mains from the inside outward in three stages. Again, do not bottom studs out. If you have converted a two-bolt main block to a four-bolt, the line bore must be line bored to size, then honed.

Check bores with a micrometer. Here is a 4.000-inch bore, which will be bored and honed to 4.030 inches. Never bore more than 4.040 inches, though some are willing to take it to 4.060 inches. If you intend to go to 4.060 inches, sonic check cylinder walls before machine work begins.

This Cleveland block has been bored to 4.025 inches. Honing takes it to 4.030 inches. Jim Grubbs of JGM Performance Engineering has his own honing process, which is based on how the engine will be used.

Mike and hone lifter bores for proper fitment and oil control. When tolerances become too sloppy, lifter bores should be sleeved and honed.

Marvin seeks perfect main cap fit by dimpling the main saddles as shown. These dimples take up gaps providing a secure fit. A snug fit prevents cap movement at high RPM.

Ford 351C/400/351M Block Specifications

Engine	Cylinder Bore Diameter (inches)	Cylinder Bore Diameter (.0003-inch Oversize)	Lifter Bore Diameter (inch)	Main Bearing Bore Diameter (inches)	Distributor Shaft Bore (inch)	Head Gasket Surface (inch)
351C	4.000 to 4.0024	4.0024 to 4.0036	0.8752 to 0.8767	2.9417 to 2.9429	0.5160 to 0.5175	.0003 in any 6-inch direction. No more than .0007 overall.
400/351M	4.000 to 4.0024	4.0024 to 4.0036	0.8752 to 0.8767	3.1922 to 3.1930	0.5160 to 0.5175	.0003 in any 6-inch direction. No more than .0007 overall.

Block Preparation

You want a block with perfectly machined surfaces that mates well and seals tight without conflict. This calls for extreme measures in machining—and painstaking attention to detail. Before you spend a lot of money on a block, it must first be cleaned and inspected, then confirmed fit for service. You're not going to find a machine shop that cleans and machines a block, then refunds your money because it is cracked, bored oversize beyond salvage, windowed by a stray connecting rod and repaired, or suffers from some other type of defect. You must first know if you have a usable block. Begin with a pressure test to confirm integrity. Then, give it a complete thermal cleaning including removing all freeze and oil galley plugs followed by a visual and magnetic particle inspection.

Go into the water jackets with a high-power magnet to catch slag and other metal debris. You will be amazed at how much you find in there from the foundry, which can cause hot spots and overheating. There have been freeze plugs found inside water jackets, knocked inside by careless rebuilders and autoworkers. Do this even if it's a new block, especially if it's a new block. Measure cylinder bore size from top to bottom, and sonic check walls and decks. While you're at it, do a pressure test. Line bore should also be checked. Check cam bore to line bore centerlines. Check the cam bore. Examine lifter bores.

Block cleaning should be an ongoing process throughout the machining phases. Have your machinist clean the block after each machining phase to ensure debris doesn't accumulate in oil galleys, water jackets, and other cavities. Not everyone agrees with this because it's labor intensive and adds to the cost; however, it is just good housekeeping. The logic here is even the smallest metal particle (grit) can and will damage moving parts. Even a hair-thin score in a journal costs you oil pressure. Oil galleys and other passages must have a thorough cleaning with long and aggressive rifle cleaning brushes again and again until you are confident all debris is gone. Another aspect of cleaning is slag and stress riser removal. Slag can impede oil and cooling system passages. Stress risers can lead to cracking.

Machine work includes cylinder boring and honing if bores are tapered beyond .0001 inch. Maximum wear limit is .010-inch over before you must go to the next oversize. Where possible, bore and hone to .020-inch oversize instead of .030 inch, which buys you more block

After all block machine work has been performed, double-check bore sizing and piston to cylinder wall clearances with a dial bore gauge. This is a good last-minute precautionary check prior to assembly.

Hone the line bore to achieve good bearing security and crush. "Crush" because you want bearings to be secure in the saddles. The caps should fit with some interference and a snug fit.

U.S. Standard Bolt Specifications and Torque Values

The information in this chart was provided by ARP Racing Products (using ARP Lube on fastener threads).

Fastener Tensile Strength	170,000–180,000 psi		190,000–200,000 psi		220,000 psi	
Fastener Diameter (inch)	*Torque (ft-lbs)*	*Preload (pounds)*	*Torque (ft-lbs)*	*Preload (pounds)*	*Torque (ft-lbs)*	*Preload (pounds)*
1/4	12	3,492	14	3,967	16	4,442
5/16	24	5,805	28	6,588	32	7,371
3/8	45	8,622	50	9,782	55	10,942
7/16	70	11,880	80	13,470	90	15,060
1/2	110	16,391	125	18,515	140	20,639
9/16	160	21,220	180	23,944	200	26,668
5/8	220	26,372	240	29,756	270	33,140

time. If wear is minimal and boring unnecessary, at least do a fine finish hone and ridge removal. The purpose of boring isn't just to take cylinders to the next oversize, but to also match each piston to a hone-matched bore. In other words, measure each piston and hone a cylinder to match, but only once dynamic balancing is complete and you have eight slugs and rods balanced to a specific location on the crankshaft. Piston rings should be end gapped and installed.

Make sure your machine shop uses a torque plate for honing, which simulates cylinder head installation and gets the bore as it will be once heads are installed. Hone without a torque plate and you have cylinders that are irregular when heads are installed and torqued. Always use a head gasket with the torque plate—it's that important. Three different stones are typically used in the honing process becoming progressively finer.

Main saddles need to be line honed until they are true. Line honing puts a nice crosshatch pattern in the bearing saddles, which provides crush and security. Main saddles require boring when they are worn beyond limits, which involves milling main cap mating surfaces, then boring and honing the installed caps. One thing machine shops rarely do is cam bore line honing. However, for good cam bearing security, ask them to hone yours. It's worth the expense to get a good crosshatch pattern. Ideally, your machine shop has the right equipment to rotate the block during the line honing process. Not many shops do this, but it's a nice feature when you can find it because it gets the main bearing saddles perfect.

When bearings are seated in saddles, bearing and saddle surfaces must be bone dry—and that includes skin oil. Touch only the edges. Never touch contact surfaces. Also examine oil galley passages for proper indexing with bearing passages. There may be misdrilled passages and the passages are drilled that way on purpose for reasons unknown beyond the factory level. Sometimes, you see only half of the oil galley and wonder how the engine survived. Ideally, you should have 100-percent alignment.

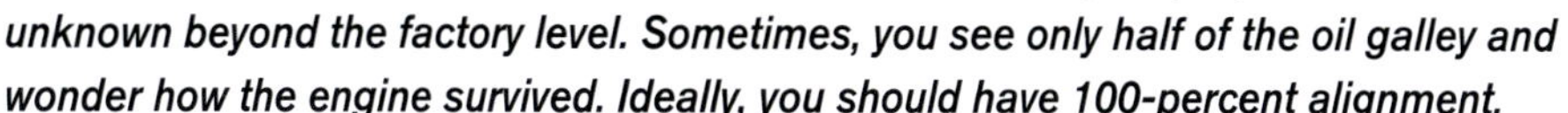

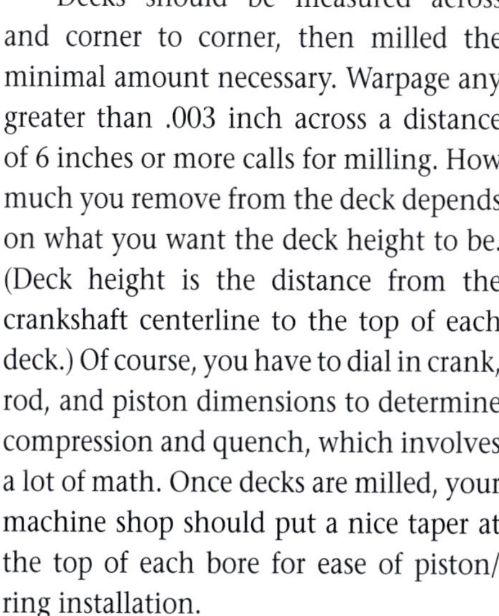

Decks should be measured across and corner to corner, then milled the minimal amount necessary. Warpage any greater than .003 inch across a distance of 6 inches or more calls for milling. How much you remove from the deck depends on what you want the deck height to be. (Deck height is the distance from the crankshaft centerline to the top of each deck.) Of course, you have to dial in crank, rod, and piston dimensions to determine compression and quench, which involves a lot of math. Once decks are milled, your machine shop should put a nice taper at the top of each bore for ease of piston/ring installation.

Once all machine work is complete and you've performed a thorough cleaning, and all oil galley and freeze plugs are installed, perform a pressure test to confirm you still have a solid block. Once the pressure test is complete, properly mask off everything that should not be painted. Once your block is in paint, spray cylinder walls and interior surfaces with WD-40 for corrosion prevention. You don't want rusty cylinder walls and bearing saddles. In a damp climate, it doesn't take long for them to get that way.

Some block cracking can be repaired via welding or JB Weld, which is a two-part catalyzed product that works well with cracked cast iron. Properly mixed and allowed time to cure, it will last the life of any engine block. For JB Weld to work effectively you need a clean surface and a crack that has been carefully stop drilled at each end. Just a small 1/16-inch hole at each end slows and stops cracking. Then weld or JB Weld the crack. I suggest against the use of JB Weld at the cylinder walls and decks where stresses can be extreme. Your machine shop can advise you; some blocks are cracked beyond repair.

Fasteners and Threads

Your block preparation should include thread chasing, which not enough of us do. Every bolt hole should be lubricated with WD-40 and chased with a thread chaser until fasteners roll smoothly. Damaged threads should be tapped or repaired with a helicoil insert. Once the threads are clear, blast them with a soapy solution and compressed air, then WD-40 in the hole for corrosion prevention. Fastener threads should also be chased while you're at it.

Use Grade 8 fasteners throughout for a high level of fastener integrity. As one example, some ARP kits don't have all of the correct fasteners, which means you need to do it piecemeal and order specific fasteners for your Cleveland. There are also AMK Products for those who wish a factory look using OEM fasteners.

Go with main studs instead of bolts in the bottom end, even with a stocker. Main studs offer greater structural integrity preventing main cap movement. Head studs make cylinder head removal difficult if they're in a car. However, if you're going to push the limits of a Cleveland block—such as nitrous, supercharging, or high RPM/high compression for extended periods—studs are the better choice. Give all fasteners a trial run through bolt holes to check for resistance. Never torque fasteners without lubrication and always torque them in three phases, then recheck.

New Cleveland Blocks

A shortage of good blocks has long presented logistics problems for Cleveland engine builders. In recent times and with better technology has come reproduction alloy and iron Cleveland blocks both domestically and from Australia. This means new and exciting options for those who want to begin with a fresh block.

Titus Cleveland Block

When MME Racing in Waldorf, Maryland, introduced the new Titus Cleveland block in cast iron and aluminum, Mark McKeown explained, "We have been pushing the envelope of the Cleveland engine for many years and have been forced to use Windsor-based blocks for some builds, including our own race car and our Engine Masters Challenge entries. We will now run our own Titus Cleveland engines in the race car and at the Engine Masters Challenge. We need a platform that we can build well over 1,100 hp from a naturally aspirated small-block to be competitive in our race car."

The Titus is exciting for Ford performance enthusiasts because Cleveland blocks are becoming more scarce every day. Though Ford Australia produced a lot of 302C and 351C engines for many years after Ford North America ended production, the global supply of good Cleveland blocks is drying up. As a result, MME Racing made the critical decision to reproduce this block, but only with significant improvements over the original.

"The Titus will allow us to build larger displacement Cleveland engines than was possible with a Windsor-based engine. I think this will open the Cleveland platform to other markets like the X275 and Outlaw Drag Radial classes using N/A, nitrous, turbo and superchargers. I believe the dirt and asphalt markets will benefit from the new capability of the Cleveland platform because this block is stronger and with greater capacity. Classes like Super Late Model are very abusive on engines and larger displacement versions have durability issues. The Titus is designed to address these issues."

What makes the Titus a good investment is greater bore capacity, a revised oiling system that corrects all of the Cleveland's notorious issues, heavier main webs, larger cam tunnel, larger one-piece rear main seal that will work with both production and aftermarket crankshafts, and is available in 9.200-inch or 9.600-inch deck heights. It has four-bolt main caps with splayed outer bolts for unequaled strength. You can order the Titus in custom deck heights as well.

"The Titus is designed to be used everywhere," Mark comments, "This is *not* a 'race only' block. It is designed to mate to stock and existing components. While it is designed to handle extreme power it will also be at home in a street car."

This is the new Titus aluminum Cleveland block from MME. The Titus has many new features including greater bore capacity and improved oil system circuitry. The cam bore is designed for stock and larger base circle camshafts.

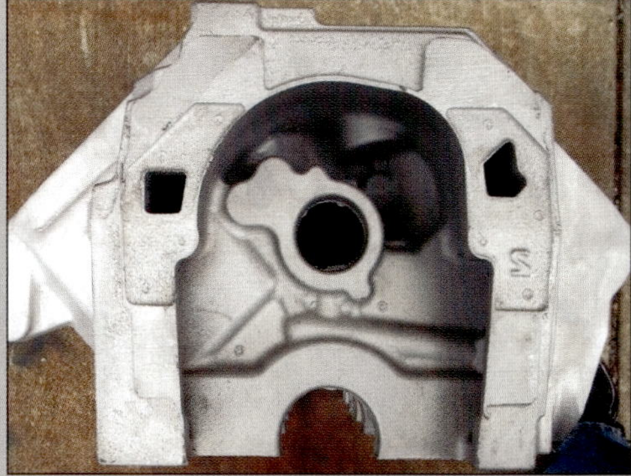

Here's the Titus block in rough cast before machine work. Two deck heights are available:9.200 and 9.500 inches. The Titus is also available in custom deck heights by special order.

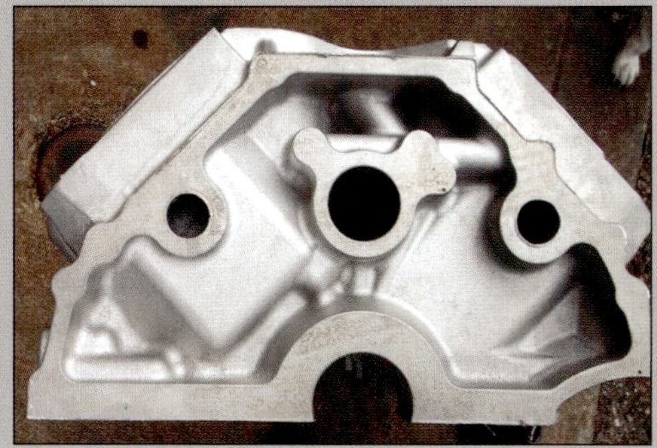

All machine work on the Titus Cleveland aluminum block will be performed by MME as it grows to include more CNC machines. Additional good news is the availability of this block in iron.

Arrow Iron Cleveland Block

Another recent reproduction Cleveland block comes from Arrow Blocks in Australia. It is a reproduction of the 351C block with a lot of nice refinements to structure, lubrication, and cooling. This adds up to thicker webs, decks, and cylinder walls along with prioritized oiling and cooling. This is a 351C block you can take to 440 ci according to *Australian Street Machine* magazine.

"After all, if you're going to go to all the trouble of casting a new block, there's no point in just copying a 40-year-old design, you might as well make it better. The Arrow is cast from high-strength, cast-iron consisting of carbon, silicon, phosphorous, sulphur, manganese, molybdenum and zinc. Its design incorporates thicker decks, siamesed bores, larger water jackets, four-bolt mains, steel billet caps, solid pan rails and priority mains oiling where pressurized oil is fed to the mains before lubricating the cam and lifters."

Because the Arrow block has a lot of refinements to structure, it is heavier than Ford's Cleveland block. There's enough cylinder wall thickness to go to 4.185 inches while being able to maintain .216-inch wall thickness.

This is the MME Titus block prior to machining in a state-of-the-art facility. Once installed in a car, it is hard to tell the Titus from a factory Cleveland block. Pricing is around $4,700.00 for the aluminum block.

Rotating Assembly

The 351C met with unfortunate timing from the start because Ford's North American corporate agenda quickly shifted from racing to lower emissions and fuel economy at the cusp of the 1970s. What this meant for an engine family long on potential was disappointing, considering what might have been. The 351C was developed during one of the meanest Woodward Avenue performance battles in Detroit history. Unfortunately, this competitive spirit ended as quickly as it began in North America.

Overnight, Ford Motor Company slashed its racing budget by a whopping 75 percent, which was devastating news for performance enthusiasts and the aftermarket. Government and the insurance industry get the blame, but it was more than that. Changing buyer trends also prompted Ford to move away from performance as baby boomers entered college and family life. Baby boomers needed more practical transportation for college and growing families. Along came Maverick, Pinto, and the Mustang II, which all sold well because they were all the right cars at the right time.

The new 351C was all dressed up for great performance with nowhere to go. In fact, Ford had to quickly develop a low-compression version of the 351C with 2-barrel carburetion and open chambers.

On the other hand, Ford Australia was just getting started with a great legacy of Cleveland power. The Aussies took the Cleveland far beyond its North American roots with a very successful family of 335 engines displacing 302 and 351 ci. The Australian 302C was a destroked 351C at 3.000 inches of stroke with a 4.000-inch bore.

Crankshaft

Where other Ford V-8 engine families had both cast and steel crankshafts, the 351C was produced in cast only. Based on years of experience with these engines, it is clear to me Ford never produced a mass-production steel crankshaft for the 351C, 400, or 351M aside for perhaps racing and rare factory experimental XE pieces. Hank The Crank began

Cleveland crankshaft identification is easy and based on codes stamped into the first counterweight. Codes 4M, 4MA, or 4MAB indicates a 351C or 351M crankshaft with a 1.750-inch throw or 3.500-inch stroke. A 351C crankshaft has a 2.750-inch main journal, which makes it a different crank than you find in the 351M, which has the 400's larger 3.000-inch main journal.

producing steel Cleveland cranks in 1974 for drag racers such as Jack Roush. The aftermarket has followed suit in the years since with a great selection of cast, steel, and steel-billet Cleveland cranks.

The 335-series factory nodular-iron crankshaft is fully capable of use in high-performance applications up to 7,500 rpm and hasn't exhibited failure issues on a grand scale. I've seen hundreds of 351C engines raced over the past 40 years without consequence. The same can be said of the Cleveland's connecting rods, which are very durable pieces with beefy large ends and 3/8-inch rod bolts.

There are three factory nodular iron crankshafts identifiable by markings, stroke (throw), and main journal dimensions. The 351C crank is marked with an identification number of 4M or 4MA. Where you must be attentive is main journal size because it's easy to unknowingly pick up a 351M crank, which has the 400's larger 3.000-inch main journals along with the 351C's 3.000-inch stroke and rod journals. The 351C has smaller 2.750-inch main journals, which means you would need the journals turned down by a competent machinist.

There's a lot of scuttlebutt about 351C, 400, and 351M crankshaft identification numbers, but basic identification has never changed in all these years. When it comes to mainstream 351C, 400, and 351M crankshafts, basic identification numbers of 4M (351C, 351M) and 5M (400) and 1K (351M only) hold true as excellent means of identification. Though you see 4MA, 4MAB, 5MA, 5MAB, the additional "A" or "B" is nothing more than an engineering revision to the casting. It does not mean Brinell tested. Any crank that has been Brinell tested for hardness gets the Brinell test mark in the first counterweight, which is little more than a small 1/4-inch dent.

We've been long taught to believe we must have a steel crank to do high-performance work. However, the 335 nodular-iron crankshaft, regardless of displacement, is a durable crank thanks to main journal sizing and the good consistency of nodular iron. Based on four decades of experience with this engine and the many people I've seen build Clevelands, this is a crankshaft with a great reputation for durability, especially if you inspect and prepare it properly.

I have to admit, although I am telling you how to treat a Cleveland's factory internals, it makes more sense these days to pump up the displacement and get more durable components in the process with a good aftermarket stroker package. But let's just say you want to keep your Cleveland all factory inside, you have a great foundation to work with. The 351C crank is an extremely durable piece that can take up to 7,500 rpm. Main thing is a detailed inspection and good prep work going in. A crankshaft's primary job is to convert heat energy into rotary motion and power. Because there are many torsional stresses on a crankshaft, a lot of

Cleveland crankshafts all look the same at a glance; however, they are quite different. There are three basic types: The 4M with a 3.500-inch stroke and either a 2.750-inch main journal (351C) or 3.000-inch journal (351M). The 400 crank has a 3.000-inch main journal and a 5M stamp. On the left here is a 351M with a 3.000-inch main journal. In the middle is a 351C with 2.750-inch main journal (both with a 3.500-inch stroke and "4M" markings). The 351M also had a "1K" mark later in production. On the right is a 400 with a 4.000-inch stroke and 5M marking. (Photo Courtesy Tim Meyer, TMeyer, Inc.)

Ford's 400 bottom end was designed with durability in mind with its 3.000-inch mains, 2.311-inch rod journals, and 4.000-inch stroke. This engine was born to make torque for full-size cars and trucks; hence the heavy-duty "5M" crank and D1AE 6.580-inch (center to center) connecting rods. Magazine tech writer and book author Richard Holdener proved you can throw nearly 600 hp at this bottom end and it stays together. (Photo Courtesy Richard Holdener)

Cleveland 335-Series Crankshaft Identification

Engine Displacement	*Crankshaft Type*	*Identification*	*Center-To-Center (inches)*	*Main Journal (inches)*	*Rod Journal (inches)*	*Stroke (inches)*
351C	Nodular Iron	4M, 4MA	1.750	2.7484 to 2.7492	2.3103 to 2.3111	3.500
351M	Nodular Iron	4M, 1K, 1KA	1.750	2.9994 to 3.0002	2.3103 to 2.3111	3.500
400M	Nodular Iron	5M, 5MAB	2.000	2.9994 to 3.0002	2.3103 to 2.3111	4.000

Brinell Hardness Testing

Brinell hardness testing was invented in 1900 by Dr. Johan August Brinell, a Swedish engineer and metallurgist. Brinell testing is little more than striking metal with a 0.39-inch (10-mm) steel ball at 6,600 pounds of force to determine how hard it is. It is a standardized form of destructive (yet non-destructive) testing to determine surface hardness. That means more than 2 tons of force with pinpoint precision, which looks like a small dent or circle in the first counterweight. Less force is required with softer iron. And where you need more force (harder iron), you use a tungsten carbide ball. Brinell hardness testing, searches for the true tensile strength of a cast/nodular iron crankshaft.

Ford conducted Brinell hardness testing on nodular iron crankshafts as a matter of practice and pulled the hardest of the lot for high-performance applications such as the Boss 351 and 351C High Output. Not all 351C crankshafts have this mark. Finding this mark proves your 351C crank has been tested, but it's not always a guarantee you've found a Boss or High Output crankshaft. I can, however, tell you the 351C's nodular iron 4M crankshaft has a proven track record as an indestructible piece.

thought needs to be given to crankshaft selection. Although the hot ticket always seems to be steel crankshafts, they're rarely necessary for a street project. Cast is good for anything up to 450 hp. If you're going to push it beyond that, you're going to want steel. It really depends on how you will treat an engine at 450 hp. If you're going to treat it to nitrous or a blower, you want steel to reduce the chance of breakage. A cast crank does well with steady, consistent applications of power. It is the shock nature of nitrous and pressurized induction that can break an iron crank. I believe you can road race an iron crank depending on how fast you want to go and how much violent twist there will be.

The thing to remember about crankshafts is that they twist and flex as combustion pulses hammer each journal and you put a load on them, which oscillates material such as rubber back and forth. Then, you load the crank with a wide-open throttle. Aside from the obvious stress, there are other loads such as oil pump and distributor, which also contribute to twist.

Twist and oscillation affect timing and power output. As pistons and rods rise to compression/ignition stroke, oscillation becomes more intense, acting on not only the crankshaft, but also connecting rods and pistons. It all moves violently with changes in power application. The crank's torsional action rebounds against the piston and rod as they ascend on the compression stroke. There's also the harmonic balancer, which acts as a shock absorber for crankshaft twist. As the crank rebounds, it works on the balancer, which softens rebound shock and reduces the risk of crankshaft breakage.

Regardless of how you look at this dynamic, cyclic issues affect crankshaft life. How do you recondition a crankshaft to make the most of its durability? I get nervous about turning a crankshaft beyond .010-inch undersize; however, crankshafts are stronger than you think. Automakers engineer tremendous strength into even the most modest cast-iron crankshafts. Crankshafts do break from time to time, but rarely due to material failure. This means you can machine your Cleveland's crank beyond .010-inch undersize without concern for failure, especially if you're building a street engine. You can comfortably turn your journals to .020-inch undersize and still have durability. Some machinists are good with .030- and .040-inch undersize, which is discouraged because it tends to negatively affect hardening.

Over the years, I've studied crankshaft failure and talked with those who have also studied it and concluded

Whether you're doing a mock-up or final assembly, journals and bearings should be generously lubed with engine assembly lube. Some builders use engine oil, but assembly lube has staying power.

most failures occur in the journal's fillet radius where heat and stress seem to occur most. If you study most crankshaft failures, look at where they fail. The fillet radius where crank journal meets the counterweight is the most common failure spot between journal and the rest of your crank. Rarely do you see a mid-journal failure or a break at a counterweight. This is why you must pay close attention to the fillet area with proper machining and finishing technique, plus the bearing's smooth and comfortable relationship with the fillet. Radiuses of both bearing and fillet must be identical for perfect mating and without stress issues. When you grind and finish a crankshaft, it is so easy to overlook the fillet radius. You spend so much time focused on journal surfaces, oil hole chamfering, and balance you forget to examine fillet radius and the bearing's important relationship with it. To add insult to injury, you sometimes install rod bearings backward, which is failure before you even get started.

A good rule to follow is to machine the crank journals to the bearings, and swap bearings around to get optimum clearances. In other words, swap bearings around to where you get the best clearances throughout. And when machining the crank, micropolish the journals to get the best oil flow and wedge. Main and rod journals get extremely hot, especially under a load at high RPM where temperatures can be as high as 350 to 400 degrees F. Oil begins to break down at 260 degrees F. Synthetic begins to break down at 300 degrees F.

Oil can tolerate extremely high temperatures for a short time, which is why steady volume across the bearing and journal is important. You want enough of an oil wedge at the journals to keep moving parts apart, yet enough flow to carry heat away from the journals. This is why the middle ground is suggested when it comes to bearing clearances.

If in the process of machining and mock-up you find excessive crankshaft endplay, King Engine Bearing has two affordable options: MaxFlange and ProFlange thrust bearings. MaxFlange is a process used on all King engine bearings. It reduces crankshaft endplay by supplying a flange on the high side of the tolerance to compensate for excessive crankshaft thrust wear.

Excessive thrust clearance is more common with manual transmission Clevelands due to clutch activity, which leans on the main thrust heavily each time the clutch is disengaged. ProFlange is a King line of bearing sets with oversize flanges, which allows the crank's thrust to be ground to .010-, .020-, or .030-inch undersize. Both approaches are designed to save crankshafts from rework or replacement.

Cast Iron

Crankshaft materials vary considerably and require a lot of thought. There's steel billet on the high end, plus forged steel, malleable steel, and nodular iron (cast iron). On stroker kit websites, you see the words, "cast steel," which is marketing jargon for cast iron. It sounds more trustworthy than "cast iron," but it is nothing more than nodular iron.

What is the difference between nodular and cast iron? They are different grades of what is essentially cast iron. Grade depends on the alloy and quenching (heat treating). The different types of iron alloy are too involved to get into here; however, here are the basics.

For example, engine blocks and heads are made from gray wall iron (ASTM A48), which has a hardness of 260 on the Brinell hardness scale. Crankshafts and camshafts are ductile or nodular iron (ASTM A339) at 310 on the Brinell hardness scale. Iron with low carbon content is known as steel.

Although it is widely believed you shouldn't race with a cast (nodular) iron crankshaft, you can race on weekends with a cast crank without consequence if you prepare accordingly. Preparation should include Magnafluxing (electromagnetic process of checking for cracks), grinding, polishing, radiusing

Though stroke is the piston's overall travel, from bottom to top, crank throw is half the stroke number. A 3.500-inch stroke adds up to 1.750 inches of throw.

Rear main seal leakage with two-piece seals can be chronic. Stagger your seal ends as shown, then dab ends with Permatex's The Right Stuff. The Right Stuff between seals and grooves is also beneficial.

Before any machine work is performed, check the crank for irregularities such as excessive runout, deep journal scoring, pitting, wear, and damage. Sometimes a nick renders a journal unserviceable if it is deeper than the minimums allow. Notice the tiny rust spots in this journal? This is another reason why journals need to be polished. Rust scores new bearings.

Crankshaft endplay is .004 to .010 inch. In high-performance applications, you want it midway between .004 and .010 inch and closer to .010 if possible. Excessive endplay beyond .010 inch is unacceptable because it adversely affects crank and rod/piston alignment.

Cranks must be thoroughly cleaned any time machining or polishing takes place. And never take for granted that a new crank is clean and free of debris.

Dynamic balancing should be performed any time an engine is rebuilt. Even with a new "balanced" stroker kit, have it balanced by a trusted professional. All 335-series Clevelands are 28-ounce offset balanced. All are externally balanced.

When you have significant differences in weight, an engine balancer may have to add Mallory metal, which adds weight to counterweights where necessary. This is where engine building gets expensive. Adding metal is exactly the opposite of removing metal via a drill bit.

The 351C, 400, and 351M all have a two-piece rear main seal. Seal end gaps should be staggered away from main cap parting gaps.

This 351C counterweight has been welded either as a repair or for dynamic balancing where metal was added.

the journals, and removing all of the stress risers (crack prevention). You also want to crossdrill where necessary and chamfer oil holes to improve oil flow at the journals. Chamfering improves oil flow to bearings and journals by reducing resistance to flow. In other words, you have a broader oil hole surface area at the journal, which increases volume.

Forged Steel

Cast-iron crankshafts are the cheapest and most common because they're easy to manufacture. Molten liquid iron is poured into a sand cast mold, cooled, heat treated, and machined to what looks like a crankshaft. Forged steel crankshafts come from a more involved process. A nearly molten steel alloy ingot is heated to approximately 2,200 to 2,600 degrees F and rammed into the shape of a crankshaft in a die at an excess of 240,000 psi. The forging is then heat-treated via a quenching process and allowed to cool before being machined into its final configuration. Once all machining is complete, the forged crank is heated to 400 to 600 degrees F to relieve stress and carefully allowed to cool. Once allowed to cool, final polishing and finish work are performed.

Forged steel crankshafts are typically made of 4340 hardened steel. Others are made of 1038 steel, which isn't as pure as 4340, but still quite effective. Specialized formulas for forged steel cranks vary from manufacturer to manufacturer. For example, Scat Enterprise's

Steel billet enters the machining process at Scat Enterprises. This is a very involved machining process; hence the cost of billet crankshafts. The key to engine component cost is time and materials. The more time involved to make a part, the more expensive it becomes.

These billet crankshafts are midway through the machining process. Notice the huge counterweights and crank snout, which have more machining phases to go.

forging process uses a pressure technique instead of a traditional "slam-bam" hammer approach to make its forged steel cranks. Instead of hammering molten 2,600-degree F metal into shape, it applies tremendous pressure to the nearly liquid metal.

Once the forging is trimmed and machined, it gets nitrided for good surface hardening. Scat manufactures some of the lightest cranks in the industry, which is what racers want. The lighter the crank as well as rods and pistons, the faster your Cleveland revs.

Eagle Specialty Products has its own unique approach to forged steel crankshafts. It's a no-twist formula that comes from a special heat-treating and shot-peening process that ensures pinpoint accuracy at high RPM. Journals are crossdrilled and chamfered for a good oil wedge between journal and bearing. A target bobweight of plus-or-minus 2 percent means less balancing time.

If you're rebuilding a Cleveland that already has a steel crank from a prior rebuild, your crank should be nitrided once all machine work and balancing is completed. This keep journal surfaces hard and less inclined to wear.

Knowing the Difference

I get asked from time to time how to tell the different between a cast and forged crankshaft. A cast crank has fewer flaws as a rule and generally has a rough surface with narrow parting lines. A steel crank has smoother surfaces and wide parting lines due to the violent forging process. If you take a small hammer and tap a forged crank, it rings like a bell with a long resonance afterward. A cast-iron crank rings, but not with the clarity and crispness of a forged crank. If you have a cracked crank, it doesn't ring at all or there is a buzzy resonance.

The billet crank begins life as a cylindrical steel ingot, which enters a labor-intensive process of many machining steps before it looks like a crankshaft. The reason you want a steel billet crank is its raw strength. It is the strongest crank you can buy for your Cleveland, especially if you intend to spin it above 8,000 rpm, use nitrous, or supercharge. The strength of a steel billet crank comes from its one-piece nature and alloy makeup, which has been machined into a crankshaft. Street Clevelands do not need a steel billet crank, which is purely a race piece for extreme-duty use.

Balancer and Flywheel

Harmonic balancers are generally elastomeric with an outer ring separated from the inner hub by a rubber shock band. Because all 335-series Clevelands are externally balanced, the balancer is part of the dynamic balancing process, as is the flywheel/flexplate. All Cleveland engines are 28.2-ounce offset balance.

I've always called this component the harmonic "balancer." However, it really is

This is the #650211 Fluidampr balancer for all Ford small-blocks prior to 1982 including the 351C. The Fluidampr balancer is a vicious fluid design that absorbs destructive vibration that can hammer a crankshaft and bearings. This damper adapts to your modifications, self-tuning in real time.

This important step is often forgotten, resulting in seal damage and leakage. Lube both the balancer hub and seal lip to ensure a smooth start-up before engine oil has a chance to get to the seal.

The ATI Performance Super Damper exceeds SFI safety standards and does an exceptional job of absorbing crankshaft torsional loads. Outer shells are available in aluminum or steel. The Super Damper is available in 28- or 50-ounce offset configurations.

Because all Clevelands are externally balanced, your balancing regimen must include a flywheel/flexplate and harmonic balancer. You can even take this to extremes and include a crank pulley, especially if you have a large one for driving accessories.

Cleveland Aftermarket Balancers

Manufacturer	Part Number	Specifics
Fluidampr	620200	6-1/4-inch diameter, no finish, 28-ounce imbalance
	650211	6-5/8-inch diameter, black zinc chromate color, external 28-ounce imbalance; non-SFI approved for street and mild race
	650231	6-5/8-inch diameter, black zinc chromate color, internal/neutral balance
Pioneer/Summit Racing	PIO-872007	6-1/2-inch diameter, nodular iron around elastomer; stock replacement balancer
	PIO-872027	6-1/2-inch diameter, steel billet, SFI Approved
ATI Performance/ Summit Racing	ATI-918900	Inner and outer shells available in aluminum or steel; has laser-engraved timing marks, black zinc chromate finish; SFI approved; takes the #916561 hub; available from Summit Racing
	ATI-918911	Inner and outer shells available in aluminum or steel; has laser-engraved timing marks, black zinc chromate finish; SFI approved; takes the #916562 hub; available from Summit Racing
Dorman/Summit Racing	RNB-594-277	Stock replacement balancer; available from Summit Racing
TCI Rattler/Summit Racing	TCI-870007	Pendulum-style dampener designed to control amplitudes of vibration and angle of crank twist; reduces vibration issues
	TCI-870010	Pendulum-style dampener designed to control amplitudes of vibration and angle of crank twist; reduces vibration issues; a racing balancer

This is a Pioneer off-the-shelf replacement balancer for the 351C, which is nothing more than a stock replacement from Summit Racing Equipment. I like the lasered-on timing marks that are easy to read. Always check the indexing of any new balancer to make sure timing marks are exactly where they belong.

Harmonic balancers tend to be overlooked; yet they're among the more important components to consider during a build-up. If you're going to spin your Cleveland above 7,000 rpm, you need an SFI-approved balancer for safety reasons.

a dampener (some call it a "damper"). It takes the destructive vibration of a spinning crank and absorbs torsional stresses from combustion pulses. Torsional stress and vibration come from torque placed on the crank as each piston rises on the compression/ignition stroke and the light-off exerts force on each journal. The piston and rod not only smack compression, but bounce off compression with combustion and linear force. Because this happens in rapid succession even at idle, it sets up a resonance, which is that weird wow and flutter you hear when two race cars roar down the track at the same time to create a musical harmony. Same thing happens to a crankshaft as well as other parts in the engine, especially at full throttle. The harmonic balancer absorbs destructive resonance by allowing a soft rebound with each pulse.

Harmonic balancers have two components designed to absorb vibration and help momentum. The outer ring and rubber elastomeric band absorb shock. In other words, as cylinders fire, the crank can twist as much as 1 to 2 degrees at wide-open throttle, which is a lot of movement. If it did this without something to absorb the twist, it could eventually break. The ring and rubber allow the crank to softly rebound from twist with less shock. There is also mass—a counterweight—that counteracts the twist. Think of the balancer's counterweight as a dampener that works hand in hand with the ring and rubber.

Because harmonic balancers have to cope with vibration, centrifugal force, and the elements of heat, ozone, and road film, they deteriorate and should be replaced from time to time. Harmonic balancers ordinarily last the life of an engine build, which means you need a new one when you build.

All 351C, 400, and 351M engines have four-bolt harmonic balancers. And in case you didn't know, Ford V-8s had three-bolt balancers prior to 1970. Beginning in 1970, all had four-bolt.

Choosing a harmonic balancer depends on how you intend to use your Cleveland. Street engines need little more than a stock steel over rubber over iron balancer. If you're going to really spin your Cleveland, you want a balancer engineered to dampen the vibration and smooth out the spin. You also want an SFI-approved balancer engineered to stay together at high RPM. Harmonic balancers dampen the "spring" effect of an engine's crankshaft.

ATI Performance pretty much pioneered the race-ready harmonic balancer. Each type of ATI balancer is engineered for a specific engine family based on a lot of research and development time for each type.

What makes the ATI dampener unique is its design using rubber O-rings, which are there to take up the inertia (the back–and-forth twisting of the crank). ATI dampeners go the distance when they're chosen based on a particular application. Choose a high-performance aftermarket balancer based on the kind of driving you intend to do. It takes a seasoned professional to see what has happened to a balancer over the course of time and use.

Fluidampr, manufacturer of high-performance balancers, says, "Torsional vibration is not a one-time occurrence. This happens across every cylinder at varying levels, with every power stroke through one revolution of the crankshaft. These occurrences are referred to as the order. In a V-8, four cylinders fire in one crankshaft rotation; hence there are four orders of torsional vibration. In a V-6, there are three orders. In an in-line four, there are two orders.

"Often the last order in the revolution contains the highest spike of damaging vibration. That is for one revolution. In a V-8 at 4,500-rpm peaks of varying vibration frequency occurs 18,000 times per minute! [four orders per revolution at 4,500 rpm]. Torsional vibration and the violent twisting and rebounding of the crankshaft happens so fast, it is not visible by the naked eye."

In other words, engines are self-destructive due to vibration issues along their crankshafts. A good harmonic balancer reduces, but never completely eliminates, torsional vibration. It reduces destructive cyclic fatigue allowing more precise engine operation along with extending crankshaft life. Despite all the best efforts of harmonic balancer manufacturers, cranks fail from time to time, with most breaking at the fillet radius.

Pistons

Piston selection boils down to what you want your Cleveland to do. When you're planning an engine, you tend

Compression comes not only from piston profile, but from everything in between BDC and TDC. Valve reliefs, no matter how small, constitute negative dish, taking away from compression. Any dome adds to compression. Then, add head gasket thickness and the area above rings and you lose even more compression.

This is a Speed Pro 4.030-inch forged piston for the 351C-2V open chamber head. All you have here are two valve reliefs in a flattop piston. The 351C-4V and 302C wedge head piston is a different experience entirely.

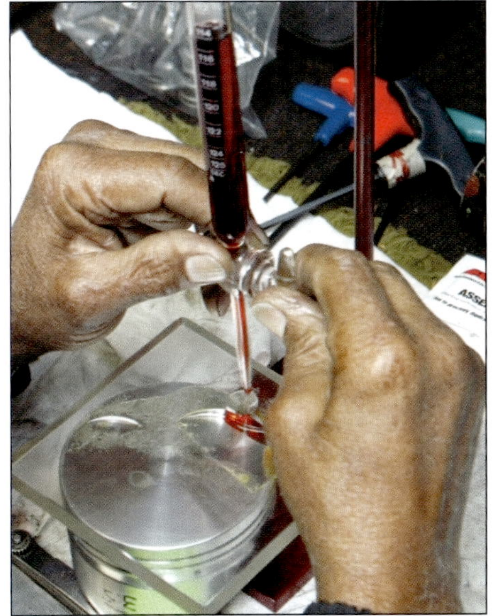

Marvin McAfee of MCE Engines calculates compression by measuring volume on everything between piston dome and chamber. Here, he measures the piston's negative volume, or dish, which takes away from compression. This piston isn't dished; however, it has valve reliefs.

You have a number of choices when it comes to piston rings, conventional, gapless, file-to-fit, ready to install. When it comes to any piston ring with an end gap, check the end gap—no exceptions. Cleveland piston ring end gaps should be .010 to .020 inch. On the wider side for high-performance applications.

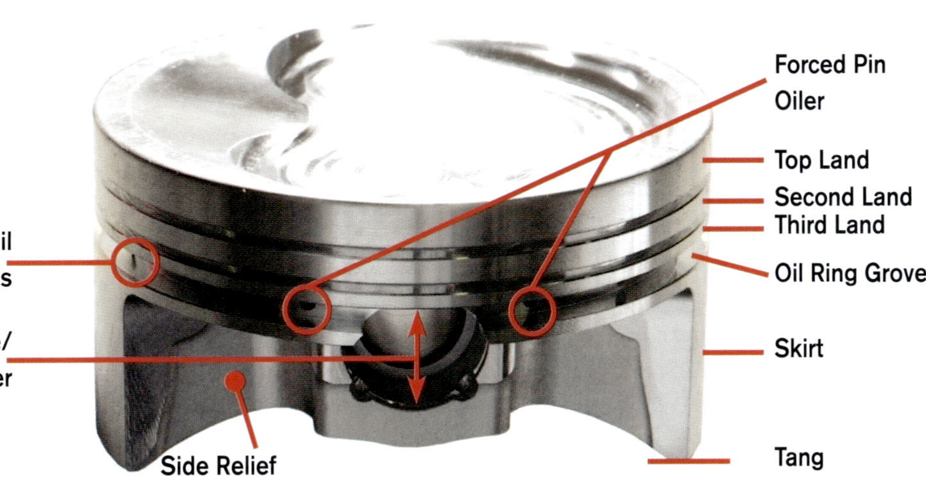

This drawing illustrates piston anatomy. This is helpful anytime you order pistons. Not all engine projects are off-the-shelf though that is the best approach. Sometimes, you have to order custom pistons. (Photo Courtesy JE Pistons)

Ring end gapping can be performed a couple of different ways. To get the ring perfectly square in the bore, you may use Summit Racing's #SME-906002 piston ring squaring tool. There's also a complete kit from Summit, the #SUM-CSUM2505 piston ring filer combo that enables you to square the ring, gap it, and file to fit. There's also Total Seal for billet piston ring squaring tools.

Although every engine builder has their own technique for piston ring installation, the best approach is a ring expander installation tool over rolling rings on. Rolling rings on can cause distortion.

Piston ring end gaps are ground to width with a manual or motorized grinder. Soften any sharp edges that can cause a ring to hang up or damage piston and cylinder wall.

Piston ring gaps should be positioned at 90-degree increments around the piston to get them off to a good start though you can expect them to move. What you hope for is that they move uniformly.

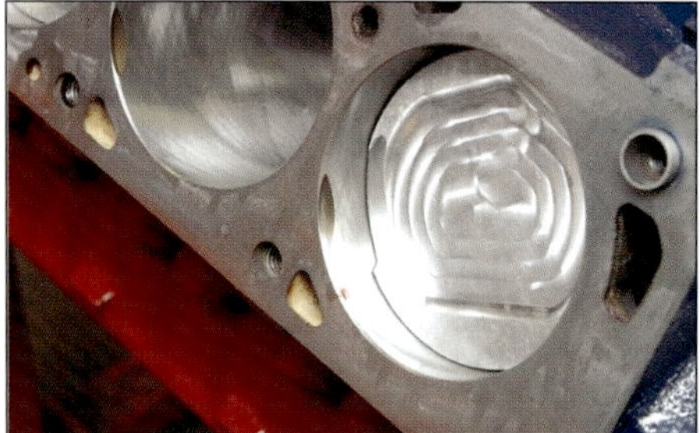

When you stroke the 351C to 408 ci with a Speed-O-Motive kit, it becomes necessary to dish pistons to keep compression conservative. Note the valve relief at the deck to clear huge 2.190-inch intake valves. Piston also has a large valve relief for the same reason.

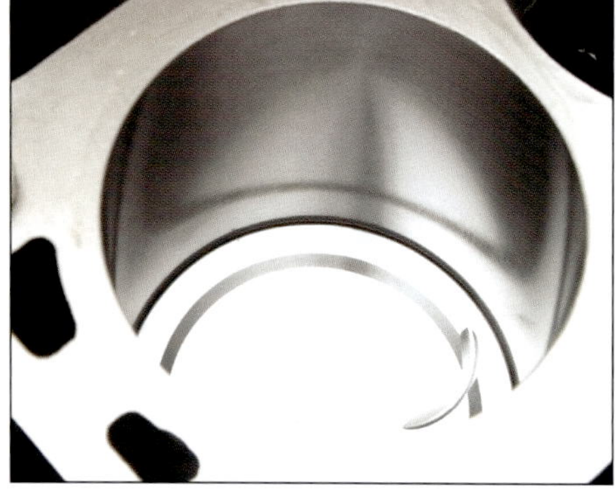

You get two elements from increased stroke—a greater air/fuel charge and the mechanical advantage of additional stroke. This is why you use a dished piston to keep compression in check.

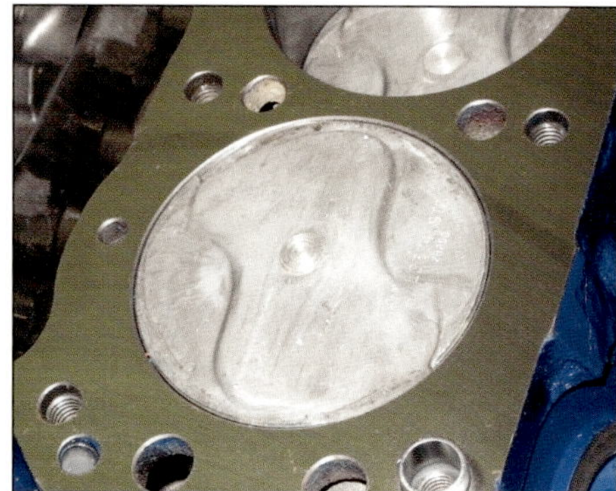

The 351C-4V piston has a dome engineered to fit the closed 64-cc wedge chamber yielding more than 11.0:1 compression. Boss 302 piston is quite similar for use with the same chamber.

to go overboard and build more engine than you actually need. It is best to watch your money and build an engine as conservatively as possible. If you're building a Cleveland for a daily driver, weekend cruiser, or tow vehicle, you don't need a steel crank, H-beam rods, or forged pistons. Even if you intend to spin your Cleveland to 6,500 rpm on occasion, you can get away with a cast crank, stock rods, and cast or hypereutectic pistons.

Choosing a piston evolves from material to dimensions, which can get tricky if you don't know what you're doing. This is why you want to be knowledgeable about crank throw, block deck height, compression height, and more. It is so easy to get this wrong and wind up with pistons that don't fit. This is why you must first select a crank and rod before settling on a piston. Manufacturers make this easy because engine kits typically include pistons. Because Cleveland engines aren't as common as Windsors and 385-series big-blocks, it's tougher to find a stroker kit with everything you need.

Cast

Cast pistons are the most basic type you can stuff into an engine. The Mahle ECOFORM cast piston is designed for modern engine building because it is a lighter piston thanks to fresh casting technology and it is more durable than your average cast piece. The Mahle cast ECOFORM pistons are 20 to 25 percent lighter than cast pistons the company was making 16 years ago. This feature enables you to get good throttle response from a Cleveland because there's less reciprocating weight to sling around.

All cast pistons have a certain amount of silicon (sand) in them for strength and hardness. The thing is, cast pistons are also brittle and can't take the kind of extreme shock loads and heat that forged pistons can. This is where you need to know up front how you're going to use your Cleveland. What you get from a cast piston is stability, with predictable expansion properties and quiet cold operation.

Forged

Forged pistons cost considerably more because they call for many more manufacturing steps to get a finished product. Once molten piston forgings are slammed (forged) into shape under very high pressure, they have to be machined through a series of complex steps.

What makes forged pistons more challenging is what the machinist has to think about during the block machining process. Because forged pistons possess greater expansion properties, the machinist has to allow for this in the way cylinders are bored and honed to size. There has to be sufficient piston to cylinder wall clearances.

The first company to develop forged pistons was Federal-Mogul's Sealed Power division in the 1960s. There were learning curves, as you saw with the Boss 302 engine in 1969–1970 with cracked piston skirts and other failure issues causing a lot of warranty claims and engine replacements. Sealed Power developed forged pistons using the VMS75 aluminum alloy, which has been a factory piston alloy for many years. The aftermarket industry utilizes the 2618 alloy for racing pistons with great success because it can withstand up to 575 degrees F. One shortcoming of 2618 is hardness. It isn't as hard as another widely used alloy known as 4032, which has higher amounts of silicon, which makes aluminum allows very hard. The 4032 piston makes more sense for street and racing use.

As always, chat with your favorite piston manufacturer for best results before making a decision. Make sure you speak with an engineer or sales person qualified to help you make a decision.

Hypereutetic

Hypereutectic pistons are a nice compromise between cast and forged. Though "hypereutectic" sounds high tech, the process has been around since 1902. Hypereutectic indicates a high-silicon cast piston, which is made of a harder material, yet without the expansion issues you see with forged pistons. Hypereutectic pistons are more durable than cast without the high price tag and those expansion issues just mentioned.

Though cast pistons have their place, hypereutectic pistons make sense as a base piston selection for any Cleveland build because they are more durable than cast yet don't have the issues you see with forged. Hypereutectic is a mixture of alloys melted together at just above the point where they become liquid. This is an oversimplification, but suffice it to say it defines how alloys are melted together temperature-wise. In other words, hypereutectic is a process of the way alloys are blended together. As I understand it from those who design pistons, cast pistons have roughly 10-percent silicon in the aluminum alloy. The hypereutectic piston has higher amounts of silicon, which calls for heat-treating until the silicon blends into the aluminum creating a harder surface. Make no mistake, a hypereutectic piston is not a forged piston nor does it have the same strength.

Connecting Rods

There were two factory connecting rods used in the 335-series engine family: one for the 351C and one for the 351M and 400 engines. The 351C rod is 5.780 inches from center to center and has a D0AE forging number. The longer 351M/400 rod is 6.580 inches center to center and has a D1AE forging number. There may be revised Ford forging and part numbers, but basic rod dimensions

Though there are a lot of opinions regarding fastener use, the lion's share of engine builders suggests replacement of all fasteners. Stud the main journals and use ARP rod bolts. Always lubricate fastener threads and use a torque wrench.

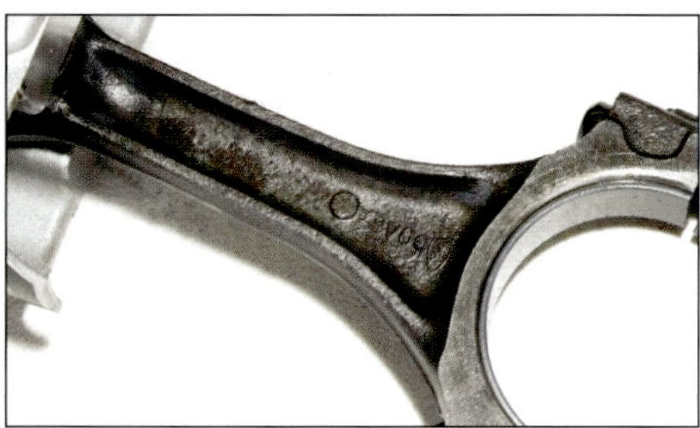
There are two factory 335-series connecting rods: the 351C and the 400. The 351C rod is 5.780 inches center to center with a .927-inch wrist pin. The 400 rod is 6.580 inches center to center with a .975-inch wrist pin and is also used in the 351M. If you see this D0AE-A forging number, odds are quite good you've found a 351C rod. The 351M/400 rod carries D1AE-AA. In any case, measure center to center and wrist pin for confirmation.

Rod reconditioning includes resizing to get the big end true again. New 3/8-inch ARP bolts are installed to make these stock rods whole again.

All 335 engines (351C, 400, 351M) have a 2.130-inch rod journal with 3/8-inch bolts. This is a Ford-tested, tough connecting rod that stands up to a lot of punishment given proper prep. Fresh ARP bolts, stress riser removal, and shotpeening makes these rods super durable.

The key to durability is precision machine and assembly work. Never take Ford's recommended tolerances as suggestions; take them as gospel. The best dimensions to go with are factory numbers. If you're going racing, open up those tolerances a little (within the factory window) to allow for heat extremes.

All bearings should be installed bone dry between the bearing and the block for security and good crush. Check oil galley and groove alignment. This should be part of your mock-up. If you have to remove bearings that have already been "crushed" with the crank installed, replace the bearings and try it again. If you reinstall bearings, you lose crush and bearing security.

remain the same. Rod journal size for all Cleveland engines is 2.130 inches, with the only difference being rod length and wrist pin size. This makes rod selection simple, with one rod for each block type.

If you're going with a stock crank and rods, connecting rods have to be inspected, reconditioned, shotpeened, and fitted with new ARP 3/8-inch bolts. This process makes your stock rods the best they can be. Reconditioning should include removal of stress risers to reduce

Rod sizing and clearancing are both crucial to internal friction and durability. You want side clearances and bearing/journal clearances to be such that you have good oil flow and heat dissipation without having too much clearance. Ford says .010- to .020-inch side clearance with a maximum wear limit of .023 inch. You want your clearances smack in the middle.

Connecting rod side clearances should be .010 to .020 inch—closer to the maximum when you're going to push it. The reason you want larger clearances is for heat and expansion room. By the same token, you don't want too much clearance so you jeopardize piston/rod to crank journal alignment.

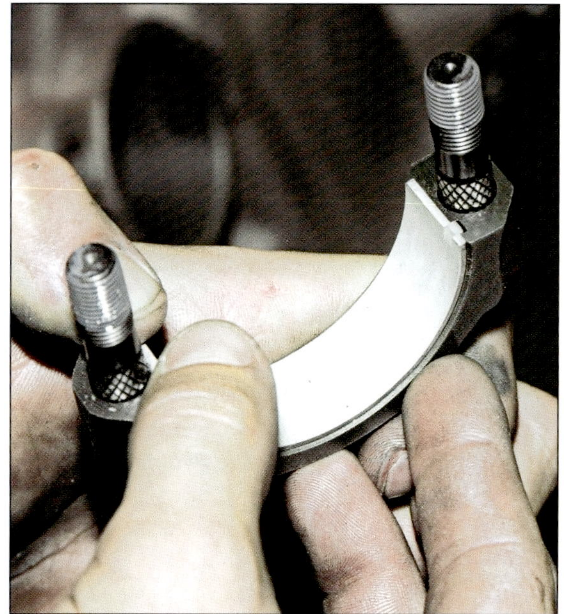

When a rod's large end is machined to specifications, you should get good bearing crush and security. Keep your oily fingers off bearing-to-bore contact surfaces.

Reconditioning connecting rods involves cutting caps and machining the large end back to original sizing (2.4361 to 2.4369 inches) per your Ford Shop Manual. Rods need to be reconditioned because the large end becomes egg shaped over time and reciprocation.

This is a heavy-duty Eagle 6.000-inch I-beam rod for the 393 Cleveland with a 3.850-inch-stroke, cast-steel crank.

H-Beam rods (left) are stronger and well suited to steel cranks. I-beam rods (right) can be applied to both cast and steel cranks.

Here is an Eagle H-beam 6.000-inch rod for the 393-ci Cleveland with a 3.850-inch-stroke, 4340 steel crank.

These Scat I-beam rods are of different lengths: 5.400 inches (left) and 5.090 inches (right). The longer the rod in relation to stroke, the greater the rod ratio. Having the longest rod possible in relation to stroke gives you greater piston dwell time at each end of the bore.

the risk of rod failure. The large end is resized and centered. The small end should be checked for irregularities. The 351C rod has a .927-inch wrist pin. The 400's is larger at .975 inch.

Displacement

Without question the greatest power investment you can make is in displacement. With displacement comes compression you can dial into your build. Displacement and compression remain the quickest paths to power. You want to keep compression conservative, around 10.0:1, if you're running pump gas. You can stroke a 351C to approximately 408 ci with some room to spare. The 400 block can be stroked to approximately 460 ci with stroker kits or a modest selection of parts.

When manufacturers started producing 351C stroker kits, the approach was to turn down main journals to 2.750 inches and get the 400's 4.000-inch stroke into a 351C; in fact, 408 ci with a 4.030-inch bore. Now that new stroker kits are being produced, it isn't necessary to find a 400 crank for your 351C unless that's what you want. And if you have a choice, don't waste your money on a 351M. Instead, take your 351M/400 block and go with as much displacement as you can, as much as 460 ci, to wake up this sleeping giant.

For all the negative talk about building a 400 Cleveland, there's a lot you can do with this engine thanks to its lighter weight and generous deck height. Within every 400 beats 500 to 600 hp and comparable torque waiting to come out. However, most people don't want that much power. Most building 400s want torque for either racing or towing/hauling. So the message here is more about torque than horsepower.

Rod Ratio

When you're looking for a stroker package, rod ratio should be a chief consideration, but not necessarily the

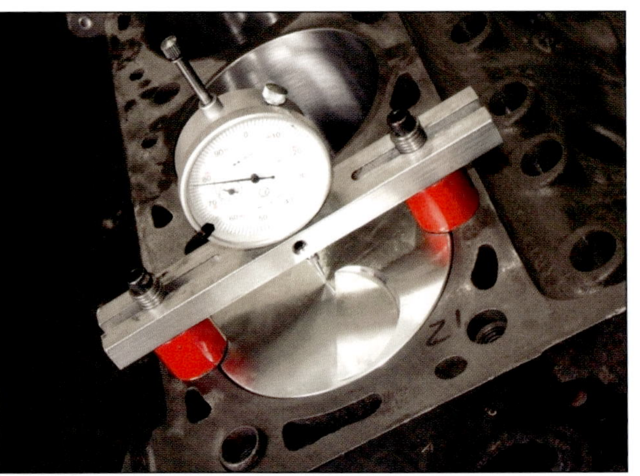

You check deck height as a part of determining compression with a dial indicator. This is also the time to determine true TDC.

When you torque fasteners, do it slowly and methodically. Torque fasteners in three phases. Never jerk a torque wrench to get your value. You want a smooth application of torque. Tighten main caps one at a time, then, check crank rotation before moving on.

All bolt threads and holes should be chased and cleaned to get accurate torque. Once clean, they must be lubricated.

only one. Rod ratio is connecting rod length divided by stroke. The distance a piston travels is cast in stone by crankshaft stroke. How quickly it travels in each direction and how long it sits at each end of the bore is determined by connecting rod length, or rod ratio. The longer a piston dwells, depending upon cam profile, the more productive your air/fuel charge. You want as much connecting rod as you can fit into the block without consequence, meaning excessive cylinder wall and bottom-end loading.

With a longer connecting rod comes mechanical advantage. To determine the maximum length of rod you can get into a block, use this formula:

Maximum Rod Length = block deck height – (compression height + 1/2 stroke length)

As much as we express disrespect for the 351M as one example, it employs one of the best rod ratios there is thanks to its long 6.650-inch connecting rod borrowed from the 400. Yet the 351M makes little sense when there's so much displacement you can cram into the 400 block.

The 400 block has plenty of room for displacement if you exercise both imagination and reality. It has been debated how much displacement you can roll into this block. One forum I visited claimed as much as 492 ci with a 4.750-inch stroke and a .060-inch overbore. I think 492 ci is a reach for the 400 block. From a durability standpoint, I'd go no greater than 4.500 inches of stroke with a 6.800-inch rod for somewhere around 450 ci with a 1.51:1 rod ratio. And if you're going to extremes, sonic check cylinder walls before making a decision.

Cleveland Rod Ratio Index

Engine	*Stroke (inches)*	*Rod Length (inches)*	*Rod Ratio*
351C	3.500	5.700	1.63:1
351M	3.500	6.650	1.90:1
383C	3.750	5.850	1.56:1
408C	4.000	6.000	1.50:1
426C	4.170	6.000	1.44:1
400	4.000	6.650	1.66:1
434	4.250	6.658	1.57:1

Cleveland Stroker Kits

Thirty years ago, you needed a lot of imagination and talent to increase a Cleveland's stroke. For a 351C, you had to turn down a 400 crank's main journals and find the right rod and custom piston, or you had to offset grind a 351C crank to get more displacement. These days, you have quite a choice when it comes to 351C and 400 stroker kits but don't waste valuable cash on parts you do not need. A steel crank and H-beam rods are good for bench racing and tough talk when you're building a street engine; however, you really don't need them. A cast-steel crank, heavy-duty I-beam rods, and hypereutectic pistons work very well in a street Cleveland. With additional stroke and displacement, you mostly get torque, which is what you want on the street.

On the stroker piston (right), the wrist pin is pushed deep into the ring lands. This configuration enables you to haul the piston deeper in the bore offering more displacement and stroke. The piston on the left is a stock version.

When you're building a Cleveland stroker, always do a mock-up first to determine clearances. All moving parts must clear by at least .060 inch.

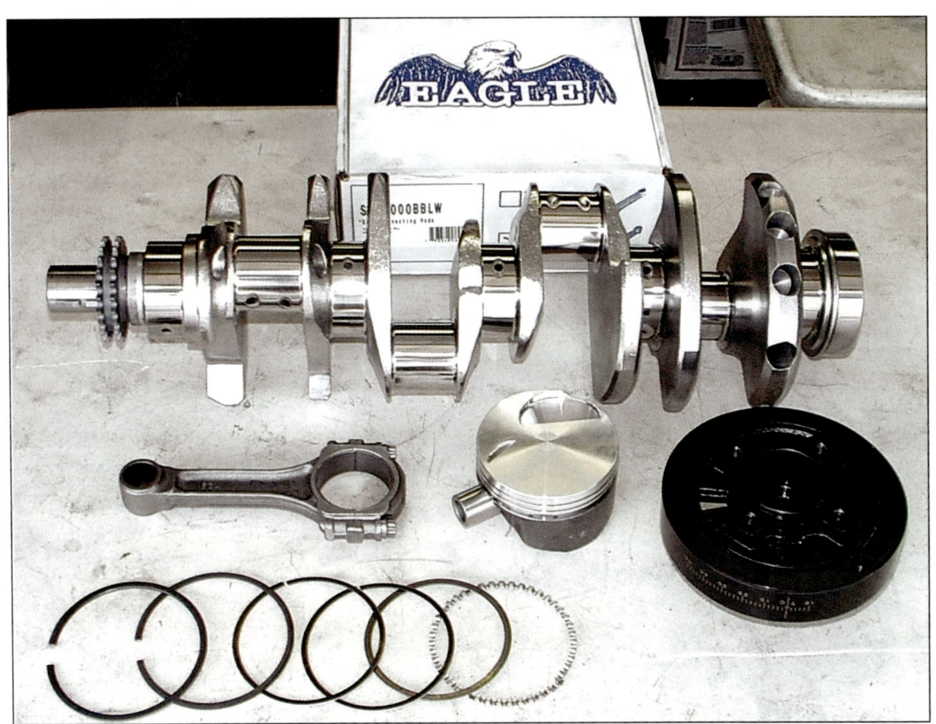

Eagle's 351C budget stroker kit (PN 16800) with a cast-steel crank and heavy-duty I-beam rods with cap screw bolts gives you generous displacement (393 to 395 ci) for approximately $1,300. You get 3.850 inches of stroke and 6.000 inches of rod (center to center) along with 3.0-cc negative-dish SRP forged pistons.

When you get down to serious weekend or full-time racing you want the steel crank, heavy-duty I-beam or H-beam rods, and forged pistons. You want parts that can take the extremes of nitrous, supercharging, or turbocharging. Any time you're pushing power numbers beyond 450 without aided induction (nitrous or blower), you need to seriously consider a steel crank, heavy-duty I- or H-beam rods, and forged pistons. You want a bottom end that stays together under most circumstances. You also want to plan ahead if you intend to pump up the power later on. If you're planning a hotter cam, bigger heads, and any form of serious racing down the road, build for these upgrades now.

Today, there are a variety of stroker kits available for the 351C and 400 engines. Good, proven sources for bottom-end kits are Coast High Performance, StrokerKits.com, Scat Enterprises, Eagle, MME Racing, and TMeyer depending on what Cleveland you're building and what you intend to do with it.

Bottom line with a stroker is: Treat it like a big-block because you now have big-block displacement, be it 408 or 460 ci. Cooling system capacity must increase along with induction, cylinder head port/valve size, cam selection, and exhaust scavenging.

Sweat the Details

There's blueprinting an engine, and then there's *really* blueprinting an engine. It isn't only about precision machine work and dynamic balance; it is getting all eight cylinders marching in unison with one another. You want identical compression ratio across the board; as close as you can get it. And you want bearing and piston/cylinder wall tolerances as uniform as possible. But, it goes

Cleveland Engine Bottom End Tolerances

Cylinder Block	Dimension (inches)
Bore Limits	4.000 to 4.036
Maximum Out-of-Round	.001
Bore Wear Limit	.005
Bore Surface Finish RMS	15 to 35 RMS
Main Bearing Bore Diameter	2.9417 to 2.9429 (351C)
	3.1922 to 3.1930 (351M/400)
Lifter Bore Diameter	0.8752 to 0.8767
Distributor Shaft Pilot Bore	0.5160 to 0.5175
Deck Trueness	0.003 in any 6-inch direction or 0.007 overall
Deck Surface RMS	90 to 150

Crankshaft	Dimension (inches)
Main Journal Diameter	2.7484 to 2.7492 (351C)
	2.9994 to 3.0002 (351M/400)
Main Journal Runout Maximum	.004 (351C)
	.002 (351M/400)
Main Journal Taper Maximum	.0003 per inch maximum (351C)
	.0005 per inch maximum
(351M/400)	
Main Journal Thrust Face Runout	.001
Thrust Journal Length	1.124 to 1.126 (351C)
	1.137 to 1.139 (351M/400)
Main Journal Finish RMS Maximum	12 journal, 20 rear (351C)
	12 journal, 25 rear (351M/400)
Connecting Rod Journal Diameter	2.3103 to 2.3111
Connecting Rod Journal Maximum Taper	.0004 per inch (351C)
	.0003 per inch (351M/400)
Crankshaft Free Endplay	.004 to .010
Crank To Rear Face Runout	.005
Flywheel/Clutch Face Runout	.010
Flywheel O.D. Runout	.018 manual, .020 automatic (351C)
	.020 automatic (351M/400)
Main Bearing Clearances	.0010 to .0015 (351C)
	.0009 to .0026 allowable
	.0011 to .0015 (351M/400)
	.0011 to .0028 allowable
Bearing Wall Thickness	.0959 to .0962 (351C)
	.0957 to .0962 (351M/400)
	Add .0010 to standard thickness

Crankshaft (continued)	Dimension (inches)
Rod Bearing Clearances	.0011 to .0015
	.0008 to .0026 allowable (351C)
	.0011 to .0026 allowable
(351M/400)	
Rod Bearing Wall Thickness	.0620 to .0626
	Add .0010 to standard thickness

Connecting Rods	Dimension (inches)
Piston Pin/Bore Diameter	.9104 to .9112 (351C)
	.9734 to .9742 (351M/400)
Rod Bearing Bore Diameter	2.4361 to .2.4369
Connecting Rod Length	5.7785 to 5.7815 (351C)
	6.5785 to 6.5815 (351M/400)
Rod Alignment/Distortion	Bend, .004; Twist, .012
Rod Side Clearance	.010 to .020; Wear Limit, .023

Pistons (stock cast)	Dimension (inches)
Piston to Cylinder Wall	.0014 to .0022
Piston Pin Bore Diameter	.9122 to .9125 (351C)
	.9754 to .9757 (351M/400)
Piston Pin Diameter	.9119 to .9124 (351C)
	.9130 to .9133 Oversize (351C)
	.9749 to .9754 (351M/400)
Piston Pin Length	3.010 to .3.040 (351C)
	3.150 to 3.170 (351M/400)
Pin to Piston Clearance	.0003 to .0005; Limit is .0008
Ring Groove Width	Top Ring .080 to .081
	Middle Ring .080 to .081
	Oil Ring .1880 to .1870
Ring Width	Top Ring .077 to .078
	Middle Ring .077 to .078
Ring Side Clearance	Top Ring .002 to .004
	Middle Ring .002 to .004
	Oil Rings Snug
Ring End Gap Width	Top Ring .010 to .020
	Middle Ring .010 to .020
	Oil Ring Rail .015 to .069
	Wear Limit for Compression Rings .006

Tips for Buying a Stroker Kit

Ronnie Besselman of Bessel Motorsports, better known as www.strokerkits.com, offers excellent advice on how to shop for a stroker kit for your Cleveland.

- Go for the longest connecting rod possible to minimize frictional losses and reduce side loading. This also makes for a quieter engine.
- Use the lightest bottom end components possible, which frees up power and improves efficiency.
- Use a windage tray and pan that keep oil away from the crank and rods (windage). You want effective lubrication. You just don't want it hindering power and efficiency.
- Remember, when you add stroke (displacement), you no longer have a 351 or a 400. You have a larger engine. Go with cylinder heads, cam profile, and headers that are up to the task.
- Be sure to tighten up cam lobe centerline to optimum by 1 degree for every 16 ci of displacement increase.
- Increase valve lift proportionately with displacement because you're moving more air.
- Increase induction capacity to keep up with displacement.
- Keep the induction system cool, which is important with a stroker.
- Increase header capacity (pipe size) at the primaries, secondaries, and collectors.

even deeper than that. Real blueprinting involves removing the ragged edges and stress risers to where you minimize the risk of scoring and failure.

You want to become a taskmaster for detail. Chase every bolt and bolt hole to get threads dead perfect and smooth because you want accurate torque readings. Once all the thread chasing and clean-up work is performed, lubricate bolt threads with SAE 30 weight engine oil or moly lube—be sure that you never fill the hole with oil. Excessive oil in bolt holes means you risk cracking the block because you cannot compress a liquid. If you torque the bolt with no way for oil to escape you will "hydraulic" the casting with an ugly crack. When you install studs instead of bolts, never bottom the stud out. Allow roughly 1/8 to 1/4 inch of gap at the bottom to allow room to eliminate this risk.

When torque is applied on a stud or bolt you want tension on the shank and threads. It is bolt or stud stretch and tension that provide clamping power on main and rod caps and other components.

Seal installation requires extreme attention to detail. Always install the harmonic balancer before the oil pan so you may inspect the lip-retention spring. If the spring pops off, the seal leaks. Seal lip and spring must always be turned inward, never outward. Springs tend to pop off during balancer installation, which is why you want an abundance of lubrication on the balancer and lip.

Placing harmonic balancers in boiling water makes the balancer expand so it can be pressed onto the crank by hand. No hammer or press-on tool is required. As the balancer cools, it contracts and becomes tight on the crank.

Choice of clutch pilot bushing or bearing boils down to what you want. Smooth clutch and transmission operation come from an input shaft that rolls smoothly in a bearing. Bushings cost less but you get what you pay for. Bushings wear out more quickly causing shaft sideplay and clutch chatter.

Lubrication

When Ford was developing its 335 Cleveland engine family, the objective was to produce a large engine family with displacements ranging from 335 to beyond 400 ci as a companion to the larger 385-series 429/460-ci big-block engines.

Although the Cleveland has been conceived to consolidate engine families/displacements and lower manufacturing costs, it was also a high-performance V-8 with its beefy bottom end, poly-angle valves, wedge chambers, huge ports, and dry-manifold induction system. To lower manufacturing costs, Ford had to reduce the number of machining and manufacturing steps, one of which resulted in fewer oil galleys. Although this really hasn't had an adverse effect on street engines, it has plagued racers and hard-core performance buffs.

The 335-series oiling system is different from the 289/302/351W small-block in that there's one less oil galley, resulting in two galleys along the lifter bores. Oil is drawn to the pump from a front or mid-sump pan, then passed to a main horizontal oil galley across the front of the block where it leads to both cam bearings and main bearing journals, then up to the lifter galleys.

The problem with this approach is oil starvation to main and rod bearing journals at high RPM. Main and rod bearings share oil with the lifter galleys. Traditionally, mains and rods always had an exclusive oil galley. Starvation really isn't a fair way to put it, however, because high-performance street Clevelands have adequate oil supply to all critical points throughout the engine proving Ford engineers did their job well. However, when you spin a Cleveland to high RPM (above 6,000), oil starvation exists at main and rod journals mostly.

When Ford developed the 427 FE side-oiler, it conceived the perfect lubrication system for a high-performance V-8 with the pressure relief valve installed in the block instead of the pump, which kept pressure and volume high throughout the system. This, of course, made manufacturing quite expensive and impractical for mass production. The 351C oiling system is typical of most mass-produced V-8s of the era with the pressure relief

One issue facing some Cleveland blocks is oil galley indexing at main bearing saddles. If your block isn't indexed at the bearing oil slots, chamfer the block oil passages to allow for larger volume.

From a practical standpoint, there's really nothing wrong with the Cleveland oiling system. It makes good use of oil galleys with uniform flow to cam bearings, main and rod journals, lifters, and valvetrain. Where it falls short is in uniform distribution to these locations at high RPM.

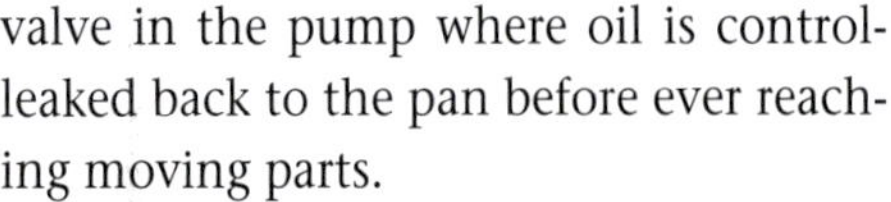

Two lifter galleys run the length of this block without the need for a third. Both are primary oil passageways for crank, cam, and lifters with an additional galley at the back of the block for additional flow.

MCE Engines carry oil system blueprinting into galleys and passages by radiusing all passages and transitions to eliminate fluid turbulence and foaming.

valve in the pump where oil is control-leaked back to the pan before ever reaching moving parts.

This problem is corrected when you limit oil flow to cam bearings and lifters and divert more of it to main and rod journals where it is needed most. While you're at it, you need to increase volume and pressure to some degree with a high-volume oil pump and some adjustment to the pressure relief valve as necessary.

Use a Melling or Ford Racing high-volume oil pump and never install it without first inspecting and blueprinting. The Cleveland's oil pump is different with its screw-in oil pick-up, another example of cost control within this engine family.

Pump Blueprinting

Marvin McAfee of MCE Engines in Los Angeles has been described by Jim Smart of *Mustang Monthly Magazine* as something of a West Coast Smokey Yunick because he looks at engines in ways most of us never have. McAfee's approach to engine building is methodical with extreme attention to detail. Without exception is his approach to the oil pump, which McAfee stresses must never be installed right out of the box.

"Blueprinting" is not simply engine tuning;. real blueprinting takes a closer look at things engine builders don't always examine. Most owners install oil pumps right out of the box assuming all bases have been covered. However, oil pumps are not foolproof. They may come out of the box with all kinds of flaws and machining errors. And unless you inspect them and measure critical clearances, you're rolling the dice on more than just an oil pump.

You don't have to take your blueprinting as far as MCE Engines does; however, there are three items you definitely need to check: G-rotor endplay, radial clearances for a full 360 degrees, and pressure relief valve function/spring pressure. If the pressure relief valve piston binds in any way, you need to chase the bore with a small ball hone until the piston glides smoothly with lubrication. If radial clearances are tight, have a machine shop examine and bore as necessary or return the pump. Rotor end clearances must fall somewhere between the minimum and maximum allowable

All pump rotor clearances must be checked. Rotor endplay should be .001 to .004 inch. Radial clearance should be .006 to .013 inch. Shaft to housing bore clearance should be .0015 to .0029 inch. If clearances are not with Ford specifications, reject the pump.

Clean up the oil pressure relief valve bore with a ball hone, then, check for freedom of valve movement. Spring pressure should be 23.6 to 24.6 pounds at 1.37 inches. If you desire more pressure, add shims one at a time.

Never use a stock oil pump shaft. Instead, order an ARP shaft (PN 154-7905) to ensure durability. The ARP shaft is made of premium aerospace grade steel and is heat-treated to 200,000 psi. If you shear an ARP shaft, you've got bigger problems than just the shaft.

measurements. If there's too much clearance, you can have the housing milled to size or return the pump and hope for a better core.

Oil Control

There are several approaches engine builders use with Cleveland oiling systems. Two are basically the same modification with slight variations in how they are performed. Another involves external plumbing, which routes oil from the front of the block to the back to improve bottom-end oiling, which isn't all that effective. Yet another approach involves lifter bore sleeves that restrict oil flow to the cam and top end, which is effective and easy to perform.

All five cam bearings are turned to the 4 o'clock position to redirect oil flow as shown in yellow.

When the Cleveland was introduced and used in NASCAR competition, an internally plumbed oiling system was used to feed journals number 2, 3, and 4 through drilled passages in the lifter galleys. But this is an unnecessary modification for a street or weekend racing engine. And if you're running hydraulic lifters, you don't want to take too much oil away from the lifter galleys.

The Cleveland oil system's main shortcoming is too much oil to the cam bearings and lifters and not enough to the main and rod journals. So you conduct modifications that get more oil to the mains and a more conservative amount to cam journals.

The easiest oil system modification is restrictor plugs between main and cam bearing journals, which limit oil flow to cam bearings and lifters while holding more oil below for main and rod journals. Of course this isn't as simple as screwing restrictor plugs in a block and moving on. You've got to know exactly what you're doing or face the consequences of oil starvation where you need it most.

Tim Meyer of TMeyer, Inc., employs one oil restrictor plug, which gets more oil at the mains and rods and less at the cam and lifters. Though he uses a very common approach to Cleveland oil control, some cam manufacturers discourage this practice due to concern about oil starvation at the cam, lifters, and valvetrain with hydraulic lifters. It has worked successfully for Meyer and without oil starvation.

In your Cleveland engine building plan, always use a high-volume oil pump and perform a detailed blueprinting before installation. Check rotor-side clearances and the pressure relief valve for proper operation. If you want more pressure, add shims to increase pressure. However, be very careful about this because you don't want too much pressure. You want a maximum of 10 psi per 1,000 rpm.

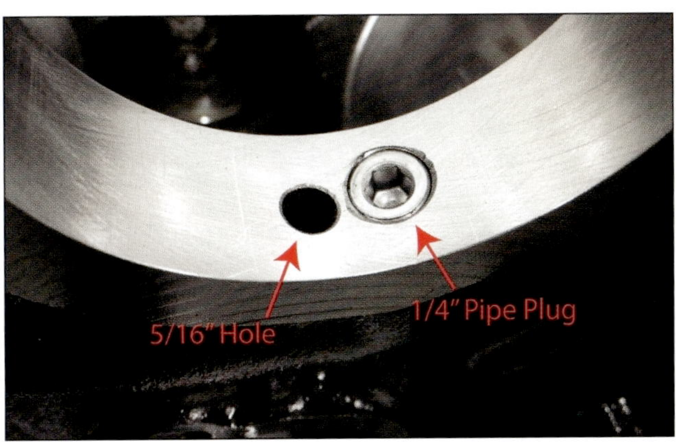

Tim Meyer's approach is to keep more oil at the crank and less upstairs with a 1/4-inch pipe plug (right) and 5/16-inch passage (center).

MCE Engines believes timing sets don't get enough oil in Clevelands or Windsors. You can go the extra mile by drilling a .020-inch oil hole in the oil galley end plug as shown, which keeps a stream of hot oil going to the timing set and doesn't hurt oil pressure. Shown here is a 351W, but it is the same for Cleveland engines.

MME Racing utilizes lifter bore sleeves to increase oil flow to mains by reducing oil flow to cam and lifters. This allows adequate oil flow to cam and lifters, improves oil control, and provides lifter stability.

Oil Pan

Choosing an oil pan is easy and depends on what kind of driving you intend to do. Drag racers need a deep-sump, high-capacity oil pan for heat transfer and lubrication no matter how wild and crazy things become. If you're going to be cutting the apexes and rounding turns, you want a high-capacity, baffled road race pan and the appropriate pick-up to keep a steady supply of oil to the pump.

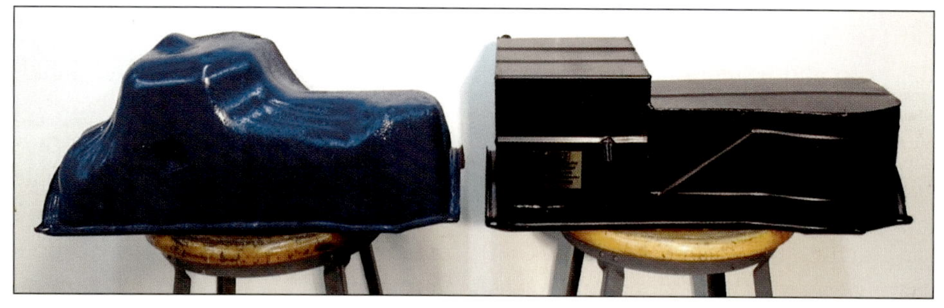

On the left is an F-Series/Bronco mid-sump Cleveland oil pan. On the right is a high-capacity version, which is also a front-sump pan used primarily in passenger cars.

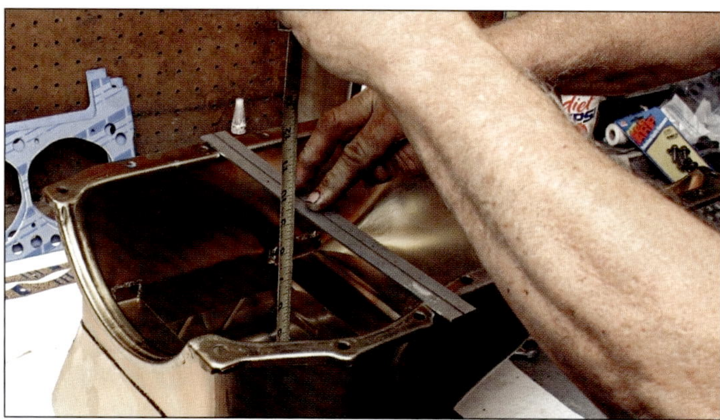

Pump pick-up and pan depth should be checked to ensure you have at least 1/4- to 3/8-inch clearance between pick-up and pan. Because the Cleveland pick-up is a screw-in pipe, you can bend it up or down to adjust clearance.

All oil galley plugs should be screw-in types using Teflon tape or The Right Stuff on the threads. Never chance using press-in plugs, even with a stock rebuild.

Cylinder Heads

The Cleveland's great success as a high-performance V-8 can be directly traced to its race-bred cylinder heads with their poly-angle valves, wedge chambers, and generous port sizing. This is a strange irony because the Cleveland's 4V heads have monster-size big-block ports that work best at 6,500 to 8,000 rpm. On the street and for occasional weekend drag racing, these ports are so large there isn't sufficient velocity at low speeds to make good low- and mid-range torque. Off the line, the Cleveland with its 7,500-rpm heads is short on twist at the green light.

To build the kind of Cleveland you want, you have to first know what you want this engine to do. Now, tell the truth. Be honest about what you want and realistically look at how you're going to get there. The best advice I can offer is to build only as much engine as you need and want.

Factory Iron Heads

Although there's some confusion over Cleveland cylinder heads, the 335-series engine family has the easiest line-up of Ford cylinder heads to understand.

- 351C-4V closed wedge chamber (bolt-fulcrum rockers)
- 351C-4V closed wedge chamber, boss/high-output head (adjustable rockers with screw-in studs)
- 351c-2v open chamber (bolt-fulcrum)
- 351C-4V open chamber (bolt-fulcrum)
- 351C Australian head (2v ports with closed wedge chamber)
- 302C Australian head (smaller, closed wedge chamber)

Although this may seem an over-simplification, lacking specifics such as casting numbers and markings, this is what you can expect to find out there at

This is the D1AE-GA 351C-4V fitted with pushrod guide plates and screw-in ARP rocker arm studs, which are modifications. The 351C-4V head has bolt-fulcrum, stamped-steel, no-adjust rocker arms. The Boss 351 head has screw-in studs and guide plates, and it has the same D1AE-GA casting number meaning both have the same head casting, but are machined differently.

The 351C-4V head made the Cleveland famous for huge amounts of high-RPM horsepower and torque. There are two types of North American 351C 4-barrel heads: closed wedge chamber and open chamber. This is the 62- to 63-cc closed-chamber wedge head.

The 351C-4V head has huge 2.50x1.75-inch drive-through intake ports designed for high-RPM use. Though the 4-barrel head is a factory iron piece installed on production vehicles, it was engineered primarily for racing. The same casting was installed on Boss 302 engines, except for water-passage differences.

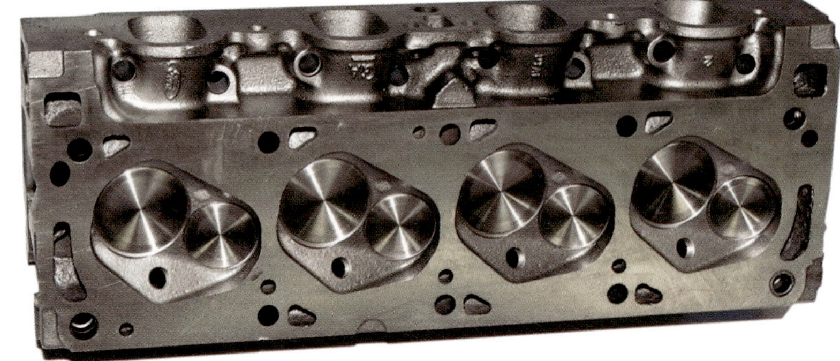

This is the D0AE/D1AE 351C-4V head with closed 62- to 63-cc wedge chambers and 2.19/1.71-inch valves.

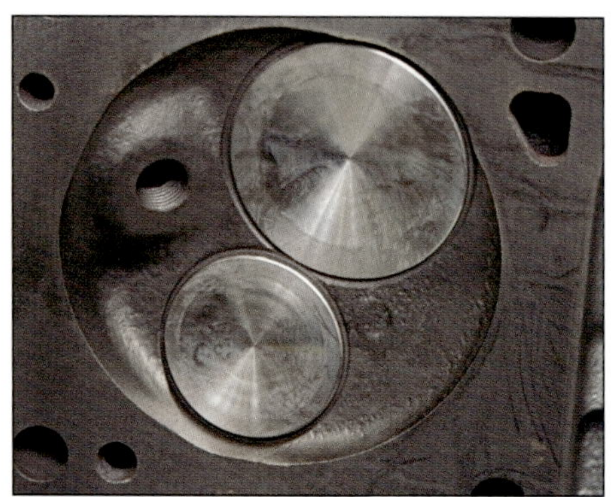

The 351C open-chamber head (2V and 4V) is a poor choice regardless of what you intend to do with your Cleveland. People associate this chamber with the small-port, 2-barrel head; however, it is also the 4-barrel head chamber for 1973–1974. This chamber offers zero quench and is prone to detonation. Valve shrouding is fair, but not much consolation when you consider the overall chamber.

Cleveland cylinder heads were among the first to have bolt-fulcrum, stamped-steel rocker arms, which had pedestals like this. It is a no-adjust design (hydraulic lifters only); just slowly tighten and torque to spec. The 385-series big-block was the first to have bolt-fulcrums in 1968.

The Boss 351 head has screw-in studs and guide plates due to the mechanical lifters; however, this is a modification you can make to any Cleveland head with a good machinist. Bolt-fulcrum pedestals are machined down to make room for guideplates, then drilled and tapped for screw-in studs.

Cleveland foundry castings have this CF logo. Though we call these engines "Clevelands," cylinder heads were also cast at the Windsor, Ontario, foundry and have a "WF" mark.

Here's a "WF" (Windsor) casting on a Boss 302 head, which demonstrates not all Cleveland heads were cast at the Cleveland facility.

Casting numbers accurately identify head castings. This is a D0ZE-6090-A Boss 302 head casting with 2.19/1.72-inch valves. It is a closed-chamber Cleveland head casting with cooling passages for the Boss 302 block and induction. Note the milled pedestals and screw-in stud holes.

swap meets and online auctions. Which heads should you pursue and which ones should you avoid? Open-chamber, Cleveland 2-barrel and 4-barrel heads, even if your Ford was originally equipped with them, should be avoided. Throw them on the shelf or into the recycle bin because they are terrible cylinder heads.

Poor quench and chamber irregularities that cause spark knock make the two open-chamber heads unacceptable for a high-performance Cleveland. They spark knock when you start the engine and they knock under hard acceleration, which makes them a poor choice for any Cleveland engine including the 351M and 400 engines. There's little or nothing you can do with these heads to gain performance or prevent spark knock. I'm puzzled every time I see these heads used for a magazine or buddy's project because they are such a poor cylinder head. Considering the great wealth of aftermarket and Aussie iron heads available for the Cleveland, there is no reason to ever use an open-chamber head.

Based on years of experience, I can tell you "4" means a 4-barrel head with large ports.

There are suitable factory iron Cleveland heads you can use with great success if you know how to work them and know how you're going to use them. The North American 351C-4V head with closed wedge chambers offers one of the best combustion chambers of its time. However, it is a medium- to high-RPM cylinder head with huge intake ports and lackluster exhaust ports with an ugly floor. It falls on its face as a street cylinder head because there's insufficient low- to mid-range torque because you're not going to get velocity at low RPM. Compression ratio is high, which means you need to lower compression via piston dimensions if running pump gas.

The best factory iron cylinder head comes from Ford Australia, which has the optimum combination of North American 4-barrel, closed wedge chambers and 2-barrel ports. This means great quench, good compression, and improved low- to mid-range torque. Torque (and velocity) comes from smaller ports, which is what you want on the street.

Powerheads Performance Engineering takes the great Aussie Cleveland head and does a nice CNC port job along with hand-finish work to set you up with deep-breathing cylinder heads you're going to like for street and weekend racing. The beauty of the Aussie iron heads from Powerheads is a broad torque curve: 2,500 to 5,500 rpm. At high RPM (5,500 to 6,500), these heads deliver. Of course it all depends on your combination of cam profile, induction, and stroke. This is why you need to know how you're going to use your Cleveland most of the time. Street drivers operate most of the time in the idle to 5,000-rpm range, which makes the Powerheads a great casting for the daily commute.

You can get into these Aussie heads from Powerheads for around $1,200 a pair. If you desire CNC port work add another $500. CNC port work depends, once again, on how you intend to use your Cleveland. If you're building a weekend drag racer that's driven during the week to work, CNC port work makes sense. If it is never raced, don't waste your money on port work.

Powerheads can set you up with turnkey CNC-ported Australian Cleveland cylinder heads with the common-sense combination of closed wedge chambers and 2-barrel ports for improved low- to mid-range torque. Once these heads are CNC ported, they get hardened exhaust valve seats and a valve job along with 16 new stainless valves and the right spring pressure for your camshaft. This particular head is an Aussie 302C with even smaller wedge chambers.

Common Cleveland Cylinder Head Castings

These are the more common Cleveland cylinder head castings you can expect to find out there. There are bound to be obscure head castings not listed here, including factory experimental castings, you're bound to see at swap meets and online auc tions. As a rule, Australian Cleveland cylinder head castings don't have Ford North America casting numbers.

Engine/Year	Casting Number	Chamber (cc)	Valve Size (Inches)	Port Size (inches)
351C 1970–1974	D0AE-E (2V)	74 to 77	2.04 Intake	2.02 x 1.65 Intake
	D0AE-J (2V)		1.67 Exhaust	1.84 x 1.38 Exhaust
	D0AE-G (4V)	61 to 64	2.19 Intake	2.50 x 1.75 Intake
	D0AE-H (4V)		1.71 Exhaust	2.00 x 1.74 Exhaust
	D0AE-M (4V)			
	D0AE-N (4V)			
	D0AE-R (4V)			
	D1AE-AA (2V)	74 to 77	2.04 Intake	2.02 x 1.65 Intake
	D1AE-CB (2V)		1.67 Exhaust	1.84 x 1.38 Exhaust
	D1AE-GA (4V)	61 to 64	2.19 Intake	2.50 x 1.75 Intake
	D1ZE-DA (CJ)	73 to 76	1.71 Exhaust	2.00 x 1.74 Exhaust
	D1ZE-B (BOSS 351)	64 to 67		
	D2ZE-A (High Output)	73 to 76	2.19 Intake	2.50 x 1.75 Intake
			1.71 Exhaust	2.00 x 1.74 Exhaust
	D3ZE-AA (CJ)	73 to 76	2.19 Intake	2.50 x 1.75 Intake
			1.71 Exhaust	2.00 x 1.74 Exhaust
400 1971–1972	D1AE-A1A	74 to 77	2.04 Intake	2.02 x 1.65 Intake
	D1AE-A1B		1.67 Exhaust	1.84 x 1.38 Exhaust
	D1AE-A1C			
	D1AE-A2C			
400 1973–1974	D3AE-G2B	74 to 77	2.04 Intake	2.02 x 1.65 Intake
			1.67 Exhaust	2.00 x 1.38 Exhaust
400/351M 1975–1982	D5AE-AA	74 to 77	2.04 Intake	2.02 x 1.65 Intake
	D5AE-A1A		1.67 Exhaust	2.00 x 1.38 Exhaust
	D5AE-A2A			
	D5AE-A3A			
BOSS 302 1969	C9ZE-A	61 to 64	2.23 Intake	2.50 x 1.75 Intake
	C9ZE-B		1.71 Exhaust	2.00 x 1.74 Exhaust
BOSS 302 1970–1971	D0ZE-A	57 to 60	2.19 Intake	2.50 x 1.75 Intake
	D0ZE-B		1.71 Exhaust	2.00 x 1.74 Exhaust
	D1ZE-A (Service Replacement)	57 to 60	2.19 Intake	2.50 x 1.75 Intake
			1.71 Exhaust	2.00 x 1.74 Exhaust
302C Australia 1972–1982		56 to 59	2.05 Intake	2.02 x 1.65 Intake
			1.65 Exhaust	2.00 x 1.38 Exhaust
351C Australia 1972–1982		64 to 67	2.19 Intake	2.02 x 1.65 Intake
			1.71 Exhaust	2.00 x 1.38 Exhaust

Port sizing on this 302C Australian head is comparable to the North American 351C-2V head. What you get with the Australian 302C head is smaller, 57- to 59-cc chambers and higher compression. Casting numbers begin with "AR" along with a North American number on the valley side of intake ports. For example, "ARD1AE" on one and "6090A" on the other stands for "AR-D1AE-6090-A.

Regardless of what you're going to do with your iron-head Cleveland, step up to hardened exhaust valve seats for durability with unleaded fuels. Here the iron seat is being cut out in preparation for a steel seat.

If you plan on stroking your Cleveland to 393 or 408 ci, the Aussie Cleveland head becomes debatable depending on how you intend to use it. With a longer stroke comes the need for more breathability. North American 351C-4V heads with their large intake ports work better with displacement in excess of 400 ci. Large ports cultivate the velocity needed with the deep draw of a long stroke, which gives you torque at lower RPM ranges.

The hardened exhaust valve seat must be driven into place before getting a nice angle cut.

Head Prep

If you're reworking factory iron heads for your Cleveland, there are all kinds of things you need to know. Have the heads Magnafluxed for cracks along with a close visual inspection before doing any machine work. Because some Cleveland head castings tend to crack, get this concern out of the way. Always install hardened exhaust valve seats so that your iron heads compatible with today's harsh unleaded fuels.

As to porting: If you clean up the bowls and smooth out the high spots you wind up with a respectable street/strip head, especially if you want a stock appearance. MPG Head Service has stamped-steel port plates, also known as port tongues, to get rid of that ugly exhaust floor rise on 4-barrel heads. This rise creates unwanted turbulence that interferes with exhaust scavenging. There's not a lot you can do with this rise because you don't want to grind off too much. Best you can do is make it a smoother ride for hot gases.

Guides, Liners and Stems

When evaluating bare heads and deciding what to do first, a few things are immediate priorities. Valveguides should always be replaced, whether you choose to use new guides or bronze liners. I know I will get arguments on this one, but bronze liners hold up better in the long term and they offer better oil control than iron or powdered-metal guides. Complete replacement of iron valveguides is a matter of personal choice, but it's also an expensive option because more labor is involved. The more affordable, less time-consuming option is bronze liners. What makes bronze liners a better value is their excellent lubricating qualities and therefore durability. Bronze liners are happy with chromed, non-chromed, and coated valvestems. All a

Apply Prussian Blue to the new valve seat in preparation for cutting, which enables the machinist to see the cut and angle. A three-angle valve job is routine to improve flow and heat transfer.

a machinist has to do is get stem-to-liner clearances healthy and you're good to go.

Bronze liners are installed in existing valveguides. All the machinist has to do is machine the guides to size and drive in the liners. Of course it is more involved than. For one thing, headwork is not for the novice. It is for the trained, competent professional machinist with the right experience and equipment.

Installing bronze liners initially calls for reaming the iron valveguide to size. The machinist uses a reamer and less than 1,000 rpm for no more than five seconds per guide before checking size. Most machinists ream the guide dry in preparation for liner installation. Once guides have been reamed, use cutting oil and a ball hone to get a good crosshatch pattern. This cleans up the guides and prepares them for the bronze liners. Liners

Even new valvestems need to be measured and dressed to allow for thermal expansion and conservative oil flow. You want enough clearance to allow oil flow without starving guide and stem.

Valve faces are painted with red dye (or Prussian Blue) and ground to a compatible angle to the seats. High-tech cutters allow a multi-angle cut without having to change cutters.

This is a custom-made go/no-go gauge made from aluminum stock that measures 1.900 inches in length, which is what MCE uses to determine installed spring height.

Spring pressure must always be compatible with your cam profile. Too much pressure and you face excessive friction and wear issues. Not enough pressure and you're looking at valve float at high RPM.

In recent years the trend has been away from umbrella valve seals and toward Teflon or Viton seals, probably because Teflon valve seals are more appropriate for racing and don't offer long-term durability. For street and racing engines, you want Viton valve seals, which offer extreme durability and oil control.

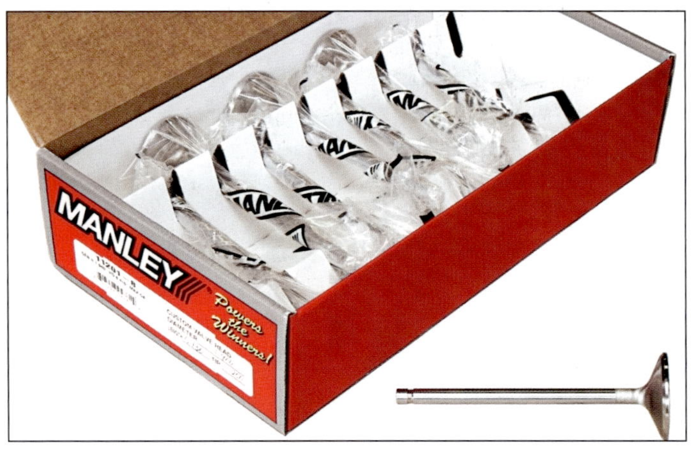

Do not reuse valves. MCE, for example, specifies Manley stainless valves. Cylinder head work includes new valves, springs, retainers, keepers, and seals.

Blueprinting includes fine-tuning valvestem to guide clearances with generous amounts of assembly lube. Clearances should be .0010 to .0027 inch intake and .0015- to .0032-inch exhaust. Valves should slip-slide back and forth with smoothness without binding. Any binding, no matter how slight, is unacceptable. Valve faces should seat with precision and pass a vacuum check when the heads are assembled.

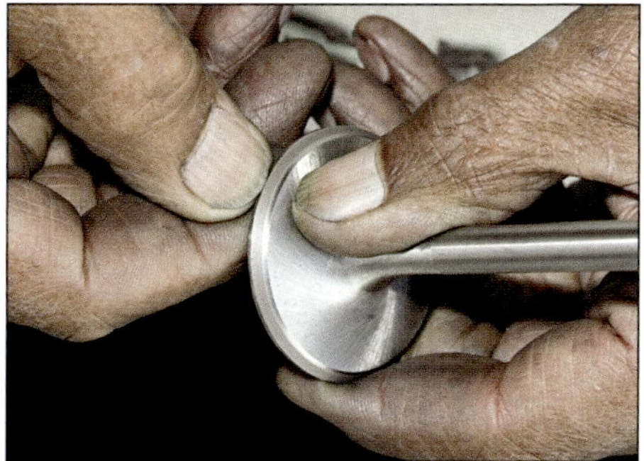

Seat contact determines both flow and cooling. The more surface contact you have between valve and seat, the better valve cooling (heat transfer). With increasing contact comes some hindrance to flow. Drag racers can get away with less valve-to-seat contact. Drivers and road racers need more contact area to aid valve cooling.

Although these look like 351C heads with closed-wedge chambers, they're actually Australian 302C heads with smaller 57- to 59-cc wedge chambers. You are unlikely to find these at a swap meet, but pay attention to chamber size and compression ratio.

are driven in with a pneumatic driver at approximately 3,000 pulses per minute. Overpower the driver and you damage the liner.

It should take a machinist roughly five seconds to install each liner. Once the liner is installed and trimmed, a carbide ball is used to permanently install the liner. Because the carbide ball is .001 inch larger than the intended finish size (known as an interference fit), it presses the liner into place, coming out on the other side. Once the liners are installed, they should be honed to size one valve at a time. With each liner, check valvestem fit and movement using lubricant, then clean with solvent to remove any metal debris. Any debris left behind causes stem or liner damage. Be thorough in your clean-up efforts, then use plenty of engine assembly lube between the stems and guides when it's time for assembly.

Another option is silicon bronze valveguides, which can be installed in iron or aluminum heads. If you're going with bronze guides, they should be knurled externally for added security. Yet another option, though strongly discouraged, is knurling iron guides internally for oil control and stem clearancing. However, this is an approach with a limited lifespan and little benefit.

Valvestems should be inspected, measured, and dressed for proper fit and oil control just as you do with guides and liners.

Valve Job

While you're reworking heads, a multi-angle valve job improves flow and durability. You can perform a three-angle, five-angle, or radius valve job. Each varies in durability. First, you need to know how much valve face contact you want with the seat. The more contact you have, the better your valve cooling and durability. However, you sacrifice flow with increasing seat contact.

For drag racing, as one example, you can get by with less seat contact (.060 inch) and better flow because power comes in short bursts and heat doesn't have a chance to build as you see in road racing or extended highway driving. If your Cleveland is going to operate for extended periods at high RPM, you want more seat width (.080 inch) and heat transfer. Ford recommends .060- to .080-inch intake and .070- to .090-inch exhaust.

Most factory valve jobs are single-angle with a lot of restriction. Engine rebuilds normally get a three-angle job (45-, 60-, 70-degree angle cuts), which is quite common for street performance applications. With a three-angle valve job, there's a bottom cut that ranges from 50 to 70 degrees depending upon the head casting and port configuration.

Machinists normally begin with a 70-degree cutter just below the valve seat to improve flow. The 60-degree cut on a three-angle valve job, reduces restriction. The valve and valve seat get a 45-degree angle cut. Contact width depends on what you want your engine to do. Normally, contact width is .080 inch.

A three-angle valve job improves flow significantly to where you can experience a solid 10- to 15-hp/torque improvement depending on technique and what is done port-wise. If you keep

Valve Job Specifications

Specifications tend to vary with aftermarket aluminum cylinder heads where expansion rates differ and component sizing may also be different. Check with each cylinder head manufacturer for specifications.

Engine Type	Intake Stem-Guide (inch)	Exhaust Stem-Guide (inch)	Valve Seat Angle & Runout (inch)
351C, 351M, 400	.0010 to .0027; .0055 maximum	.0015 to .0032; .0055 maximum	45 Degrees; .016 maximum

Engine Type	Valve Guide Bore Diameter (inch)	Stem To Rocker Allowable (inch)	Stem To Rocker Desired (inch)
351C, 351M, 400	.3433 to .3443	.100 to .200, Lifter Collapsed	.100 to .150, Lifter Collapsed

Engine Type	Intake Stem Diameter (inch)	Exhaust Stem Diameter (inch)	Intake Valve Head Diameter (inches)	Exhaust Valve Head Diameter (inches)	Valve Face Angle (degrees)
351C-4V	.3416 .3446 .3566 .3716	.3411 .3441 .3561 .3711	2.183 to 2.198	1.705 to 1.715	44
351C-2V, 351M, 400	.3423 .003 Oversize .3453 .015 Oversize .3573 .030 Oversize .3723	.3418 .003 Oversize .3448 .015 Oversize .3568 .030 Oversize .3718	2.032 to 2.050	1.650 to 1.660	44

Engine Type	Spring Pressure (pounds at inches)	Wear Limit (pounds at inches)	Valve Spring Free Length (inches)	Assembled Height (inches)
351C-2V	76 to 84 at 1.820 199 to 221 at 1.420	68 at 1.820 179 at 1.420	2.070	1 13/16 to 1 27/32
351C-4V	85 to 95 at 1.820 271 to 299 at 1.320	79 at 1.820 244 at 1.320	2.050	1 13/16 to 1 27/32
351C-BOSS High Output	88 to 96 at 1.820 299 to 331 at 1.320	79 at 1.820 269 at 1.320	2.030	1 13/16 to 1 27/32
351M at 400	76 to 84 at 1.820 215 to 237 at 1.320	68 at 1.820 183 at 1.390	2.060	1 13/16 to 1 27/32

valve-to-seat contact around .060 inch for the intake valve, the news is even better. For cooling, minimum exhaust valve seat contact width should be .080 inch; however, this depends on how your engine will be used. Short blasts, such as in drag racing or marine use, can get away with a .060-inch contact width. Otherwise, .080 inch.

Should you go to larger valves during the machine work? This depends upon how much room you have for larger valves. Ford was mighty generous with Cleveland valve sizing at 2.09/1.73 inches. Valve shrouding becomes an issue if you try to go larger with factory iron heads. You also want at least .060-inch distance between intake and exhaust valves.

With original-equipment umbrella valve seals, expect to machine your heads for more modern Teflon or Viton valve seals. To accommodate Teflon or Viton valve seals, heads have to be machined at the valve guides to .530/.500-inch outside diameter. Another consideration is valvespring cups, which keep valvesprings stable and reduce wear and tear at the head. Once your valve job is complete, make sure your machine shop checks each valve for freedom of movement before assembly.

Just about any high-quality, stainless valve works well in Clevelands. If you're racing, use the lightest valve possible to reduce internal drag. Street engines can live with any high-quality stainless valve. When valves, guides, seats, and ports are machined and properly set up, it is time to check and mill deck surfaces to get a perfect mating surface. Milling deck surfaces, reduces deck thickness and combustion chamber size, which increases compression and makes valve-to-piston clearances tighter. This is why you should wait to do head work until the block is ready for mockup. You must know all the dimensions between the piston and combustion chamber. Heads need to be measured across and diagonally. If warping varies more than .003 inch in any direction beyond 6 inches, mill the deck .005 to .010 inch. Before milling, sonic check deck thickness and be sure you have enough deck. Keep in mind you may have heads that have already been milled. If you mill away too much, you have a doorstop.

If you're working with Cleveland heads with bolt-fulcrum rocker arms, consider screw-in adjustment rocker arm studs and guide plates. This is a modification any competent machine shop can do. Pedestals are milled flat the appropriate amount (thickness) to make way for guide plates and studs. Holes are drilled out and tapped for studs.

Cylinder Head Sources

There was a time when all you had to choose from for Clevelands were factory iron heads you could spice up with some port work. Today, a large variety of great aluminum castings is available.

Note that all specifications are subject to change. Contact each manufacturer for details before ordering or buying.

Cylinder Head Innovations

The most common high-performance cylinder heads out there are the iron and alloy castings from Cylinder Head Innovations (CHI) in Australia, which are available from a number of sources in the United States in a wide variety of configurations. CHI has invested tremendous amounts of time in Cleveland head technology and come up with one of the best cylinder heads ever for the Cleveland and Windsor engine families. This cylinder head has gone to the Engine Masters Challenge and competed successfully on a grand scale. CHI tells me (at press time) no other cylinder head manufacturer has won the Engine Masters twice.

CHI has taken the Cleveland head and made the most of its great potential with right-sized ports large enough to flow generous amounts of air and hot gases, yet small enough to make velocity. With velocity comes torque, and torque is what you want for street and weekend racing. If you're going road racing, torque is what thrusts you out of turns and down straights. In drag racing, torque helps in coming off the line under hard acceleration. And with the right head, cam, and induction combination, torque hands off to horsepower at high RPM.

There are three basic types of CHI heads: 2V, 3V, and 4V. The 2V head, as its designation indicates, has the 351C-2V (2-barrel) port configuration. The 4V head has 351C-4V port sizing. The 3V head has the airflow potential of the 4V head with 2V port sizing. It's a great compromise between 2V and 4V.

Among CHI believers are engine builders Jon Kasse and Darin Morgan who have been able to massage these legendary cylinder heads and make a lot of power. CHI heads are completely manufactured in house from foundry to finished product. This enables CHI to maintain high quality standards. No fewer than five CHI heads are available for the 335-series Cleveland engine family. Within those head types, there are plenty of options.

CHI 3V Iron Head: The CHI 3V cast-iron Cleveland head is an iron version of the aluminum 3V with the same chamber, valve sizes, and port configurations. CHI conceived the 3V iron head for racing classes where aluminum heads are not permitted, yet you get the same benefits of the alloy head.

The 3V iron head can deliver upwards of 500 hp and comparable torque with standard displacement. If you dial in more displacement, horsepower and torque increase accordingly. The iron 3V head is available on a very limited basis for racers primarily. In truth, this is not a head for the average street enthusiast. Why order iron when you can shave weight (and heat) and have aluminum?

CHI Street Master 2V Cylinder Head: The CHI 2V 190-cc cylinder head works in perfect harmony with 351C-2V intake and exhaust manifolds. The 2V Street Master flows 300 cfm at .600-inch lift. Because the 2V head has the 3V (68 to 70 cc) or 4V (74 cc) chambers, you get great swirl and quench. With these features, detonation becomes a thing of the

CHI 3V Iron Head

Intake Valve Size	2.070 inches
Exhaust Valve Size	1.650 inches
Intake Port Volume	190 cc
Intake Port Flow at .600 inch	290 cfm
Exhaust Port Volume	N/A
Exhaust Port Flow at .700 inch	222 cfm
Chamber Size	68-70 cc

CHI Street Master 2V

Intake Valve Size	2.070 inches
Exhaust Valve Size	1.650 inches
Intake Port Volume	190 cc
Intake Port Flow at .600 inch	300 cfm
Exhaust Port Volume	N/A
Exhaust Port Flow at .700 inch	222 cfm
Chamber Size	3V, 68 to 70 cc; 4V, 74 cc

CHI 3V 185 cc	
Intake Valve Size	2.070 inches
Exhaust Valve Size	1.650 inches
Intake Port Volume	185 cc
Intake Port Flow at .600 inch	290 cfm
Exhaust Port Volume	N/A
Exhaust Port Flow at .600 inch	222 cfm
Chamber Size	3V, 60 to 64 cc; 4V, 74 cc

CHI 3V 208 cc	
Intake Valve Size	2.070 inches
Exhaust Valve Size	1.650 inches
Intake Port Volume	208 cc
Intake Port Flow at .600 inch	314 cfm
Exhaust Port Volume	N/A
Exhaust Port Flow at .600 inch	219 cfm
Chamber Size	3V, 68 to 70 cc; 4V, 74 cc

CHI 3V 225 cc	
Intake Valve Size	2.150 inches
Exhaust Valve Size	1.650 inches
Intake Port Volume	225 cc
Intake Port Flow at .600 inch	322 cfm
Exhaust Port Volume	N/A
Exhaust Port Flow at .600 inch	219 cfm
Chamber Size	3V, 68 to 70 cc; 4V, 74 cc

CHI 3V 260 CNC	
Intake Valve Size	2.190 inches
Exhaust Valve Size	1.650 inches
Intake Port Volume	260 cc
Intake Port Flow at .800 inch	370 cfm
Exhaust Port Volume	N/A
Exhaust Port Flow at .800 inch	230 cfm
Chamber Size	3V, 68 to 70 cc

past. The 2V's 220-cfm exhaust ports are designed to work with 2V or 4V exhaust manifolds and headers. Where the head meets the block, you get 5/8-inch deck thickness. These heads are available in stud or bolt-fulcrum configurations. They're also available bare or assembled.

CHI 3V 185 cc: The 3V 185-cc cylinder head is in a unique class among Cleveland cylinder heads. Correct port sizing makes this cylinder head an exceptional pick because it is the smallest Cleveland head currently on the market. The 3V 185-cc head is well suited to stock-displacement bottom ends where you'd like to make up to 500 hp along with comparable torque. Intake ports are engineered to deliver the sweet combination of good low- and mid-range torque coupled with high-RPM horsepower. By downsizing the 4V port to 185 cc, you get the best of both worlds: low-end torque and high-end horsepower. The key to power is in high velocity at low-RPM ranges, which is where torque comes from.

CHI 3V 208 cc: The 3V 208-cc cylinder head was developed by Dave Storlien for the 2004 Engine Masters Challenge. The objective was 410 ci and revs up to 6,500 rpm with power in the 500- to 550-hp range. The 208-cc intake port features a minimum cross section of 2.300 inches with the tallest roof of CHI's 3V head family. It has the most generous short-turn radius of all the 3V heads. The 208-cc intake manifold that goes with this head has fuel injection bosses cast in for port injection or nitrous. Intake port flow is a generous 314 cc at .650 inch. Exhaust flow is 223 cc, also at .650-inch lift.

CHI 3V 225 cc: This head replaces the older 218-cc design. It really is a serious street/race head for more than 400 ci and more than 600 hp. These 225-cc intake ports have a minimum cross section of 2.400 inches. What you get from these intake ports is shear volume—340 cfm at .700-inch lift; in the real world, 322 cfm at .600-inch lift. Exhaust flow is 219 cfm at .600-inch lift. In dyno testing, this has proven to be 740 hp and 640 ft-lbs of torque with 4.125 inches of stroke with a 6.125-inch rod along with 12.0:1 compression. Of course your results will vary.

CHI 3V 260 CNC: The manufacturer says this is the "ultimate race Cleveland cylinder head." What makes it a great head is revised intake and exhaust ports, some 370 cfm of intake flow, and CNC port design. Intake ports are .060 inch

CHI 4V 228 cc	
Intake Valve Size	2.190 inches
Exhaust Valve Size	1.650 or 1.710 inches
Intake Port Volume	228 cc
Intake Port Flow at .700 inch	325 cfm
Exhaust Port Volume	N/A
Exhaust Port Flow at .700 inch	222 cfm
Chamber Size	68 to 70 cc

Kaase C-400 2.850	
Intake Valve Size	2.190 inches
Exhaust Valve Size	1.650 inches
Intake Port Volume	N/A
Intake Port Flow at .800 inch	400 cfm
Exhaust Port Volume	N/A
Exhaust Port Flow at .800 inch	253 cfm
Chamber Size	45 cc

Few aftermarket performance companies have done more for Cleveland engines than CHI. And few have spent more time making these heads even better than Jon Kaase of Kaase Racing Engines, which offers the Kaase C-400 head for all Clevelands.

Kaase C-400 3.100	
Intake Valve Size	2.150 inches
Exhaust Valve Size	1.650 inches
Intake Port Volume	N/A
Intake Port Flow at .750 inch	400 cfm
Exhaust Port Volume	N/A
Exhaust Port Flow at .750 inch	253 cfm
Chamber Size	45 cc

higher than the 3V 225 cc. At .600-inch lift, I witnessed 340-cfm intake and 223-cfm exhaust. At .800-inch lift (where this head really lives), I saw a whopping 370-cfm intake and 230-cfm exhaust. The 3V 260 CNC is not a street head because it is more at home at 760 hp.

CHI 4V 228 cc: This is the cylinder head for those who desire a factory-style casting. "Designed around our 3V 218-cc intake port, we spent many hours reshaping the entry of our port to accommodate factory and aftermarket intake manifolds," CHI comments. "Careful attention was paid during development not to increase volume any more than necessary to keep velocity high." These heads are machined to accept 2.190-inch intake and 1.650-inch exhaust valves. If you want a larger exhaust valve, these heads can be machined to accept 1.710-inch valves at no extra charge.

Jon Kaase Racing Engines

Jon Kaase easily has the greatest understanding of Cleveland heads out there because he has been able to take the CHI head and massage it to where it is the undisputed champ for airflow and power. Kaase has been working with CHI and other Cleveland cylinder head castings for years and knows how to shape ports to where they give up impressive numbers.

Kaase C-400: This head offers real Pro-Stock cylinder head technology, making it the most advanced Cleveland head ever to hit the market for racing. This may sound like a sales pitch, but it is not. When you study the numbers on the flow bench and in dyno cells, the C-400 is an unbeatable cylinder head for Cleveland and Windsor small-blocks alike.

The C-400 is available from Kaase in at least two CNC ported variations: the 2.850-inch, which means a 2.850-inch minimum intake port cross section, and the 3.100-inch, which means a minimum 3.100-inch cross section. The 2.850-inch 3V C-400 head is engineered to work with the 3.500-inch 4500 CHI intake manifold atop a 408-ci Cleveland. It is designed for more than 700 hp. The 3.100-inch port head is engineered for the new CHI 4.200-inch manifold. At .750-inch intake-valve lift, the 2.850 head flows 400 cfm. The result in actual dyno testing has been 800 hp and nearly 600 ft-lbs of torque.

The C-400 head has an all-new combustion chamber, not to mention revised

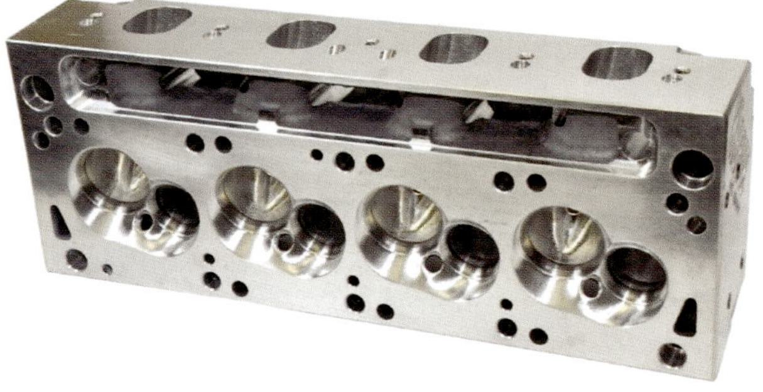

The C-400 head from Kaase is the most advanced Cleveland cylinder head ever made. It is available in two CNC-ported versions. The C-400 2.85 has a minimum 2.850-inch cross section across its intake ports. The C-400 3.1 has a minimum of 3.100 inches. These generous intake ports offer in excess of 400 cfm at .700-inch valve lift thanks to Kaase's handiwork. Ports are raised for improved flow tied to redesigned 45-cc combustion chambers. CHI induction works very well with the C-400 heads and is available with 4150/4160 and 4500 flanges.

On the hot side, the C-400 brings improved exhaust scavenging thanks to its raised port angle. You're going to need a custom piston with these heads with 1.200-inch compression height. CP Pistons offers a piston design (available from Kaase) that works with these heads. Relocated valve positions call for longer valvestems. "Although this cylinder head is designed with shaft-mounted rockers in mind, standard Cleveland roller rockers do work with this cylinder head and stud girdles need slight modification on the intake side for them to fit," Victor Moore of Kaase comments.

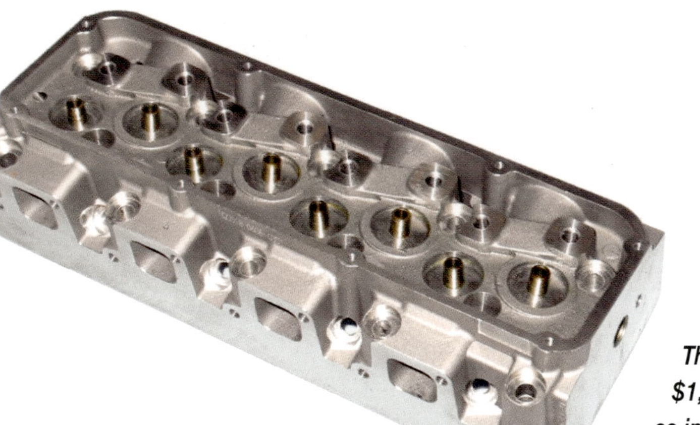

Street/Track Boss

Intake Valve Size	2.190 inches
Exhaust Valve Size	1.710 inches
Intake Port Volume	205 cc
230-cc CNC Ported Intake Port Flow at .600 inch	312.5 cfm
341.2-cfm CNC Ported Exhaust Port Volume	105 cc
125-cc CNC Ported Exhaust Port Flow at .700 inch	215.5 cfm
240.6-cfm CNC Ported Chamber Size	67 cc

The Superboss is a good cylinder head for the money at roughly $1,600 in street form with 2.19/1.71-inch valves, 67-cc chambers, 205-cc intake runner, 105-cc exhaust, and 7/16-inch screw-in studs.

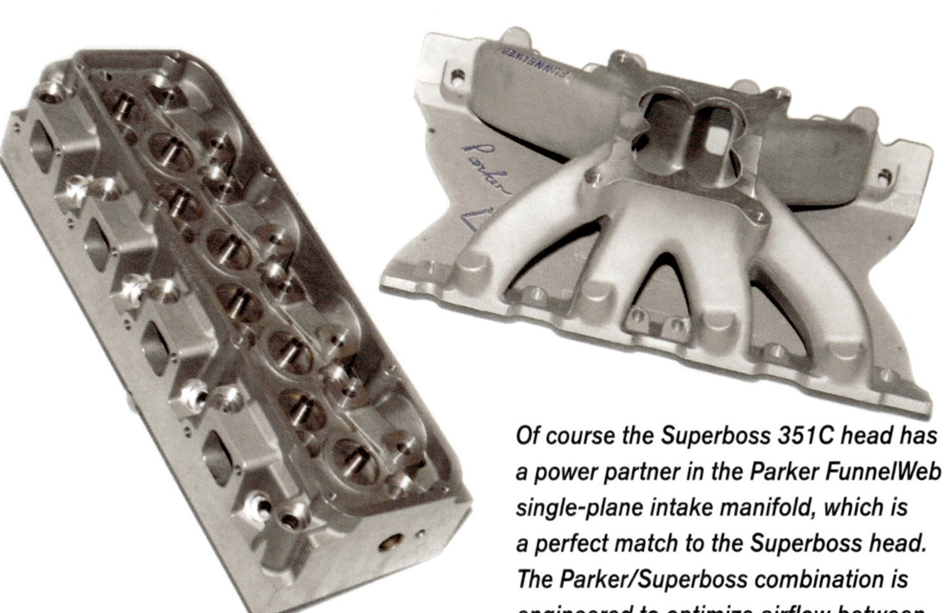

Of course the Superboss 351C head has a power partner in the Parker FunnelWeb single-plane intake manifold, which is a perfect match to the Superboss head. The Parker/Superboss combination is engineered to optimize airflow between induction and intake port.

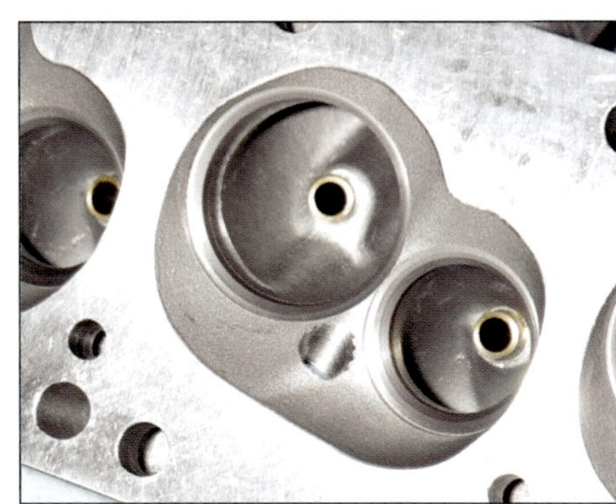

The Superboss 351C chamber offers great quench, minimal valve shrouding, and makes the most of its size. Intake ports flow 312 cfm at .600-inch lift out of the box and 341.2 cfm with optional Powerheads port work. Exhaust is 215 cfm out of the box at .660-inch lift and 240 cfm with optional Powerheads port work.

intake and exhaust port layouts. What this means for you is the need for a custom piston with a specific compression height. CP Pistons has this custom piston already available. These heads are engineered for shaft-mounted rocker arms though you can go with stud-mounted rockers with a girdle.

Powerheads Performance Engineering

Ralph Pici of Powerheads has always managed to keep a low profile in the industry. However, he's one of the sharpest engine builders and head porters I've ever worked with. Ralph understands how to get power through common-sense port and bowl enhancement—making the most of flow and knowing how it behaves.

Powerheads is well known for CNC port work on factory cast-iron heads. However, did you know Powerheads also sells new cylinder heads for the 351C and 351W engine families? The Superboss 351C aluminum cylinder head from Powerheads is available two ways: Street Boss and Track Boss.

Street Boss is an out-of-the-box aluminum cylinder head with 2.190/1.710-inch intake/exhaust valves and 67-cc chambers. Track Boss is the Street Boss head casting with CNC port and hand-finish work plus stainless-steel valves, dual valvesprings, 7/16-inch screw-in rocker studs and guide plates, and Viton seals. Both heads are a great value. The Street Boss is $1,595. For another $600, you get CNC port and finish work.

Powerheads Iron Side: Powerheads was originally founded in 1995 to do affordable CNC porting on factory iron cylinder heads including

Cleveland. Of particular interest these days is the imported Australian Cleveland cylinder head with good-old-fashioned hot rodder port sizing and cutting. The Aussies had enough sense to match the 4V wedge chamber with 2V intake and exhaust ports to achieve a great cylinder head good from 2,500 to 6,500 rpm, which makes it the best factory Cleveland head out there. And Powerheads is the place to find it.

The exhaust clearly shows the difference between the 351C-4V head (top) and MPG CHI head (bottom). Though the 4-barrel heads have larger exhaust ports, they're restrictive with that hump in the floor. The MPG CHI head has smaller exhaust ports, yet they're not restrictive, offering better velocity and scavenging.

MPG Head Service enjoys a wealth of NHRA racing experience and success. The MPG 3V cylinder head for Clevelands is basically a CFI head with a tremendous amount of port work. These guys have performed quite well at the Engine Masters Challenge.

Scott Main of MPG placed the 351C-4V head (top) alongside the MPG CHI head (bottom) for a port comparison. The CHI head has "right sized" intake ports that afford you velocity and lower engine speeds, which translates to torque. These heads are happy at low- to mid-range RPM and go gangbusters at high RPM.

The North American 351C-4V head is a great casting if you intend to operate your Cleveland in the 3,500- to 7,500-rpm range. It is also a good cylinder head for a engine with more than 400 ci because you're hauling more volume through those huge ports. The downside to the 351C-4V head is its exhaust ports, which have an ugly speed bump that disrupts flow and causes turbulence. Powerheads CNC port work improves 4V intake and exhaust flow if you're going to operate at high RPM or move a lot of displacement.

Remember, any open-chamber Cleveland head is unacceptable because there's no quench and these poorly thought out chambers are prone to detonation. It doesn't matter how effective the smaller 2V ports are, it's those awful open chambers that don't get the job done.

So what about Aussie Cleveland heads from Powerheads? If you're seeking a stock external appearance or are faced with a limited budget, iron Aussie heads are the best choice. A stock pair of Powerheads Aussie Cleveland heads retail for $1,195, or $1,695 CNC ported. In any case, all are fitted with stainless swirl-polished valves, hardened exhaust seats, screw-in rocker studs with guide plates, dual springs, new bronze guides, and Viton seals.

MPG Head Service/ Cam Research Corporation

Many credible engine builders believe in CHI cylinder heads and are doing a lot with them. MPG Head Service/Cam Research (outside Denver) is one of them. In 2006, MPG went to the Engine Masters Challenge with a 409-ci Windsor and made 680 hp and 480 ft-lbs of torque with MPG's CHI 3V head. You might be tempted to ask, What does this have to do with Clevelands? The answer

MPG/CHI 3V

Intake Valve Size	2.160 inches
Exhaust Valve Size	1.650 inches
Intake Port Volume	218 cc
Intake Port Flow at .600 inch	343 cfm
Exhaust Port Volume	N/A
Exhaust Port Flow at .600 inch	N/A
Chamber Size	64 cc

Ford Australia Cleveland

(by Powerheads)

Intake Valve Size	2.190 inches
Exhaust Valve Size	1.710 inches
Intake Port Volume	N/A
Intake Port Flow at .600 inch	191.5 cfm
253.0-cfm CNC Ported Exhaust Port Volume	N/A
Exhaust Port Flow at .600 inch	172.5 cfm
209.0-cfm CNC Ported Chamber Size	60 cc

is "plenty" because bore and stroke are similar, along with rod ratio and cylinder head. The 409-ci Windsor (#31384715 Dart Block) made 680/480 using this proven 3V cylinder head recipe. That year, MPG accumulated 993.90 points right behind Jon Kaase Racing Engines with 1,043.20 points in First Place.

The MPG CHI head isn't an extensively ported casting; instead it has a mild port and bowl work where it is needed to clean up airflow. MPG applies special thermal coating to intake runners to help reduce intake temperatures, which improves power because cooler air and fuel are denser. Exhaust ports are raised .400 inch to improve scavenging. MPG/Cam Research takes the raw CHI 3V castings and fits them with its own stainless valves for better flow. Where the mixture becomes fire, a heart-shaped 64.5-cc wedge chamber features a good light-off and the absence of detonation thanks to great quench.

This is how far chamber design has come in 40 years. On top is the classic Cleveland wedge chamber. On the bottom is the MPG CHI high-swirl chamber, which is smaller with better quench. Couple this with excellent port design and massaging and you have the recipe for power.

Scott Cook Motorsports

Australia has embraced the Cleveland engine family like no other place on Earth including the United States. Scott Cook is another Aussie with vision and enough imagination to conceive and cast his own Cleveland cylinder heads, which have CHI 3V-style chambers and port configuration while retaining the Cleveland's external appearance. Bolted on, they look like a factory Cleveland 4V head; no one knows they are there once painted. If unpainted, they're a great-looking casting to bolt on top of your Cleveland.

Cook claims with confidence these heads are performers right out of the box with no port work necessary. Of course that's a matter of personal opinion and choice once your Scott Cook heads arrive. The company is not currently offering a 4V port; however, Cook ultimately expects to have one.

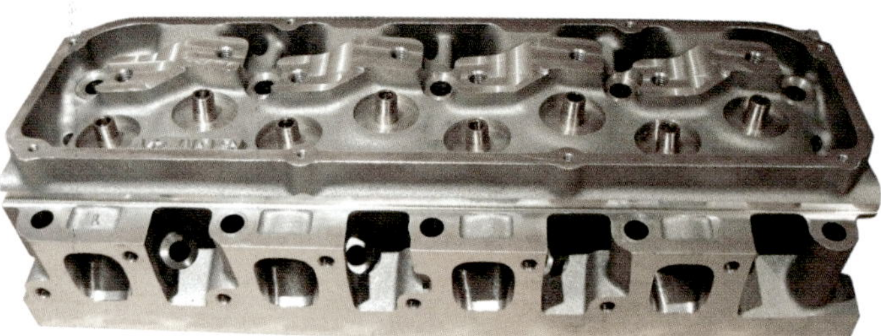

The Scott Cook head isn't a high-port head—yet it has the same basic port and chamber configuration as the successful CHI 3V head. This head accepts a 2.08/1.87-inch valve package for improved flow.

Here's the new Scott Cook aluminum head, which is configured like the CHI head with minor casting changes to give it a more factory appearance.

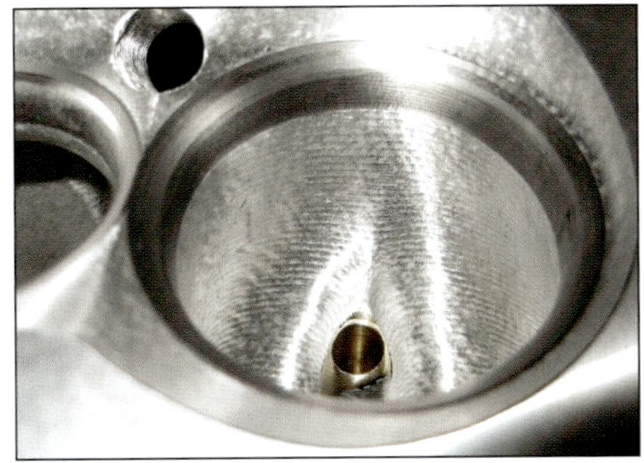

This port and bowl work on a Scott Cook head has minimal or no valve shrouding and buttery-smooth CNC bowl work for improved flow. These ports flow well right out of the box. However, you can get even more improvement with finish work in the bowls.

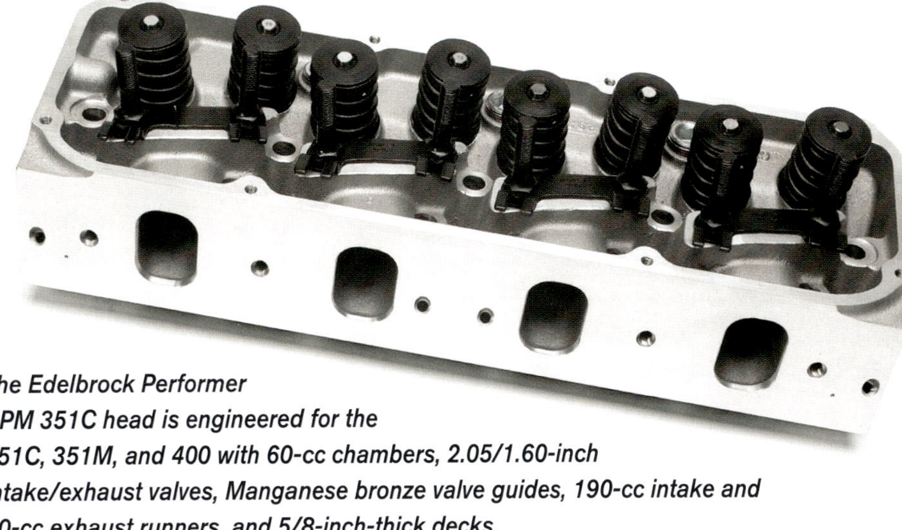

The Edelbrock Performer RPM 351C head is engineered for the 351C, 351M, and 400 with 60-cc chambers, 2.05/1.60-inch intake/exhaust valves, Manganese bronze valve guides, 190-cc intake and 90-cc exhaust runners, and 5/8-inch-thick decks.

Somewhat confusing is that the Scott Cook head has what the Aussies call a "stuffed" 4V port instead of a full 4V port. The "stuffed" port is engineered with mid-range torque in mind.

The jury is still out on whether or not this is the best approach. So far in dyno and track testing, the Scott Cook Cleveland head has performed very well. On top of a 393-ci stroker, prototype heads produced 602 hp at 6,500 rpm and 505 ft-lbs at 5,600 rpm. These are baseline numbers from testing, but by no means the best they can do. There's more testing to be done.

Exhaust port sizing is just right at 90 cc. This is basically the same size and positioning as the 351C-2V head for good velocity and scavenging. Headers bolt right up to the Edelbrock head.

Edelbrock Corporation

Edelbrock has an affordable cylinder head for the 351C, 351M, and 400 engines. The Edelbrock Performer RPM for 335-series engines has well-thought-out "compact charge," kidney-bean-shaped combustion chambers with intake and exhaust port runners based on the factory 351C-2V cylinder head. Instead of a dysfunctional open chamber, it has the good quench and squeeze of a 60-cc chamber that gets rid of destructive detonation for two reasons: great quench/anti-detonation characteristics and great heat dissipation through aluminum, which keeps combustion temperatures down.

Scott Cook Cleveland

Intake Valve Size	2.190 inches
Exhaust Valve Size	1.625 inches
Intake Port Volume	225 cc
Intake Port Flow at .800 inch	358.7 cfm (standard chamber), 372.5 cfm (shallow chamber)
Exhaust Port Volume	N/A
Exhaust Port Flow at .800 inch	240 cfm
Chamber Size	58 to 64 cc (standard chamber), 40 to 45 cc (shallow chamber)

Edelbrock Performer RPM

Intake Valve Size	2.050 inches
Exhaust Valve Size	1.600 inches
Intake Port Volume	190 cc
Intake Port Flow at .600 inch	265 cfm
Exhaust Port Volume	90 cc
Exhaust Port Flow at .600 inch	165 cfm
Chamber Size	60 cc

The Edelbrock Performer RPM 351C has these cozy, kidney-shaped, 60-cc chambers for good squeeze and great quench. Valve size is 2.05/1.60 inches, which is on par with the factory iron head; however, it has better flow and port angle. An optimized spark plug location gives you adequate header clearance and puts the firing tip right in the middle of the action.

Trick Flow Specialties

There are many power players in the Cleveland head industry. As you might expect, Trick Flow Specialties could never stay out of this game because it's just too much fun—taking the race-proven Cleveland head concept to the limit with a better alloy casting known as "PowerPort" available in two configurations: 190 and 225 cc.

Trick Flow says, "Ford's 351 Cleveland was an engine that made big promises. The 2V version featured small port heads optimized for low-speed torque. The 4V heads, however, had huge ports that boosted top-end horsepower. What Ford did not do was make a version of the Cleveland that combined the torque of the 2V heads and the high-RPM rush of the 4V head design."

Trick Flow responded to the North American Cleveland head's shortcomings and is producing a great cylinder head that lives up to the proven Trick Flow name. The PowerPort Cleveland 190 and 225 cylinder heads, available in a variety of configurations, feature all the great nuances of Ford's 351C-2V head, yet with a better exhaust port and compact wedge chambers that deliver outstanding quench and anti-detonation characteristics.

Exhaust ports are raised .100 inch for improved scavenging, yet they accept off-the-shelf headers and manifolds. Oil return drains are much improved over factory castings getting oil back to the pan as quickly as possible. All the lumps, bumps, and turns have been taken out of the intake ports for better flow. These high-tech castings are fitted with 7/16-inch rocker arm studs from ARP along with pushrod guide plates that are good to go. There is a choice of 1.530- or 1.460-inch spring installed heights. Viton valve seals deliver controlled oil flow to stems and guides along with excellent wear qualities.

Pro Comp USA

The Pro Comp Cleveland cylinder head is a copy of the highly successful Australian CHI 3V casting. Reviews are

Trick Flow PowerPort 225

Intake Valve Size	2.080 inches
Exhaust Valve Size	1.600 inches
Intake Port Flow	N/A
Intake Port Volume	225 cc
Exhaust Port Volume	115 cc
Exhaust Port Flow	N/A
Chamber Size	60 cc

Trick Flow PowerPort 190

Intake Valve Size	2.080 inches
Exhaust Valve Size	1.600 inches
Intake Port Flow	N/A
Intake Port Volume	190 cc
Exhaust Port Volume	112 cc
Exhaust Port Flow	N/A
Chamber Size	62 cc

Because Trick Flow Specialties has always been successful at making Ford power, it's no surprise it has come up with a pair of right-size cylinder head packages for the 351C, 351M, and 400 engines. There are two sizes: 190 and 225 cc (intake port volume). The 190-cc heads have 112-cc exhaust ports and 62- or 72-cc wedge chambers with 2.080/1.600-inch valves. Larger 225-cc heads have larger 115-cc exhaust ports with 60-cc chambers and 2.080/1.600-inch valves. Trick Flow stays conservative with valve sizing because that's where the torque is.

Intake port sizing is generous with the Trick Flow heads and depends on what you want your Cleveland to do. If you're running high displacement, such as a 408C or a 430+ 400, the 225-cc port and 60-cc chamber should make you happy. If displacement is conservative, consider the 190-cc port for better low- to mid-range torque.

Pro Comp	
Intake Valve Size	2.190 inches
Exhaust Valve Size	1.710 inches
Intake Port Volume	220 cc
Intake Port Flow at .800 inch	284.9 cfm
Exhaust Port Volume	90 cc
Exhaust Port Flow at .800 inch	193.7 cfm
Chamber Size	74 cc

It's easy to feel good about Trick Flow's low-restriction, 112- and 115-cc exhaust ports because they're based on Ford's 2V head. They have, however, been raised .100 inch to give hot gases more of a straight shot without causing header fitment problems. Bowls are nicely blended to reduce restriction and turbulence.

mixed about this cylinder head because it is inconsistent. Some like it; others would never buy another one. However, because it is affordable, it is a hot seller.

I decided to take a closer look at what people are doing with this head and what their experiences have been. Richard Holdener, respected author and technical writer, conducted a 400 dyno test with the Pro Comp head with remarkable results in *Muscle Mustangs & Fast Fords* Magazine. Holdener didn't just install these heads right out of the box. He had Bryce Mulvey do a precision valve job on new Pro Comp heads, which involved port and bowl work that netted 348-cfm intake and 252-cfm exhaust. With greater airflow you can get more power with milder cam timing. And with displacement of 400 ci and higher, you get torque without the need for a lot of throttle.

When Holdener went to the SuperFlow 902 dyno with his tall-deck 400 topped with these Pro Comp heads and a CHI single-plane intake, he managed to get 529 hp and 506 ft-lbs of torque. The CHI single-plane was one of two manifolds used, the other being the Edelbrock Performer Air Gap dual-plane. With the Edelbrock dual-plane, he saw 489 hp and 502 ft-lbs of torque. Where his efforts really differed was where peak torque happened, considerably lower with the dual-plane thanks to its longer runners. (Holdener has proven the success of the Pro Comp head with port massaging and a good valve job. See Chapter 11 for more details on his efforts.)

Air Flow Dynamics

Australian Air Flow Dynamics (AFD) has been making cylinder heads for many years and is using that experience to produce a great one for the 335 Cleveland V-8s. AFD has engineered this cylinder head to produce a broad torque curve, which makes it an exceptional street and race head; good for up to 7,000 rpm. A high-swirl chamber is available in a variety of sizes depending upon your bottom end and compression needs. These heads are fitted with phosphorus bronze valveguides, 7/16-inch screw-in ARP rocker studs and Comp Cams guide plates, stainless valves, and hardened Durabond Diamond valve seats.

On the exhaust side, the AFD 2V Cleveland head has round ports for improved scavenging. Yet you can use existing off-the-shelf headers or manifolds with good compatibility. Intake ports have been extensively modified for improved flow. And it isn't so much about volume, but more about how air and fuel flow from manifold into intake port. When you get intake and exhaust flow in synch coupled with the right cam profile, you cannot miss. Exhaust scavenging is just as crucial as intake flow if you want to make real power.

When AFD conducted initial dyno testing with these heads, it learned they

AFD 4V and SP4V Cleveland

Intake Valve Size	2.150 or 2.190 inches
Exhaust Valve Size	1.625, 1.650, or 1.710 inches
Intake Port Volume:	235 cc
Intake Port Flow at .700 inch	330 cfm
Exhaust Port Volume	115 cc
Exhaust Port Flow at .800 inch	221 cfm
Chamber Sizes	48, 54, 58, 64 cc; 70, 75 cc CNC ported only

AFD 2V Cleveland

Intake Valve Size	2.125 inches
Exhaust Valve Size	1.625 inches
Intake Port Volume	200 cc
Intake Port Flow at .650 inch	298 cfm (standard), 319 cfm (ported)
Exhaust Port Volume	115 cc
Exhaust Port Flow at .650 inch	189 cfm (standard), 218 cfm (ported)
Chamber Sizes	54, 57, 60, 64, 68, 75 cc

made excellent street torque and horsepower. At 7,000 rpm, AFD witnessed 555 hp from 383 ci. Peak torque was 482 ft-lbs at 5,300 rpm. Induction was an Active 2V and 950-cfm carburetion. These numbers make the AFD a good street/strip head.

Another dyno test showed even better results with a 393-ci stroker: 666.1 hp at 6,900 rpm along with 534.8 ft-lbs of torque at 5,400 rpm. This was performed with a Parker Funnelweb 2V and 950-cfm carburetion.

The AFD 4V head is a step up in terms of power and performance because it's a nice balance of 2V and 4V heads. It delivers at high RPM with 4V-style performance while acting more like a 2V at low RPM. What you get for your money is better exhaust flow thanks to AFD raising the port .080 inch, which enhances torque. Peak horsepower in testing has been 598.6 at 7,000 rpm, with torque topping out at 502.1 ft-lbs at 5,300 rpm.

Another item to check is valve-to-valve clearance. The minimum should be .060 inch to allow for thermal expansion when things get hot. You can stack two .030-inch gauges to verify clearance.

Regardless of what gasket manufacturers tell you about not needing head retorquing, you should always retorque your heads. Do it in three stages, and lube the threads with engine oil. Once the engine has had a good warm-up and break-in, retorque your cylinder heads.

When you're setting up guide plates, don't tighten them until you've mocked up the valvetrain (rocker arm, pushrod) and dialed in your geometry. Once you have good rocker arm geometry all the way through the complete range of travel, check pushrod to guide plate clearances and torque down the plates.

CHAPTER 6

Camshaft/Valvetrain

Camshaft and valvetrain components directly determine how reliably an engine performs throughout its service life. Before choosing a camshaft and valvetrain, you must first understand how they work and how you want your engine to perform. Are you building a driver where low- and mid-range torque are important or are you building a high-revving racing engine that makes peak torque at high RPM?

Any camshaft manufacturer's catalog lists dozens of camshaft types for the same type of engine. This chapter helps you sort through what all the terms mean and how they affect your engine's performance and durability.

Street Cams

In my experience, the best street-performance cams are ground with a lobe separation between 108 and 114 degrees. Keeping lobe separation above 112 degrees improves drivability because the engine idles smoother and makes better low-end torque. There's also more vacuum at idle for accessories and power brakes. This is what you want from a street engine. Anytime lobe separation is below 108 degrees, idle quality and streetability suffer. But there's more to it than just lobe separation. Compression and cam timing must be considered together because they always affect each other. Valve timing events directly affect cylinder pressure and ultimately working/dynamic compression. Long intake-valve duration reduces cylinder pressure. Shorter intake duration increases cylinder pressure. Too much cylinder pressure can cause detonation (pinging). Too little and torque is lost. Cam manufacturers figure stock compression ratios into their camshaft selection tables, which makes choosing a camshaft easier than it's ever been. Follow the cam manufacturer recommendations and you will be pleased with the result most of the time.

Getting into roller technology is expensive, but a great lifelong investment in what you gain in performance and huge frictional reduction. This is a small base circle roller cam designed to clear rod bolts in a stroker.

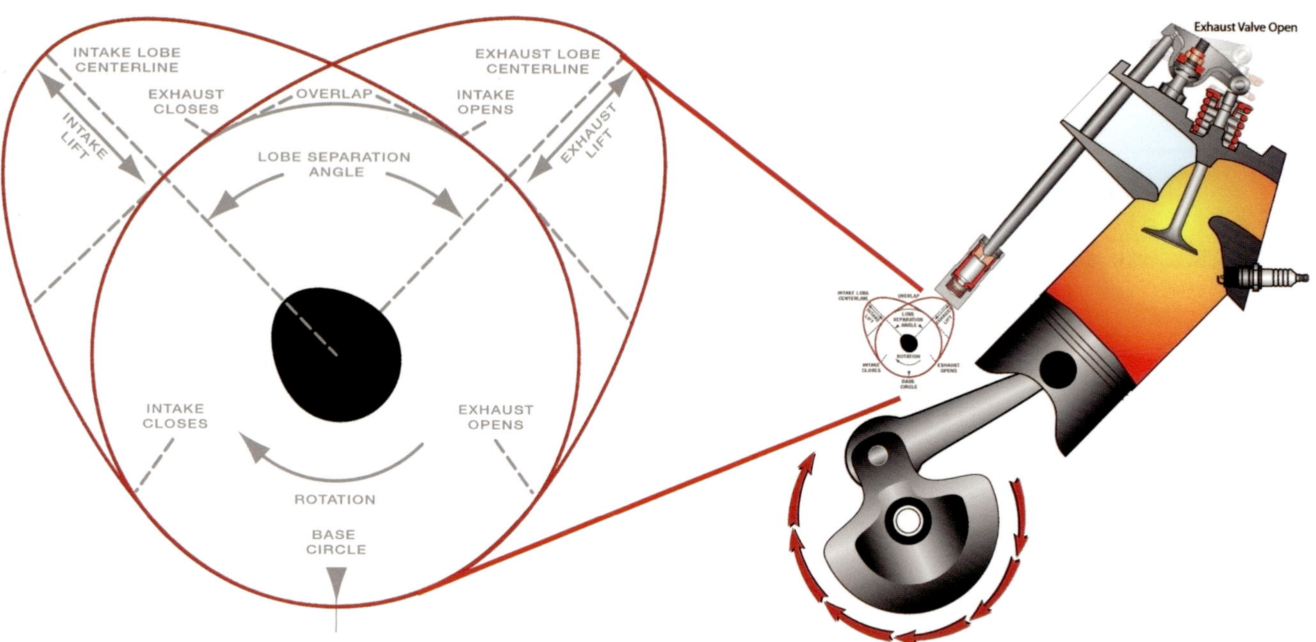

This Comp Cams illustration shows the dynamics of what a camshaft does. This applies to Clevelands, as well as nearly all OHV V-8 engines. (Photo Courtesy Comp Cams)

An engine's "personality" comes from cam profile: lift, duration, lobe separation (lobe centers), valve overlap. (Photo Courtesy Comp Cams)

Flat-tappet cams, though popular because they are affordable, have drawbacks. They're limited in performance potential because you can't go with the kind of aggressive ramp (valve opening and closing) you see with roller cams. They also wear significantly more than a roller cam because there is more friction. This means more internal friction and stolen power.

Flat-tappet technology is affordable, but presents long-term losses such as internal friction and profile limitations. Friction reducers include dual-roller timing sets and roller-tip stamped-steel rocker arms.

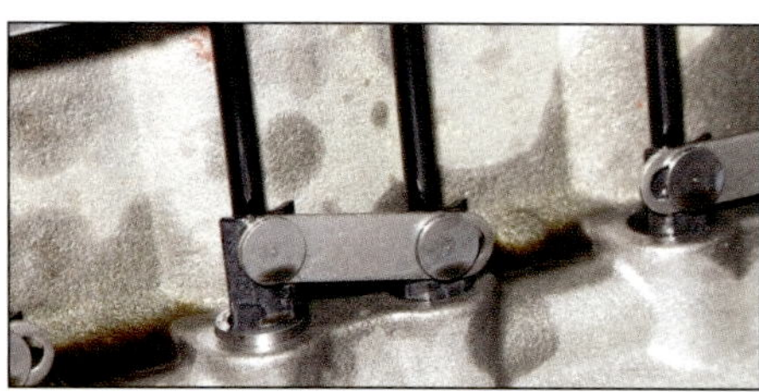

Linked roller tappets are expensive, but less troublesome than spider types with fewer parts. The beauty of a roller cam is how aggressive you can go and keep a civilized idle and cruise.

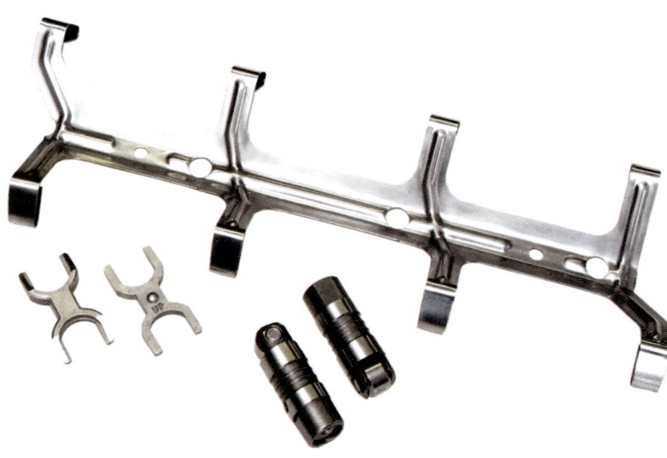

The spider-style, roller-tappet system is borrowed from Ford's 5.0L and 5.8L roller-tappet V-8s that arrived in the mid 1980s. It is both affordable and effective consisting of the spider (retain) assembly and dog bones (to keep tappets squared).

You don't have to drill the block for spider retaining bolts and mollies. This retrofit kit consisting of mollies and bolts enables you to lock the spider at oil drainback holes.

A roller cam is a great internal friction reducer because it eliminates the drag of 16 tappets and lobes. Though this is more expensive, it is a great investment in engine life and performance. How much power is lost to friction? For every bit of friction lost, power is gained.

Cam Speak

The following is a brief explanation of some camshaft terms. All of these factors influence how an engine performs.

Adjustable Valve Timing is being able to dial in a camshaft by adjusting valve timing at the timing sprocket. Advance valve timing and you increase torque, but lose horsepower. Retard valve timing and it loses torque, but gains horsepower. It's called compromise.

Base circle of a camshaft is the portion of the lobe that doesn't generate lift. The bottom-most portion of the lobe is called the heel.

Duration is the amount of time the valve is open beginning when the valve unseats. In other words, it's the number of degrees the camshaft rotates when cam lift begins. Duration typically begins at .004 inch of cam lift or when the lifter begins to ride the ramp coming off the base circle. "Duration at fifty" means duration begins at .050 inch of cam lift. It is the industry standard for determining camshaft lobe duration. It is what you see when you're reading camshaft specs.

Exhaust Centerline is basically the same as intake centerline. It is when the exhaust valve reaches maximum lift before top dead center (BTDC), also measured in degrees.

Flank is the ascending or descending portion of the lobe past the base circle nearest maximum lift.

Flat-tappet camshafts work differently than roller camshafts, which means you have to think differently with each type. Flat-tappet camshafts limit what you can do with lobe profile if you want streetability. If you want an aggressive profile with flat tappets, you can only go so far with a street engine or suffer with poor drivability (rough idle, low manifold vacuum). If you want an aggressive profile in a street engine, step up to a roller camshaft, which can handle the aggressive profile better using roller tappets.

Intake Centerline is the position of the camshaft in relation to the crankshaft. For example, an intake centerline of 114 degrees means the intake valve reaches maximum lift at 114 degrees after top dead center (ATDC).

Lift is the maximum amount a valve-lifter/pushrod combination can be raised off the base circle. Lift is measure in thousandths (.000) of an inch. Lobe profile determines how quickly this occurs; it can either be smooth or abrupt.

Lobe Separation (also known as valve overlap) is the distance (in degrees) between the intake lobe peak and the exhaust lobe peak. Lobe separation generally runs between 102 and 114 degrees (camshaft degrees).

Ramp is the ascending or descending side of the cam lobe coming off the base circle when lift begins to occur.

Valve Overlap is the period of time when both the intake and exhaust valve are open to allow for proper cylinder scavenging (also known as lobe separation). Overlap occurs when the exhaust valve is closing and the piston is reaching top dead center (TDC). The intake charge from the opening intake valve pushes the exhaust gases out. Camshaft grinders can change valve overlap to modify the performance of a camshaft. Sometimes they do this rather than change lift or duration.

Lift and Compression

Be conservative with your cam specs if you want reliability and an engine that lives a long time. Choose a conservative lift profile (.500-inch lift). High-lift camshafts beat the daylights out of a valvetrain. And they put valve-to-piston clearances at risk. Watch duration and lobe separation closely, which help you be more effective in camshaft selection. Instead of opening the valve more (lift), you want to open it longer (duration) and in better efficiency with piston timing (overlap or lobe separation).

Always bear in mind your induction, heads, and exhaust. The savvy engine builder understands that in order to work effectively, an engine must have matched components. Cam, valvetrain, heads, intake manifold, and exhaust system must all work as a team or you're just wasting time and money. If you're going to use stock cylinder heads, your cam profile need not be too aggressive. Opt for a cam profile that gives you good low- to mid-range torque. Torque doesn't do you any good on the street when it happens at 6,000 rpm. Choose a cam profile that makes good torque between 2,500 and 4,500 rpm. Otherwise, you're just wasting engine.

One thing to remember with camshaft selection is how the cam works with your engine's cylinder heads. Take a close look at valve lift with a particular cylinder head and determine its effect. Some camshafts actually lose power with a given head because there's too much lift or duration. This is why you want to understand a cylinder head before choosing a camshaft. You want to seek optimum conditions with any cylinder head/camshaft combination. This means doing your homework before making a decision.

What type of fuel do you intend to run in your engine? This also affects camshaft selection. You can actually raise compression if you're running a mild camshaft profile or using a higher octane fuel. Camshaft timing events must be directly tied to compression ratio. The longer the duration, the lower cylinder pressure and working compression. The shorter the duration, the less air brought into the cylinder, which also affects compression.

Your objective needs to be the highest compression possible without detonation, which harms the engine. With this in mind, you want the most duration possible without compression extremes. Duration is what gives you torque, as long as compression is sufficient.

Valve Overlap

Valve overlap is the period between exhaust stroke and intake stroke when both valves are slightly off their seats. This occurs to improve exhaust scavenging and cylinder filling. It improves exhaust scavenging by allowing the incoming intake charge to push remaining exhaust gases out by the closing exhaust valve. With the exhaust valve completely closed, you wouldn't get scavenging. The greater the overlap in a street engine, the less torque the engine makes down low where you need it most. This is why you want less valve overlap in a street engine and more in a racing engine, which makes its torque at high RPM. Increased valve overlap works best at high RPM.

Street engines need 10 to 55 degrees of valve overlap to be effective torque powerhouses. When valve overlap starts traveling above 55 degrees, torque on the low end falters. A really hot street engine needs more than 55 degrees of valve overlap, but not much more. For example, racing engines need 70 to 115 degrees of valve overlap because that is what you need at high RPM.

For a street engine, valve overlap should maximize torque, which means taking a conservative approach in the first place. Push overlap as far as you can without compromising torque. You also have to figure in lift and duration with valve overlap to see the complete power picture.

Lobe Separation Angle

Lobe separation angle is another area of consideration in street cam selection. This camshaft dynamic is chosen based on displacement and how the engine will be used. Rule of thumb is this: Consider lobe separation based on how much displacement and valving you're going to be using. The smaller the valves, the tighter (fewer degrees) the lobe separation should be. However, tighter lobe separation does adversely affect idle quality. This is why most camshaft manufacturers spec their cams with wider lobe separations than the custom grinders.

Duration

Duration in a street engine is likely the most important dynamic to consider in the selection process. Why increase duration whenever less lift is desired? Because your airflow gets into the cylinder bore two ways: lift and duration. You can open the valve more and for less time to get more airflow. Or you can open the valve less and keep it open longer via duration to get more airflow. Each has a different influence on performance.

Duration is determined by the size of the cylinder head and amount of displacement, and how the engine will be used. Excessive duration hurts low-end torque, which is what you need on the street. So balance must be achived by maximizing duration without losing low-end torque. This is done by using the right heads with proper valve sizing. Large valves and ports don't work well at all for street use. Mix in too much duration and you have a real slug at the traffic light.

So what does this tell you about duration? You want greater duration whenever displacement and valve sizing go up. Increasing duration falls directly in line with torque peak and RPM range. And this does not mean you necessarily gain any torque as RPM increases. It means your peak torque simply comes in at a higher RPM range. For example, if your engine is making 350 ft-lbs of torque at 4,500 rpm and you increase duration, you may well be making that same amount of torque at 5,200 rpm. In short, increased duration does not always mean increased torque.

Compression has a direct effect on what duration should be. When you're running greater compression, you have to watch duration closely because it can drive cylinder pressures too high. Sometimes you curb compression and run greater duration depending on how you want to make power. When you have greater duration, the engine makes more power on the high end and less on the low end. This is why you must carefully consider duration when ordering a camshaft. Higher compression with a shorter duration helps the engine make torque down low where you need it most in a street engine. The thing to watch for with compression is detonation and overheating. Maximum street compression is around 10.0:1.

Valve Lift

Think about valve lift as it pertains to an engine's needs. Small-blocks generally need more valve lift than big-blocks. As you increase lift, you generally increase torque. This is especially important at low- and mid-RPM ranges, where it counts on the street. Low-end torque is harder to achieve with a small-block because these engines generally sport short strokes and large bores. Your objective needs to be more torque with less RPM if you want your engine to live longer. Revs are what drain the life out of an engine more quickly.

To make good, low-end torque with a small-block, you need a camshaft that offers a combination of effective lift and duration. As a rule, you want to run longer intake duration to make the most of valve lift. You get valve lift via the camshaft to be sure. But, rocker arm ratio is the other half of the equation. The most common rocker arm ratio is 1.6:1, which means the rocker arm gives the valve 1.6 times the lift as at the cam lobe. When you step up to a 1.7:1 ratio rocker arm, valve lift becomes 1.7 times, which you find at the lobe.

Camshaft Wear

It is best to spec a cam on the conservative side, especially if you're building an engine for daily driving and weekend race use. Whenever you opt for an aggressive camshaft with a lot of lift, you're putting more stress on the valvestem, guide, and spring. The constant hammering of daily use with excessive lift is what kills engines without warning.

Taking this excessive wear logic a step further, it is vital that you ascertain proper centering of the rocker arm tip on the valvestem tip when you're doing valvetrain setup. This is performed by using the correct-length pushrod for your application. Use a pushrod checker to properly configure your Cleveland's rocker-to-stem geometry.

A pushrod checker is little more than an adjustable pushrod used to determine rocker arm geometry. If the pushrod is too long, the tip is under-centered on the valvestem, causing excessive side loads toward the outside of the cylinder head. If the pushrod is too short, the rocker arm tip is over-centered, causing excessive side loading toward the inside of the head. In either case, side loads on the valvestem and guide cause excessive wear and early failure. This is why you want the rocker arm tip to be properly centered on the valvestem for smooth operation.

One accessory that reduces valvestem tip wear and side loading is the roller-tip rocker arm. Roller-tip rocker arms roll smoothly across the valvestem tip, virtually eliminating wear. Stamped-steel, roller-tip rocker arms are available at budget prices without the high cost of extruded or forged pieces.

Dual-Pattern Camshafts

A dual-pattern camshaft runs different profiles on the intake and exhaust side to meet individual need. You run dual-pattern profiles whenever you're pushing up the revs. Typically, a dual-pattern camshaft runs a shorter exhaust-valve duration due to less time required to scavenge the exhaust gases at high RPM. It is also beneficial whenever you're running nitrous or supercharging/turbocharging where exhaust scavenging is rapid and furious where you need more duration.

Another reason for running dual-patterns is Ford's traditionally restrictive exhaust ports. Though the 351C-4V is blessed with generous intake port sizing, it is cursed with restrictive exhaust ports, which call for a dual-pattern cam profile. Intake needs to behave differently than exhaust. This is where you need more duration on the exhaust side in an effort to improve scavenging.

Race Cams

Building an engine for racing is different than building a street engine. Camshaft profile in a racing engine depends upon the type of racing you're going to do, vehicle weight and type, even the type of transmission and rear axle ratio.

Drag racing mandates a different camshaft profile than road or circle track racing. A short-track racing engine needs to be able to produce huge amounts of torque in short order, for example. The same is true for a drag racer. These differences teach us something about engine breathing. Breathing effectiveness is determined by camshaft profile.

Lobe Separation

Lobe separation for the drag racing camshaft should be between 104 and 118 degrees, which is actually a broad range because drag racing needs can vary quite a bit. This is where you must custom dial in your application with a camshaft grinder. Most camshaft grinders have computation charts that show the right cam for a particular application. As your needs change, so must the camshaft profile.

If you're going road racing, lobe separation becomes more specific, in the 106-degree range. Some cam grinders push lobe separation higher for the circle track engine, depending on conditions. Generally, the higher the lobe separation, the broader the torque curve (more torque over a broader RPM range).

Lifters

Four basic lifter (tappet) types are used in Clevelands: flat-tappet hydraulic and mechanical, and roller-tappet hydraulic and mechanical. Flat-tappet lifters were original equipment in all 335-series Cleveland engines. Roller tappets were increasingly used in Ford

Why Degree a Camshaft?

Making power isn't just about adding displacement, large-port heads, a big carburetor, and a lumpy camshaft, it is about the physics of packaging and tuning your engine properly. Why degree camshafts after they're installed in an engine? What does it accomplish?

Degreeing a camshaft is a quest to learn the truth about power and how to get more. The most basic reason for degreeing a camshaft is to determine you have the correct grind for the job and that your cam matches the card. Camshaft grinders today employ very advanced technology. As a result, very few faulty camshafts ever make it to the consumer. However, camshafts do get mispackaged and improperly ground sometimes, which means you could receive a completely different grind than appears on the cam card and packaging. This is why you should fact check during cam installation.

When you degree a camshaft, you're determining valve timing events as they relate to crankshaft position. The crankshaft makes two complete revolutions for every one revolution of the camshaft. One full revolution of each is 360 degrees. This means the crank turns 720 degrees and the cam turns 360 degrees. Think of rotation like a pie. Half a turn is 180 degrees. A quarter of a turn is 90 degrees.

Duration is the number of degrees of rotation the camshaft makes from the time the valve begins to open until the time it closes. When you see 244 degrees of duration, it means there are 244 degrees of camshaft rotation from valve unseat to valve seat. Valve overlap (or lobe separation) is the number of degrees between maximum valve lift intake and maximum valve lift exhaust. With all this in mind, you can degree the camshaft timing events in time with piston travel.

A camshaft is degreed by bolting a degree wheel to the crankshaft, cranking piston number-1 to top dead center (TDC), finding true TDC, and installing a timing pointer. You can purchase a degree wheel kit from Summit Racing Equipment (#SUM-G-1057).

You can find TDC with a Summit bolt-on piston stop that bolts to the deck (#SUM-900188) or screws into the spark plug hole (#SUM-900189). I suggest doing this with the cylinder head removed, which provides the greatest accuracy because you want true TDC.

Here are the steps for this process:

1. Turn the crankshaft clockwise until piston number-1 comes up to TDC and you are smack in the middle of crank rollover with the rod at 12 o'clock.
2. With the cylinder head installed, hold your thumb over the spark plug hole and listen to the air being forced out by the piston.
3. Both timing marks on the crank and camshaft sprockets should be in perfect alignment at 12 and 6 o'clock.
4. Install the degree wheel and align the bolt-on timing pointer.

With all of this accomplished, piston number-1 should be at TDC, with the degree wheel and pointer at zero degrees. This is true TDC and becomes your base point of reference. Everything from here on out is before top dead center (BTDC) or after top dead center (ATDC).

The intake valve opens at a given number of degrees ATDC and closes at a given number of degrees BTDC. The exhaust valve opens at a given number of degrees BTDC and closes a given number of degrees ATDC. Much depends upon valve overlap.

factory V-8 engines after 1985, which is when aftermarket manufacturers began to make them available. More and more engine builds are witnessing the use of roller tappets because there's less friction, smoother operation, and the ability to run a more aggressive profile without the drawbacks of a radical flat-tappet camshaft.

Roller tappets are more costly than flat tappets due to tighter tolerances and a greater number of parts. Their cost puts them outside of the budget-engine category, but they're worth every penny in what they save in wear and tear. They also give you an advantage if you run a more aggressive camshaft profile.

Although hydraulic lifters saw more widespread use beginning in the 1960s, their use dates back to the 1920s. Hydraulic lifters don't require periodic adjustment as do mechanical or solid lifters. As the camshaft and valvetrain wear, hydraulic lifters expand with the wear via oil pressure to take up clearance. This keeps operation quiet and reliability sound.

Hydraulic lifters do well until cam-lobe and valvestem wear is so excessive the lifter can no longer take up the clearance. Then you hear the telltale "click" or tapping of rocker arm noise, especially when the engine is cold. Sometimes rocker arm click is a faulty lifter (leaking hydraulic pressure) or an excessively worn rocker arm. The first indication of an excessively worn rocker arm is the "clicking" that occurs at any engine temperature. It can also mean oil starvation at the rocker.

To find bonus power, you have to reduce friction everywhere it exists. This is a Torrington thrust bearing for small-block Fords including the Cleveland, which reduces internal friction at the cam sprocket.

The Torrington needle-bearing, cam-sprocket thrust includes its own machined-steel cam plate for excellent wear and fit. Always check cam endplay and sprocket to thrust clearances.

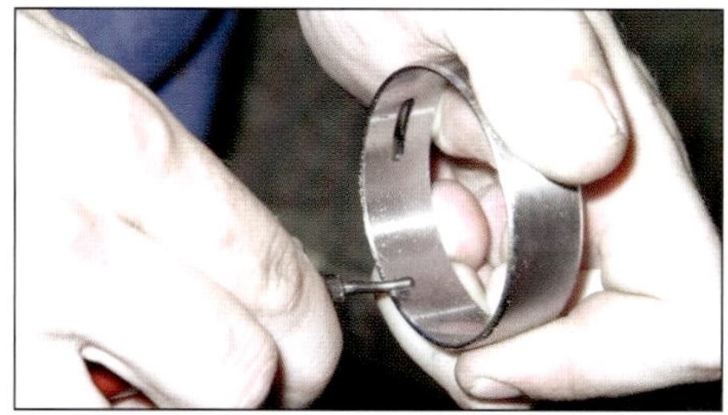

JGM Performance Engineering stresses the need to trim ragged edges from cam bearings to prevent journal scoring. Not all agree with this approach; however, it has worked very well for JGM. Cam journal scoring, no matter how slight, hurts oil pressure.

Friction reduction and cam timing accuracy are gained from the use of a dual-roller timing set. It's always important to save money; however, friction reduction is a great investment in engine life and efficiency.

Gear drives have been around for a long time and they deliver pinpoint valve timing accuracy; however, they're expensive and can be noisy. This really is a personal choice depending on what you want your Cleveland to do. Gear drives are best left to racing because they are impractical for the street even though they sound cool.

This is a two-piece Ford fuel pump eccentric for the 351C, which offers reduced internal friction.

Lifter and cam-lobe wear and failure are rarely caused by a manufacturing defect. They fail because you don't give them a good start when it's time to fire the engine in the first place. Flat-tappet camshafts must be broken in properly or failure is inevitable. Moly coat must be applied to the cam lobe and lifter face when you're installing a flat-tappet camshaft. The engine must be operated at 2,500 rpm for 20 to 30 minutes after the initial fire-up to properly wear in the lobes. Synthetic engine oil should not be used until after the break-in period. During this period, check the pushrods for rotation.

Roller tappets don't require break-in because rollers and cam lobes enjoy

Adjustable timing sprockets enable you to tune your Cleveland's valve timing events. This is best done during engine buildup and degreeing, though it can be done in the car.

Advance the cam 2 degrees and gain torque depending upon how your cam compares with the cam spec card. Retard timing to gain horsepower. By the way, check valve to piston clearances as a precaution before buttoning up.

Retard cam 2 degrees and gain horsepower but lose torque. Again, check those valve to piston clearances. The downside to adjustable cam sprockets at the crank is the limitation of 2-degree increments.

Here's another type of adjustable cam sprocket; small eccentrics are swapped in to advance or retard the cam sprocket. There are usually five eccentrics in the kit to fine-tune your valve timing.

All engine builds should include degreeing the camshaft because you want to know exactly what you have right out of the box. Begin cam degreeing at zero at TDC and record valve timing events. When you advance valve timing, you gain low- to mid-range torque. When you retard valve timing, you gain horsepower on the high end. Make these adjustments in 2-degree increments and check valve-to-piston clearances.

JGM Performance Engineering uses a Comp Cams billet degree wheel, which is easy to see and use. You can turn the crank by the wheel or use a 1/2-inch-drive ratchet as shown.

a good relationship to begin with. The lobes are already hardened and the rollers provide a smooth ride. Flat-tappet mechanical camshafts are good for high-revving engines where the inaccuracies of hydraulic camshafts (lifter collapse) are unacceptable. Mechanical camshafts give you accuracy because there's nothing left to chance. The lift moves with the cam lobe with solid precision. Given proper valve-lash adjustment, mechanical lifters do their job very well. The thing is, mechanical flat and roller tappets have to be adjusted periodically, which can be annoying on a daily driven street engine. This is where you need to do some soul searching before selecting a camshaft.

Valvetrain

At 6,000 rpm, valves slam again their seats 3,000 times per minute. Exhaust valves not only reciprocate vigorously at half the speed of the crankshaft, they're subjected to combustion temperatures of approximately 1,800 to 2,000 degrees F. Lifters, pushrods, rocker arms, and valvesprings take a like amount of punishment without the levels of heat valves experience. Of all your engine's components, valvetrain components are the most likely to fail. Many a broken valvespring or failed keeper has brought down the mightiest of engines. This is why your attention to this area is vital.

Jim Grubbs of JGM Performance Engineering likes to soak lifters in hot oil with a moly additive to ensure deep-penetrating lubrication on start-up.

A valvetrain's greatest ally is stability. Valvetrain systems must have matched components for stable operation. This is why camshaft manufacturers have increasingly gone to camshaft kits in recent years to help you choose the right combination of components. Camshaft companies make it easy to package your valvetrain system. Packaging a valvetrain depends on how you want your engine to perform.

Three-piece (left) versus one-piece (right) pushrod? Use a one-piece pushrod with .080-inch wall thickness even with a stock Cleveland because you want durability, and this is cheap life insurance.

If you're building a street engine that will be operating in the 2,500- to 5,500-rpm range, camshaft specifications need

Proper valvetrain setup is about doing the math accurately because you don't want to mess this up. Cam profile and valvespring pressure must match. Too much spring pressure and you lose power and eat up the cam. Not enough spring pressure for the profile and you float valves at high RPM. You also want proper installed height void of coil bind.

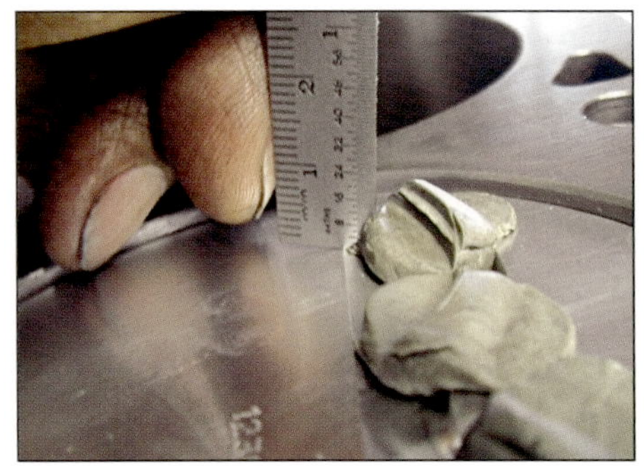

When degreeing a cam, don't forget to temporarily bolt on the cylinder heads and do a mock-up to check valve to piston clearances. Some builders check just one bore while others check all of them. Unless clearances are dangerously close, you probably don't need to check all eight bores. Minimum piston-to-valve clearance should be at least .060 inch.

More aggressive cam profiles call for greater spring pressures where you double or triple the number of springs. This is a Crane double spring with a dampener.

to have conservative torque because you want the engine to make good low-end torque for the street.

Lifters, pushrods, rocker arms, and springs need to follow suit. Run a spring that is too soft for your camshaft profile and your engine experiences valve float (not enough spring pressure to close the valves quickly) at high RPM. Likewise, run a spring that's too stiff and you can wipe the cam lobes from excessive pressure against the lobe. This is why running matched components is so important.

Once valve-to-piston clearances are confirmed, check for coil bind at maximum lift. You want a minimum of .060 inch before you get into coil bind. You need more room, on the order of .100 inch.

Blueprint every valvespring by removing ragged edges for buttery smoothness, then give them an anti-friction coating and generous amounts of engine assembly lube. This ensures a good start-up without scoring.

Rocker Arms and Pushrods

The rocker arm and pushrod transfer the cam lobe's energy to the valvestem. Think of the rocker arm as the camshaft's messenger because the rocker arm multiplies lift, which makes the valve open farther than the camshaft's lobe lift. Rocker arm types range from stock cast affairs all the way up to extruded and forged pieces with roller bearings and tips. Forged or extruded roller rocker arms are quite costly, which generally leaves them out of a budget engine program. However, this doesn't mean you have to settle for stock cast or stamped-steel pieces either.

Valvespring pressure and cam profile must coincide with each other. The best advice I can offer is to go with the spring pressure your cam manufacturer specifies or to go with a complete kit with matched springs. Shown here is a mild spring with a dampener for stability and heat dissipation. This is a spring you would expect to see with a mild flat-tappet or roller cam.

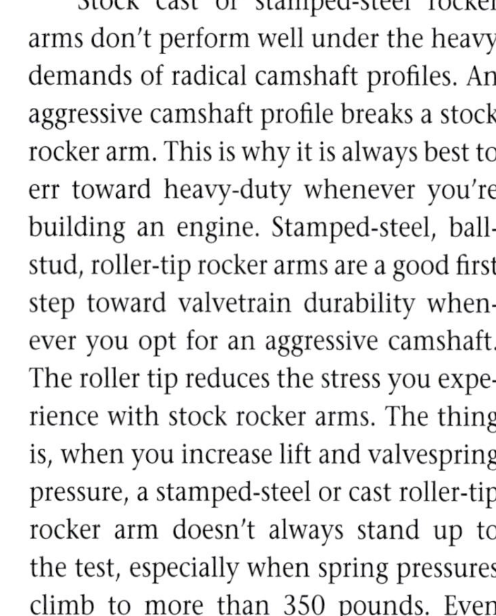

Stock cast or stamped-steel rocker arms don't perform well under the heavy demands of radical camshaft profiles. An aggressive camshaft profile breaks a stock rocker arm. This is why it is always best to err toward heavy-duty whenever you're building an engine. Stamped-steel, ball-stud, roller-tip rocker arms are a good first step toward valvetrain durability whenever you opt for an aggressive camshaft. The roller tip reduces the stress you experience with stock rocker arms. The thing is, when you increase lift and valvespring pressure, a stamped-steel or cast roller-tip rocker arm doesn't always stand up to the test, especially when spring pressures climb to more than 350 pounds. Even the best stamped-steel, roller-tip rocker arm will fail when overstressed.

When lift and spring pressures go skyward, you want a roller-pivot, roller-tip, forged rocker arm for your budget engine build. Going that extra mile with a super-durable rocker arm ensures longer engine life, especially if you're going to drive it daily. For the weekend racer, stepping up to a better rocker arm is like writing a life insurance policy because marginal rocker arms do not

This is a good mock-up where valve-to-piston clearances and true valve lift are checked using a dial indicator.

stand up to the high-revving task. Roller-pivot, roller-tip rocker arms also ensure valvetrain precision and accuracy when the revs get high.

Crane Cams, Comp Cams, or Ford Racing are good sources for rocker arms and pushrods. These companies all have a lot of valuable experience with valvetrain components and offer wide selections. Always run the same brand of rocker arm and camshaft.

When it comes to valvetrain adjustment, Clevelands have flexibility in adjustable aftermarket studs where adjustable studs were not originally used. Early small-block Fords (1962–1967) had adjustable, ball/stud-mounted rocker arms. From 1968 to 1977, they received no-adjust, positive-stop rocker arm studs which are undesirable for the performance buff. From 1978 to present, the rocker arm stud was replaced with a new-design, stamped-steel rocker arm, fulcrum, and bolt that mount atop a boss. Clevelands differ from other small-block Fords in that they never had a stud-mounted rocker on common examples. Only the Boss 351 and 351 High Output had stud-mounted adjustable rockers.

Clevelands were originally fitted with two types of rocker arm packages. Most had this bolt-fulcrum, stamped-steel rocker arm package, which is not adjustable. The bolt-fulcrum rocker arm first saw use on the 385-series 429/460. A 1971 Boss 351 or 1972 High Output has screw-in studs and adjustable rocker arms with guide plates.

The 335-series small-block engine family (351C, 351M, 400M) had two types of rocker arm arrangements from the factory. The Boss 351 (1971) and 351 High Output (1972) had adjustable, stud-mounted rocker arms. The rest had bolt-fulcrum style, no-adjust, stamped-steel rocker arms as found on small-block Fords 1978-up.

Valve-Lash Adjustment

If you're building a Cleveland with a bolt-fulcrum rocker, there is no valve-lash adjustment. However, bolt-fulcrum rocker arms sometimes require pushrods of varying lengths to get into proper adjustment. If you have a noisy rocker arm, confirm lifter status before doing anything else. A collapsed lifter causes excessive rocker arm noise. According to Ford you are allowed 5 to 55 seconds of lifter leakdown time. A damaged or

Friction and wear reduction begin with a roller-tip rocker such as from Comp Cams, which has a 1.52:1 ratio. If you're on a limited budget, this is a good rocker. The key to durability is to get your rocker arm geometry just right. You want the roller-tip to be dead-center on the valvestem with the valve fully open.

Here's the bolt-fulcrum rocker setup with roller tip from Crane. You want a steel fulcrum regardless of how you intend to build your no-adjust valvetrain.

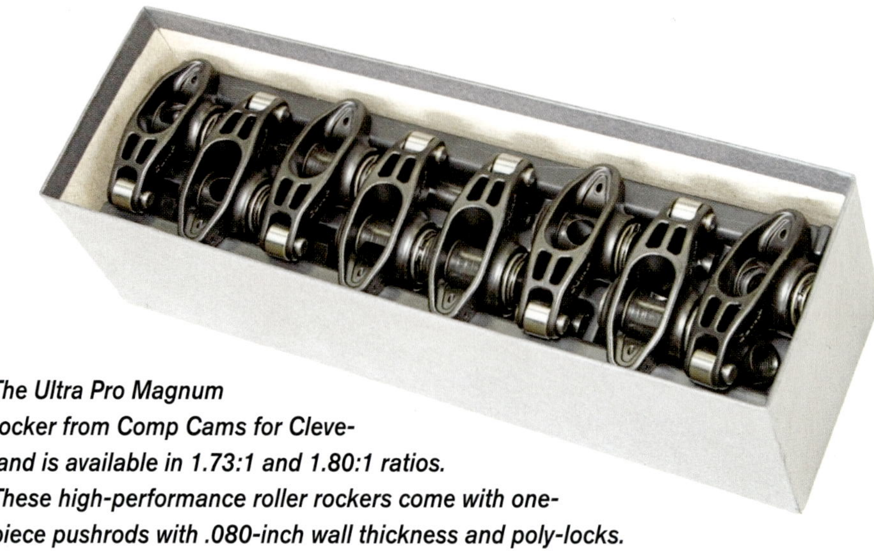

The Ultra Pro Magnum rocker from Comp Cams for Cleveland is available in 1.73:1 and 1.80:1 ratios. These high-performance roller rockers come with one-piece pushrods with .080-inch wall thickness and poly-locks.

excessively worn rocker arm can make noise, as does a loose fulcrum-retaining bolt. Ford suggests a .060-inch-longer pushrod to help take up excessive clearance.

Many go with an adjustable stud-mounted rocker arm with mechanical or hydraulic tappets. There's endless discussion about how to adjust valve lash on hydraulic-lifter Clevelands. However, adjustment is nothing more than common sense. Hydraulic-lifter pistons have a very limited amount of travel or preload: .020 to .060 inch. On top, that means approximately 1/4 to 3/4 turn at the rocker arm. When adjusting valve lash, you want the lifters smack on the cam lobes' heels (valves closed) on compression stroke. But honestly, cam manufacturers offer even more precise advice: Slowly turn the crank until each valve closes completely, then, make your adjustment.

Turn the pushrod with your fingertips while tightening the rocker arm adjustment nut. When the pushrod becomes ever so slightly resistant to your fingertips, turn the adjustment nut 1/4 to 1/2 turn. Though Ford suggests 3/4 turn with some applications, this is too much. If you're running poly locks, tighten the Allen screw lock. Do this in the engine's firing order, one cylinder at a time.

You don't know if you are successful until you fire the engine and it is at operating temperature. If there's significant rocker arm noise, there's too much lash and you need to go a little tighter. Some aftermarket rocker arms, such as the Comp Cams Pro Magnum or Ultra Pro Magnum, make a soft clicking sound, which makes a Cleveland sound more like it has mechanical tappets, but is of no consequence.

With roller or flat mechanical tappets, valve-lash adjustment is simple. As with hydraulic tappets, follow the firing order with both valves just closed. Valve lash between rocker arm tip and valvestem is .022-inch cold for both intake and exhaust. When you start the engine, you should hear uniform rocker arm chatter. Any loud clicking is excessive valve lash.

Proper valve adjustment is crucial to both performance and durability. A valve that doesn't seat from over-tightening ultimately burns and fails, not to mention misfires and rough operation. Valves need contact with the seat not only for the obvious (compression) but also for heat transfer to the seat and water jacket. The .022 inch the rocker arm has at the valvestem gives you the necessary allowance for safe operation.

This rocker arm stud girdle (PN 1135) by Joma is available from MPG Head Service. Stud girdles provide extraordinary valvetrain stability by securing all studs and limiting movement.

Pushrod Length

Proper pushrod length is a very serious consideration for any engine builder. It can mean the difference between long engine life and having to pull heads in a few thousand miles. A pushrod that's too long pushes the rocker arm tip under-center, causing excessive side loading to the valvestem and guide. Likewise, a pushrod that's too short does the same thing on the opposite side. A pushrod checker (found at your favorite speed shop) helps you make the right decision for not much money.

When checking pushrod length, the rocker arm tip should be close to center on the valvestem tip and dead-center with the valve fully open. Remember, the rocker arm tip is going to walk across the valvestem tip when you come up on the high side of the cam lobe.

Take a black felt-tip marker and darken the valvestem tip. Then install the rocker arm and pushrod. Hand crank the engine and watch the valve pass through one full opening and closing. Get down along side the rocker arm and valvespring and watch the rocker arm travel. Then inspect the black marking for a wear pattern. This shows you exactly where the rocker arm tip has traveled across the valvestem tip.

The pattern should be centered on the valvestem tip. If it runs too much toward the outside of the valvestem tip, the pushrod is too short. If it runs toward the inside of the valvestem tip, the pushrod is too long.

Valve-lash adjustment begins at cylinder number-1 with both valves just closed. Twirl the pushrod with your fingertips while slowly tightening the rocker adjustment until there is slight resistance. Slowly tighten the adjustment clockwise 1/4 to 1/2 turn. Lock the adjustment down.

Valves and Springs

Valves and springs play an important role in power and reliability. Weak spots in either area can rob you of power or lead to engine failure. This is why choosing the right valves and springs is so important. Most cam manufacturers offer a variety of valvespring combinations designed to work well with the camshaft you have chosen. In fact the best way to shop for and buy a cam is to purchase a camshaft kit, which includes valvesprings, retainers, and keepers matched to your camshaft profile. You match a cam and springs because you want a compatible spring for the profile. More radical cams call for stiffer springs. Milder camshaft grinds need less valvespring pressure. Too much spring pressure can wipe the cam lobes. Too little can cause valve float (valve seating doesn't keep up with the revs) at high revs.

Choosing the right valvespring is strictly a matter of following a camshaft grinder's recommendations. Most springs are applicable to hydraulic or mechanical lifters. Some are specific only to roller camshafts. Crane Cams, for example, offers dozens of different valvespring types.

When you opt for a camshaft kit, there's comfort in knowing the manufacturer has matched the springs to the camshaft profile. Most of the homework has been done for you. There won't be concern about coil binding, or too much or too little spring pressure.

The best time to check for coil bind is when you're degreeing the camshaft. Do this before permanently bolting on the heads. Most cam grinders tell you the recommended installed spring height and seat pressure. Correct installed height and spring pressure are achieved with the use of shims as necessary. Coil bind is checked by measuring coil spacing with the valve at maximum lift. There should be no less than .060 inch between the coils at full valve lift. Retainer to valve guide clearance at full lift is the same; no less than .060 inch. This clearance is vital because coil bind or retainer contact with the head causes valvetrain failure. The .060 inch you give it allows for thermal expansion of metal parts and any camshaft aggressiveness and spring movement at high revs.

Another consideration is piston-to valve-clearance whenever you're installing a camshaft with greater lift and duration. The most common practice is to press modeling clay into the piston valve reliefs, then temporarily install the head and valvetrain, then turn the crank two complete revolutions. If you feel any resistance, back off and remove the head. Chances are at this point you have valve-to-piston contact. Forcing the crank bends the valve and/or damages the piston. If no resistance is felt in two full turns of the crankshaft, remove the head and examine the clay. Slice the clay at the valve relief and check the thickness of the clay. This is your valve to piston clearance, which should be no less than .060 inch.

INDUCTION

Clevelands can be fitted with any type of induction system including electronic-port or throttle-body fuel injection. Although the 351C was introduced as a high-performance engine in 1970, Ford never fitted this engine with a Holley or Carter performance carburetor due to tougher federal emissions standards. All 4-barrel Clevelands were fitted with the Autolite/Motorcraft 4300 (351C-4V) or 4300D (Boss 351 and 351C High Output).

Carburetion

Induction begins with a carburetor and there are a lot of them to consider these days because the market is competitive and plentiful. Holley remains the carburetor of choice but there are nice alternatives from Demon, Edelbrock, Summit Racing, Quick Fuel, and Proform. Holley has been smack in the middle of racing and street performance since the 1950s and manufacturing carburetors for more than a century.

Serviceability is what makes Holley performance carburetors appealing to performance enthusiasts. Jet, power valve, and metering block swaps are easy though admittedly messy at times. Accelerator pump adjustment is simple. Vacuum and mechanical secondary dial-in takes a little practice.

Carburetor design consists of basically two types: One is Holley based with two removable fuel bowls and metering blocks with a central air horn and throttle baseplate. The main metering circuit consists of changeable jets. Some models have interchangeable air bleeds. The other design is Carter AFB/AVS based with a throttle baseplate, main body, and air horn with a metering rod style of main metering circuit.

Of course, there are also Ford original-equipment carburetors, which (in the Cleveland years 1970–1982) weren't much to talk about. Clevelands were equipped with Autolite/Motorcraft 2100/2150 2-barrel carburetors and 4300 and 4300D 4-barrels. The 2100/2150 has always been a reliable carburetor; however, it is in no way a performance carburetor. The 4300 was designed with a focus on emissions reduction and was never really intended to be a performance carburetor, though it was a 4-barrel. The 4300 has always struggled with drivability problems—surging, hesitation, flat spots. The late Jon Enyeart of Pony Carburetors knew and understood the 4300 and 4300D carburetors. Despite their poor reputation for performance, he always knew how to get them

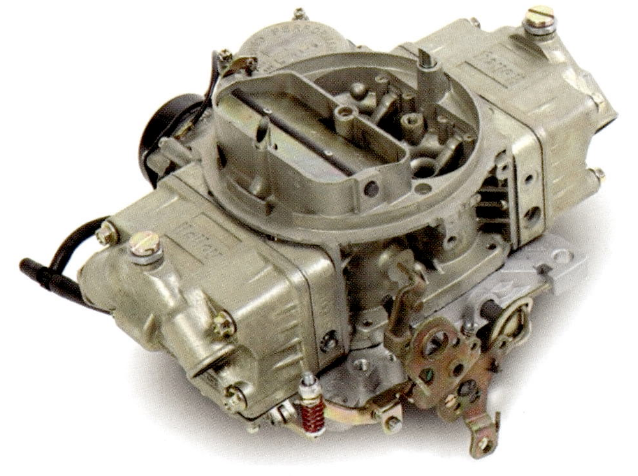

This is the Holley 4160 carburetor with vacuum secondaries and a fixed secondary metering plate.

working properly. But, unless you're building a stocker, the 4300/4300D should never be a consideration because they're just too problematic.

Cleveland 4-barrel power comes from the Autolite/Motorcraft 4300 carburetor. Though the 4300 was original equipment on a lot of Clevelands, it was never meant to be a performance carburetor. Introduced in 1967 and equipped with small primaries and larger secondaries, the 4300 was designed to be a low-emissions carburetor from the start. Unless you are forced by state motor vehicle emissions laws, go with a Holley 4160 or Autolite 4100.

Selecting a Carburetor

It is easy to think a larger carburetor, more aggressive camshaft, and large-port heads make more power, but this isn't always true. Induction, camshaft, and heads should always synch with your driving agenda. If you're building a driver, you're going to have to compromise to some degree in terms of performance if you want reliability and fuel economy. You compromise because radical engines don't do well for the commute or vacation trip. They also struggle to pass a smog check, depending on where you live.

Environmentalists and performance enthusiasts don't get along, but it is your responsibility as an engine builder to build and tune your engine for the cleanest emissions possible. This doesn't mean you have to buy catalytic converters, a smog pump, and an EGR manifold. It does mean you need to package your induction and ignition systems for optimum emissions performance at the tailpipe.

Too much carburetion is not practical for everyday street use where clean emissions and fuel efficiency are important. You want carburetor size and engine purpose to be compatible for optimum performance and cleaner emissions. If you think this clean emissions issue is a lot of bunk, consider the last time you were behind a hopped-up vintage muscle car or street rod in traffic. The

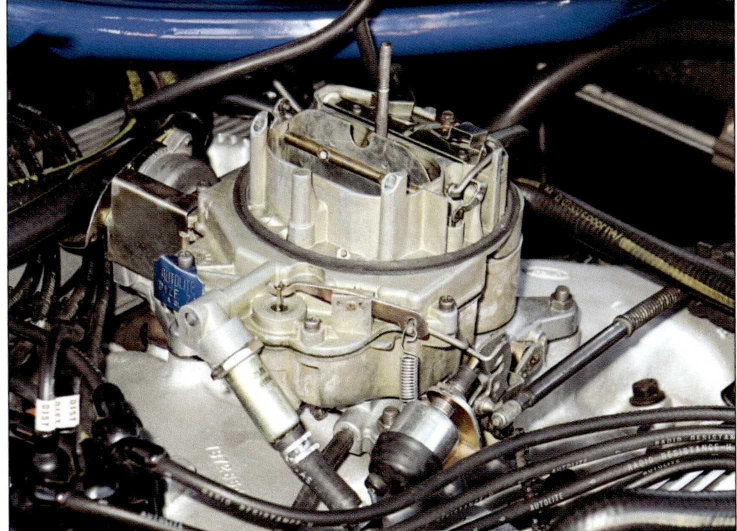

This is an Autolite/Motorcraft 4300D spread-bore carburetor, which is similar to the Rochester Quadrajet and Holley spread-bore carburetors with very small primaries and huge secondaries with a focus on wide-open throttle performance. The Holley 4165 spread bore is a suitable replacement carburetor for the 4300D.

Here's Holley's "1850" 4-barrel carburetor, which is a 4160. It really isn't a performance carburetor, but more of an Autolite 4100/4300 replacement.

Holley's HP Series high-performance carburetors are calibrated right out of the box and ready for action. The HP incorporates popular hot rodding tricks such as the flush air horn (no choke), screw-in air bleeds, sculptured venturi, high-flow metering blocks, stainless throttle plates, Dominator-style fuel bowls, spun-in boosters, and a throttle body/baseplate. Sizes range from 300 to 1,000 cfm. I've been involved in a number of builds and test small-block Fords with this carburetor and the results have been extraordinary.

The many available tuning kits make the venerable Holley the most tunable American carburetor ever. Racers worldwide count on Holley. If you are serious about performance, arm yourself with a jet kit, power valves, hard and soft parts, and gaskets.

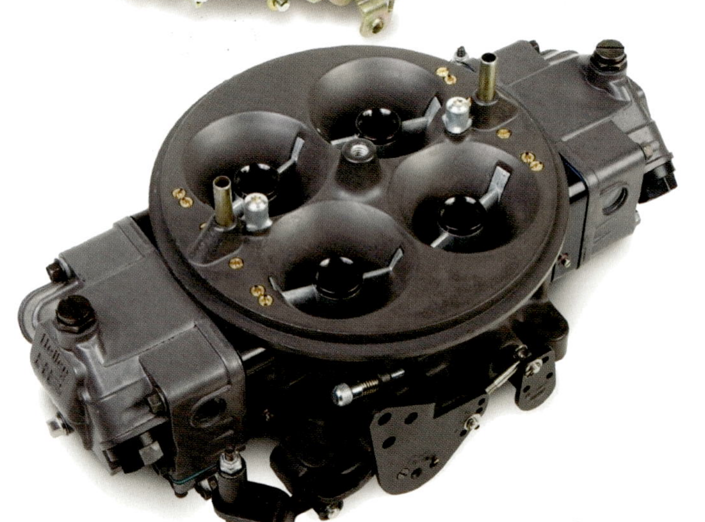

The stadium-size Holley Dominator is strictly a racing carburetor. What makes the HP Ultra Dominator different is its aluminum construction. It's lighter by 3.8 pounds. The HP Ultra, whether it is the Dominator or conventional 4150, has nice engineering upgrades such as greater fuel capacity, bowl drains, larger accelerator pumps, sight glasses, bowl baffling that reduces aeration, fully adjustable secondary linkage, pinned annular boosters, swappable air bleeds, billet metering blocks with lightweight slotted mixture screws and easy to change jets, and 12-hole booster inserts. Sizes range from 750 to 1,250 cfm.

Demon Carburetors is no longer a Barry Grant company, but instead owned by the parent company of Holley. Barry Grant engineered these great carburetors, which have a lot of the same nuances as Holleys. However, Grant refined Holley's approach creating a great performance carburetor. Feelings about these carburetors are mixed. Some love them. Some hate them. The Demon is one of many Holley clones.

If you're partial to Carter AFB and AVS carburetors, Edelbrock's Performer Series carburetors are going to be to your liking. These carburetors use a different approach to fuel metering with graduated rods instead of different-size main metering jets like a Holley. Edelbrock carburetors cost a little more than Carters, which are manufactured by Weber these days. All the same old AFB/AVS rules apply, whether they say Edelbrock or Carter or Weber.

obnoxious exhaust gases high in hydrocarbons made your eyes water, didn't they? And consider this, if your vehicle falls under the guidelines of state emissions laws and smog checks, the law doesn't give you a choice. Clean up your exhaust emission or face revocation of your license plates in some states.

Carburetor Sizing

One of the biggest mistakes enthusiasts make is over-carburetion. Engines don't need as much carburetion as you might think. The formula is simple, and without a lot of complex engine math. Over-carburetion on a street engine is a waste. It wastes fuel and pollutes the air. Too much fuel can be as bad for an engine as not enough fuel. Too much fuel washes precious lubricating oil off the cylinder walls and fouls the spark plugs. Your performance objective should also include being environmentally responsible. Plan and tune for cleaner air, not just power. Performance today is both efficiency and power. With efficiency, you get power and cleaner air.

Carburetor sizing is something not enough of us get right. However, it is very important to performance and durability. Before you can determine what size carburetor is needed, you have to know the maximum airflow your engine requires. This may seem a simple task, but it isn't. Doing the math of computing carburetor size is only scratching the surface. You also need to know how the engine will be used, the engine's operational window, and the number of cylinders.

Use the following formulas to calculate your engine maximum airflow:

Flow Rating (cfm) at 3.0 in/Hg ÷ 1.414 =
Flow (cfm) at 1.5 in/Hg

Flow Rating (cfm) at 1.5 in/Hg ÷ 1.414 =
Flow (cfm) at 3.0 in/Hg

These formulas are based on presumed maximum vacuum attainable under load at wide-open throttle. In theory, an engine doesn't realize manifold vacuum of more than 1.5 in/Hg with a 4-barrel carburetor, or more than 3.0 in/Hg with a 2-barrel carburetor. Let's face it, carburetor manufacturers and car magazines can suggest carburetor sizing based on generalized information. However, every engine is different even if both are identically equipped.

Carburetor airflow ratings don't always match the amount a given carburetor flows. So carburetor sizing guidelines aren't always absolute, but instead suggestions to get you in the neighborhood. Sizing depends on displacement, volumetric efficiency, vehicle type, weight, and size, not to mention transmission gearing and axle ratio. So let's keep it simple: All you need to know is your maximum RPM and your engine displacement. This basic formula fits most plans:

CFM Requirement =
(Engine Displacement x Maximum RPM)
÷ 3,436

For example: 351 ci x 6,500 rpm ÷ 3,456 =
660 cfm

Most high-performance street Clevelands need no more than a 650-cfm 4-barrel carburetor. It is when you get into high RPM and greater displacement that you need a larger carburetor (more CFM). For example a 400 is going to make most of its power in the form of torque between 2,000 and 5,000 rpm. You're not going to need much more than 600 to 650 cfm. If the plan is to take the 400 over 6,000, you need 700 to 750 cfm. At 700 cfm, you get torque. At more than 750 cfm, you get high-RPM horsepower.

On the dyno, air/fuel ratio and volumetric efficiency (VE) reveal a lot about an engine. VE is the percentage of the theoretical maximum amount of air and fuel you can draw into an engine during two complete crankshaft revolutions. What does this really mean? It means if you take a 400-ci engine and turn the crank two revolutions, you should get 400 ci of air.

Unfortunately, this doesn't happen in the real world. In fact, VE varies a lot throughout RPM ranges under load in dyno testing. Most engines experience a VE number of 70 to 80 percent at top engine speed. Racing engines at high revs average 85 to 90 percent VE. And if you're really on top of your game as an engine builder and tuner, you can achieve 90 to 110 percent at high RPM with a racing engine.

If you know the VE you can multiply it by the CFM number (calculated above) to see your revised CFM requirement. Here's another example:

(400 ci x 6,500 rpm) ÷ 3,456 =
752.31 cfm x 1.1 VE = 827.54 cfm

So in theory, an 800- or 850-cfm carburetor would be the right size; however, there are other variables you

Street Engine Carburetor Sizing

Displacement (ci)	*Suggested Carburetor Size*
310 to 355	500 to 600 cfm (600 to 650 cfm if fitted with high-performance camshaft and heads)
355 to 383	600 to 650 cfm (650 to 700 cfm if fitted with high-performance camshaft and heads)
393 to 450	650 cfm (700 to 750 cfm if fitted with high-performance camshaft and heads)

experience in the real world that either raise or lower this number. A few of them inlcude header tube size and length, collector size, exhaust pipe size, intake manifold type, cylinder heads, ambient temperature and humidity, and engine temperature.

Math formulas are one thing, but what happens when you put your Cleveland on a dyno? Reality happens when you load your engine and open the throttle. These math formulas change significantly when operating under hot conditions. You will probably experience disappointing numbers with hot conditions or high-altitude because heat and lower atmospheric pressure/oxygen levels hinder power.

Carburetor Sources

Choosing a carburetor manufacturer depends on what you want the carburetor to do. Carter, Edelbrock, and Holley remain the most common types of carburetors. The difference is that Carter and Edelbrock carburetors use metering rods and jets for a more graduated form of fuel metering. Holley-based carburetors use metering jets in a block with a vacuum-actuated power valve, which depends on manifold vacuum to meter fuel as the throttle is opened and RPM increases. Specialty carburetors such as Webers and even the rare Autolite in-line fours call for rare and expensive intake manifolds, which means you need to give induction a lot of thought before taking the plunge.

Holley Carburetors

George M. Holley founded the company with his brother Earl in 1899 as the Holley Brothers Company. In the beginning, Holley was about motorcycles mostly, and automobiles. By 1904, the Holley brothers were seriously in the carburetor business with the original Iron Pot single-throat carburetor. In time, Holley carburetors were original equipment on a wide variety of new automobiles, especially Fords. Holley's first 4-barrel carburetor was the 2140 in 1953 on Lincolns, then the infamous 4000 "Teapot" in 1955.

The traditional Holley 4150 twin-bowl, 4-barrel performance carburetor dates back to 1957 when it was first installed on new Fords as original equipment on the 312-ci Y-Block V-8. Holley's relationship with Ford is well documented. Ironically, Ford never installed a Holley on a factory Cleveland engine, yet the venerable Holley has always been good for enhancing Cleveland performance. One excellent example is the Holley 4165 spread-bore as a 4300D replacement atop spread-bore Clevelands. The 4165 outperforms the 4300D and is far easier to tune and maintain. There's also the Holley 2300 2-barrel carburetor in a variety of sizes ranging from 350 to 650 cfm, which is actually the primary side of a 4150.

Most people probably go with an aftermarket intake manifold designed for the Holley 4150/4160 carburetor flange or similar aftermarket replacements. If you opt for Holley carburetion, understand the differences between them.

The 4150 carburetor, which arrived first in 1957, has adjustable metering blocks for both primary and secondary circuits. The 4160 carburetor has an adjustable primary metering block and a non-adjustable secondary metering plate. There are single-pumpers and double-pumpers meaning a primary accelerator pump (single pumper) or a double pumper, which has both primary and secondary accelerator pumps.

Vacuum secondaries are appropriate for street performance Holleys. Vacuum secondaries come into play as you lean on the throttle under hard acceleration. Vacuum secondary operation depends on spring pressure and intake manifold vacuum at wide-open throttle. Too much spring pressure and your secondaries loaf or do not open at all. Too little, and they open too quickly causing a significant flat spot.

Mechanical secondaries are race oriented. Mechanical secondaries open immediately with a wide-open throttle. You rarely see mechanical secondaries without a secondary accelerator pump.

The 4150/4160 carburetors have undergone a lot of changes since their debut. Each has been offered as original equipment on a variety of factory high-performance engines, including Ford. When you're searching for a good, used Holley 4150/4160, be sure you know what you have in your hands. Swap meets are loaded with all kinds of 4150/4160 carburetors from Holley's good old days.

The Holley HP Series performance carburetors are likely the best Holley ever, thanks to fresh technology and manufacturing techniques. The main body has contoured, symetrical venturi inlets for reduced disruption of airflow, screw-in air bleeds you can swap, improved sealing, power valve-blowout protection, Dominator-style fuel bowls, spun-in boosters, high-flow metering blocks, stainless-steel throttle plates, and a new throttle-body design. Holley HP Series carburetors are available in sizes ranging from 350 to 1,000 cfm.

Edelbrock Corporation

Edelbrock carburetors are based on the time-proven Carter AFB/AVS designs and do very well in street/strip performance applications with Edelbrock's own performance manifolds (as well as with other manifolds).

Because Edelbrock carburetors function with metering rods instead of power valves, they're unaffected by induction backfire. Edelbrock carburetors are factory calibrated to run right out of the box, though you can count on tuning to your elevation and performance agenda.

There are two basic types of Edelbrock carburetors: The Performer Series and the Thunder AVS Series. Sizes for both range from 500 to 800 cfm. Because they are constructed of aluminum, they transfer heat very well.

The Thunder AVS allows for a smooth transition from primary to wide-open secondary operation thanks to the Qwik-Tune vacuum secondary air valve, which allows for more precise tuning.

Demon Carburetion

This company is now a division of Holley, yet its carburetors are still uniquely Demon. It has eight carburetor catagories: 2-barrel Road Demon, Road Demon Jr., Road Demon, Street Demon, Speed Demon, Mighty Demon, Race Demon, and King Demon.

The Road Demons are street carburetors in five sizes: 350- and 500-cfm (2V) and 525-, 625-, and 725-cfm (4V). Most street Clevelands are happiest with the 625- and 725-cfm carburetors. Each Demon arrives equipped for Ford kick-down linkages, which is true for most aftermarket carburetors. And like their Holley counterparts, they're easy to tune.

The Speed Demon is a more aggressive street/strip Demon with vacuum secondaries in sizes ranging from 575 to 850 cfm. This is likely the most desirable Demon for a street/strip Cleveland because it offers both street and race nuances.

Mighty Demon and Race Demon are race oriented and affordable alternatives if you're on a tight budget. They offer many of the same tuning features as the Holleys. Mighty Demons are available in sizes ranging from 650 to 850 cfm. Race Demons, from 500 to 1,000 cfm.

The King Demon is in Holley Dominator territory, and strictly a racing carburetor for the mightiest of Clevelands. It comes in 1,000 to 1,190 cfm and fits 4500-size flanges.

Proform

Proform Street Series performance carburetors are similar to the Holley 4150/4160 with a lot of the same design features, including cathederal-style fuel bowls, billet flange, fuel-bowl sight glass, secondary jet extensions, swapable air bleeds, and die-cast construction. The Proform Street Series is a good carburetor for the money, available in sizes ranging from 600 to 750 cfm.

Proform Street Replacement carburetors, which are similar to the Street Series, are drop-in replacements for the 4150/4160 Holley carburetors available in 570 to 770 cfm. These are 100 percent aluminum construction with replaceable air bleeds, fully adjustable metering blocks on both sides, cathederal-style fuel bowls, vacuum secondaries, and electric choke.

Proform Race Series carburetors are on a par with Holley's HP Series, with mechanical secondaries, double-pump design, fully adjustable metering blocks, cathederal-style fuel bowls, interchangeable air bleeds, and billet baseplates. Race Series carburetors are available in 650 to 1,050 cfm.

You may also build your own Proform carburetor from a plethora of parts and kits available from Proform.

Exotic Ford Carburetion

Ford is well known for exotic induction systems most never get to see, such as the Autolite inline 4-barrel carburetor as well as Weber twin-throat designs. The Autolite inline four, such as the 427-ci FE-series SOHC and a host of other efforts, was created to give Ford the edge while in theory remaining within the rules of sanctioning bodies such as NASCAR and SCCA. It was never easy or simple for Ford to compete in sanctioned competition because Ford always tended to be ahead of its time.

The Autolite inline four, the Cross Boss, was conceived by Ford engineers in order to live within the SCCA's single 4-barrel carburetor ruling while giving the Boss 302 a distinct advantage in competition. Ultimately, there were two versions of the Autolite inline four serving two different racing purposes: one for road racing and one for drag and general-purpose racing.

The D0ZX-9510-A inline four has huge 1$^{11}/_{16}$-inch throttle bores and flows 850 cfm at wide-open throttle. This one is for road racing. The D0ZX-9501-B is a monster behemoth with 2½-inch throttle bores and 1,400 cfm at wide-open throttle. This one is more for drag racing and

Exotic Ford fuel systems have been available for Clevelands through the years including the Autolite inline 4-barrel racing carburetor. The inline four was produced in two sizes: the 850-cfm for road racing and the huge 1,400-cfm drag racing four-throater. This is not a street carburetor. Here's the 850-cfm (part number D0ZX-9501-A) on top of a combo Cross Boss 302 (D0ZX-9C483-A and D0ZX-9425-A).

other types of competition. Of course these carburetors need intake manifolds to be of any benefit. At first, the inline four was mated to a special Boss 302 manifold and named "Cross Boss." It had a two-piece top (D0ZX-9C483-A) and bottom manifold (D0ZX-9425-A) with a straight shot into each intake port. In time, there were more variations for more and more applications, such as the FE big-blocks, Clevelands, and others.

In the early 1970s, Ford's own Ak Miller conducted 351C testing with a pair of inline fours to see how they compared with a pair of comparably sized Holleys on top of a tunnel-ram manifold. Bottom line was the Holleys performed well at low RPM because they offered more torque. The Autolites did poorly down low, but came on like gangbusters at high RPM where they were designed to live. The Autolite inline four had great potential as a legendary racing carburetor. However, when Ford got out of racing in 1970, the inline four fell off the priority list and wasn't developed any further.

Weber Induction

The Weber IDA, IDF, and DCOE carburetors have seen use on everything from Ferraris to Volkswagens. For one thing, these are good-looking, twin-bore carburetors that have experienced great success as performance pieces around the world. However, they are not for everyone. You must know what you're doing or you can count on a frustrating experience trying to tune them. Webers do not come cheap nor do the intake manifolds that support them.

The beauty of Webers is how well they mix fuel and air before it all reaches the venturi. Another positive is how tunable the Weber is with a wide variety of jets and venturis available to get it right where you want it. Weber caught the close attention of the late Carroll Shelby who decided to place a quartet of these carburetors on top of Ford's 260-ci V-8 in the early 1960s. giving Ford's small-block a 30 hp advantage. Since that time, Webers have seen widespread use on all Ford V-8s, including the 351C. The nice thing about the Weber is its air/fuel distribution; each bore has its own bore (or eight throttle bores for eight cylinders), offering perfect fuel distribution.

The Weber works much the same way as any carburetor with a float bowl and main metering jets. Once fuel passes through jets, it then passes through emulsifier tubes where it is mixed with air and atomized into the venturi. At this point it passes through the throttle bore. There is an idle circuit function when throttle plates are closed.

Weber carburetors do not have a choke, but instead have a fuel-enrichment system that functions when the engine is cold. Like most carburetors, Webers have an accelerator pump, which sprays raw fuel into the throttle bore when the throttle is advanced. The trick with Webers is getting them in synch with one another. There are four of them to get in synch, which could take up an entire book in itself.

The Weber IDA is more a racing carburetor due to its larger float bowls offering great on-demand performance. The IDF is a better street carburetor with a smaller float bowl, which tends to keep the fuel cooler because it is constantly on the move. The IDF offers a central fuel-bowl configuration in a compact design.

Redline, Inc., reintroduced the 48 IDA twin-throat carburetor, which has a reputation for great low-speed to main metering circuit operation, which makes it a great road-racing carburetor. Redline has improved the 48 IDA to race specifications originally instituted by Carroll Shelby.

Intake Manifold

Intake manifold selection depends on how you intend to build and use your Cleveland.

Dual-Plane

Street engines operating between 2,000 and 5,500 rpm generally call for a dual-plane intake manifold, which offers longer intake runners that enhance low- to mid-range torque. Classic dual-plane manifolds offer a nice combination of good, low- to –mid-range torque while coming on strong at high RPM. Vintage Cobra high-risers, Offenhausers, Edelbrocks, Weiands, and Shelby manifolds are good examples. Edelbrock's Performer RPM and Weiand's Action Plus manifolds

Weber carburetion has been a "look at me" Ford mainstay since the 1960s. Carroll Shelby was probably the first to put Weber carburetion on a Ford in his 260 Cobras. These are Weber IDA twin-bore carburetors, which are as popular as IDF carburetors, which are very similar in appearance.

Cleveland Intake Manifold Information

Manufacturer	Model	Type	Specifics
Blue Thunder	4145	Dual-Plane	Good low- to mid-range torque coupled with high-RPM power; great street/strip manifold
	4146	Dual-Plane	For 4500 carburetor flange
Edelbrock	Performer RPM #2171	Dual-Plane	For 351M and 400 only with 351C-2V heads; non-EGR raw cast aluminum
	Performer RPM #21711	Dual-Plane	For 351M and 400 only with 351C-2V heads; non-EGR polished
	Performer RPM #21713	Dual-Plane	For 351M and 400 only with 351C-2V heads; non-EGR black powdercoat
	Performer RPM #3771	Dual-Plane	For 351M and 400 only with 351C-2V heads; EGR polished
	Performer RPM Air Gap #7564	Dual-Plane	For 351C only or 351M/400 with spacers; for 2V or 4V head with 138 x 204-inch port exits; excellent strip and strip manifold thanks to long and generous intake runners and heat separation
	Torker 351 #2760	Single-Plane	For 351C only with 4V head (3,000 to 7,000 rpm); does not clear Pantera; does not fit 351C-2V head
Ford Australia	73DA-9425-AB or D0AZ-9424-C	Dual-Plane	Factory iron 4V manifold
Holley	Street Dominator	Single-Plane	For 351C-2V spread-bore
	Street Dominator	Single-Plane	For 351M and 400 spread-bore
	Strip Dominator	Single-Plane High-Rise	For 351C-4V spread-bore
Offenhauser	360 Equaflow #5964	Dual-Plane	For 351C-4V with 4150/4160 flange
	360 Equaflow #5965	Dual-Plane	For 351C-4V with 4500 Dominator flange
	360 Equaflow #5966	Dual-Plane	For 351C-4V with spread-bore flange
	Dial-A-Flow #6127	Single-Plane	For 351C-4V heads with 4500 Dominator flange
	Dial-A-Flow #6128	Single-Plane	For 351C-2V heads with 4500 Dominator flange
	Dual-Port #6110-DP	Dual-Plan, Split-Port	For 351C-2V with 4150/4160 flange; dual-port design has long primary runners and short secondary runner; long runners for torque and short runners for high rpm power
	Dual-Port #6111-DP	Dual-Plane, Split-Port	For 351C-2V with spread-bore flange; does not fit the Motorcraft 4300D
	Dual-Port #6013-DP	Dual-Plane, Split-Port	For 351C-4V with 4150/4160 flange
	Dual-Port #6014-DP	Dual-Plane, Split-Port	For 351C-4V with spread-bore; does not fit Motorcraft 4300D
	Port-O-Sonic #6120	Single-Plane	For 351C-4V with 4150/4160
	Port-O-Sonic #6121	Single-Plane	For 351C-4V with spread-bore
	Port-O-Sonic #6122	Single-Plane	For 351C-2V with 4150/4160
	Port-O-Sonic #6120	Single-Plane	For 351C-2V with spread-bore
Parker	Funnelweb	Single-Plane	For 351C-2V and 4V; refined plenum with cloverleaf shape for smooth airflow
Pro Comp	#3517	Single-Plane	For 351C-2V and 4150/4160
Scott Cook	SC-351-HD	Dual-Plane	For 351C-4V head; same as D0AE-9424-L iron manifold except it is aluminum; fits 4150/4160
Shelby	#9250	Dual-Plane	For 351C-4V and 4150/4160
	#351D-9424-D	Dual-Plane	For 351C-4V with 4500 flange
Trick Flow	Track Heat #TFS-51600111	Single-Plane	Strictly high-RPM, 3,000 to 8,000 rpm, or stroker; has bungs for injectors; raised plenum floor for improved velocity and fuel atomization
Weiand	Action Plus #8010	Dual-Plane	Idle to 6,000 rpm, good low- to mid-range torque, standard Holley flange, 185 x 132-inch intake port for 351C-2V heads
	X-CELerator #7516	Single-Plane	1,500 to 7000 rpm, fair low- to mid-range torque, mostly a high-RPM street/strip manifold, 202 x 148-inch intake ports for 351C-2V heads
	X-CELerator #7517	Single-Plane	1,500 to 7,000 rpm, fair low- to mid-range torque, mostly a high-RPM street/strip manifold, 244 x 156-inch intake ports for 351C-4V heads
	HI-RAM #1994	Tunnel Ram	3,200 to 9,000 rpm, for racing and high-RPM only, 236 x 163-inch intake runners

It is one thing to choose the right carburetor and another thing to pick the right carb and manifold combination. Use dual-planes for driving and low-end torque, and single-planes for high-RPM use. This is a single-plane Edelbrock Torker 351, which is not a good street manifold, but good for drag racing and high RPM. This manifold lives at 3,000 to 7,000 rpm. It does not fit the 351C with 2-barrel heads.

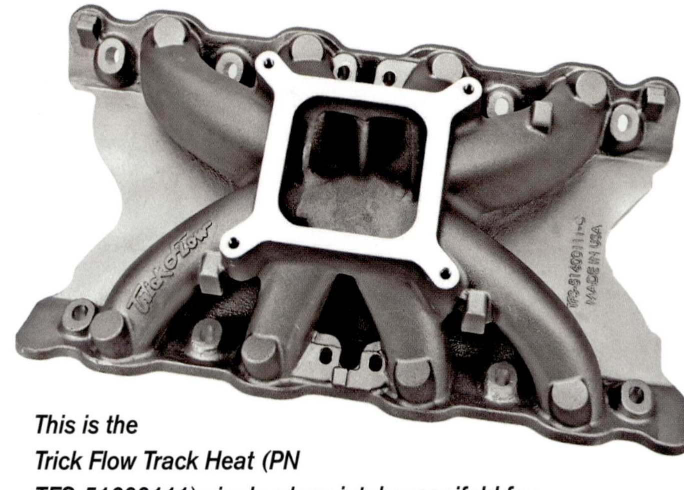

This is the Trick Flow Track Heat (PN TFS-51600111) single-plane intake manifold for the 351C (9.200-inch deck height block) with 2.100x1.500-inch intake ports. This is a street/strip manifold designed for high-RPM use at 3,000 to 8,000 rpm, which is where it lives. What you get from this manifold is peak torque in the 4,500- to 5,500-rpm range and peak horsepower from 6,000 rpm up. Best carburetor for this manifold is the Holley 4150 double-pumper.

Edelbrock has answered the call of Cleveland quite well in recent years. The Performer LB 351C-4V manifold is designed for 351C engines with the factory 4-barrel heads. What you get from this dual-plane manifold is the Holley 4150/4160 baseplate flange pattern and long, high-ceiling intake runners that improve low- to mid-range torque. Valley width is 6-31/32 inches for the 1970–1974 351C only. There's also the Performer 400 non-EGR and EGR manifolds for the 351M and 400 engines with long runners for good low- to mid-range torque, which are compatible with 2-barrel heads. Valley width is 8 17/32 inches for the tall-deck 351M and 400.

have taken this old-school, high-ceiling runner approach and refined it for even better performance across RPM ranges. Plenums and runners are engineered to create less turbulence, which improves velocity and fuel atomization.

Single-Plane

When most people think "street" they tend to think dual-plane. However, if you're adding displacement via stroke, you have to start thinking of your engine as you would a big-block. You no longer have a 351, but instead a 383, 408, or 430. With stroke comes more torque as well as horsepower because you're moving more air/fuel through those ports. This is why a single-plane, straight-shot style may work better than a long-runner, dual-plane. Often it is a matter of trial and error. You may have to try both to determine which works best for your Cleveland.

Power Curve

Dual- and single-plane manifolds offer different power curves. The dual-plane offers a broader torque curve, from 2,000 to 5,000 rpm. The single-plane moves your torque curve higher and increases horsepower, especially with a stroker. Dual-plane manifolds work best for straight street use. Single-planes are more for high RPM and high displacement, where you're seeking more horsepower as well as torque.

Dual-plane high-rise manifolds don't always have to be new. Vintage aftermarket dual-plane, high-rise manifolds yield the benefits of low-end torque and high-RPM breathability and can be found at swap meets all over the place. They do well on the street in stop-and-go driving, and they yield plenty of power when it's time to rock.

Cool Air

Long intake runners and a dual-plane design are two reasons you can achieve good low- and mid-range torque from a carbureted engine. You also want cool air, both ahead of the carburetor and beneath it. To get cool air before the carburetor, you need to source cool air from outside. Underhood air is much hotter

Edelbrock took 351C induction a step further with its Performer RPM Air Gap 351C dual-plane manifold (PN 7564). The Air Gap isolates runners from engine heat, which helps control induction air temperature. Runners are generous in size and offer length, which means great low- to mid-range torque. The Air Gap is designed for Edelbrock's own Performer Cleveland heads plus factory 2- and 4-barrel heads.

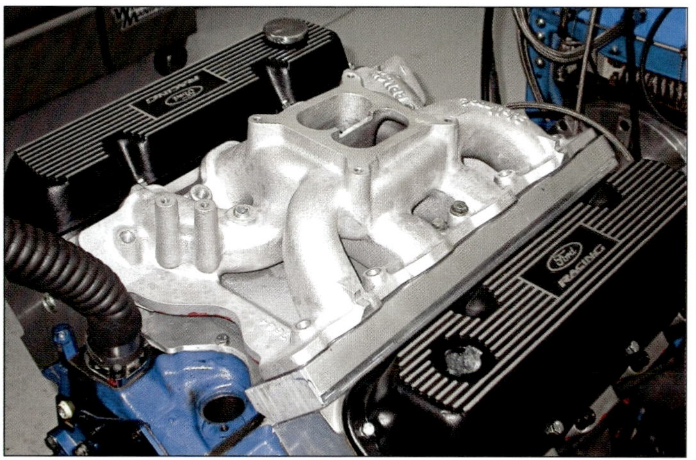

Magazine tech writer Richard Holdener was curious about what could be done with a 400, so he put one to the test at Westech Performance Group using a variety of approaches. Richard quickly put to rest the idea you can't do anything with the tall-deck 400 Cleveland. He fitted this one with Pro Comp heads, Edelbrock Air Gap induction, and a Holley HP 750-cfm carburetor (to name the things you can see) and made 489 hp and 502 ft-lbs of torque. Richard stresses the 400 is the legendary 351C with a raised deck and 4.000 inches of stroke; so why the bad rap? This engine can make real power given cylinder heads, induction, and a hot cam.

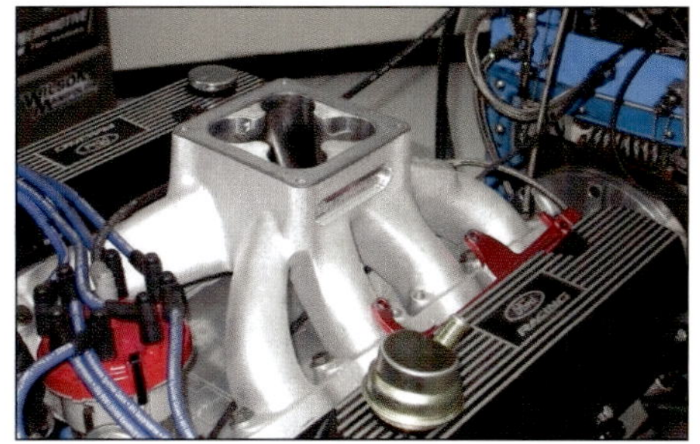

When Richard Holdener installed this single-plane CHI manifold, an 1,150-cfm Holley Dominator, and a custom-ground cam from Cam Research, Westech's dyno measured 568 hp and 542 ft-lbs of torque.

Australian Scott Cook is reproducing 351C-4V iron manifolds identical to original castings: D0AE-9425-L complete with casting date codes and other markings including Cleveland foundry.

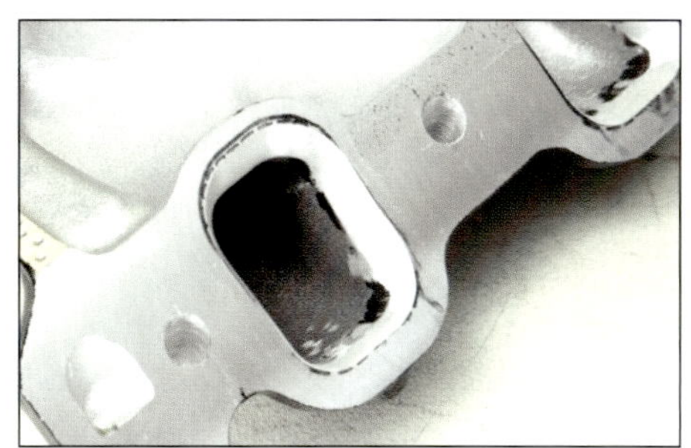

Port matching is an important key to power. Port mismatches lose power due to turbulence at the manifold and head. Even if port mismatch is slight, you can take an intake manifold gasket and blend the ports. The gain is significant.

than the ambient air outside. If you can drop the intake air temperature by 50 to 80 degrees F, it makes a considerable difference in thermal expansion inside the combustion chamber. You can net nearly 10 percent more power this way.

You get cooler air with a hood scoop or a ram-air scoop at the leading edge of the vehicle. Ram air can be sourced through the radiator support or beneath the front bumper. Ram-air kits can be sourced from Summit Racing Equipment or your favorite speed shop.

Getting cool induction air after the carburetor takes closing off the manifold heat passages from the exhaust side of the cylinder head. You do this by installing the manifold heat block-off plates included in most intake manifold gasket kits. Manifold heat is needed only when the outside air is really cold. A cold intake manifold does not allow the fuel to atomize as well as it does in a hot manifold, which causes hesitation and stumbling.

A low-restriction air cleaner that effectively filters out dirt while allowing healthy breathing at the same time is best. Reusable, washable air filters from K&N, AEM, Spectre, aFe, Injen, and others meet the challenge effectively, but

Another mistake I see from time to time is gasket, manifold, and head mismatch so that oil is drawn into the intake port from the valley. A very thin film of Permatex The Right Stuff along the bottom like this eliminates risk of port contamination.

There are many theories on whether or not carburetor spacers help. I know from years of watching dyno testing that spacers do make a difference in power; not so much at the high end, but at the low to mid range where they enhance torque. If you have hood clearance, go with 1/2 to 1 inch and watch the difference in torque. This is the HVH Super Sucker from MPG Heads/Cam Research, which is sculptured internally to improve fuel distribution into the plenum. The manufacturer claims up to 47 hp possible.

MSD's Atomic EFI throttle body injection system is an efficient power-adder drop-in replacement for your carburetor. It fits onto a standard Holley 4150/4160 flange and can be installed in a day with fewer connections and hand-held tuning you can do yourself. No laptop required.

they don't come cheap. They can be washed and reused, which actually saves you money in the long term. Some don't even have to be oiled, which means all you have to do is wash, dry, and reinstall. A reusable fabric/fiber air filter is money well spent in terms of performance and longevity.

Electronic Fuel Injection Sources

Aftermarket electronic fuel injection has been available for carbureted engines for quite some time, but not without its teething problems and systems that have been hard to calibrate and tune. In more recent times, the aftermarket has come out with plug-and-play electronic engine control systems that make fuel injecting your Cleveland a weekend task where you can be back on the road Monday with fuel efficiency, power, and a cleaner burning package.

MSD Ignition

MSD Ignition introduced new Atomic EFI system for carbureted V-8 engines with the Holley 4150/4160 square flange, including 351C, 351M, and 400. All you need is a basic knowledge of automotive electricity and fuel systems. No special modifications are required except for a single, welded, oxygen-sensor bung. Electrical and fuel system modifications are simple and accomplished with hand tools.

Atomic EFI incorporates fuel rails into the throttle body to feed four 80-pound injectors and annular rings designed to make the most of fuel atomization. The throttle position sensor (TPS) is automatic and self-calibrating. The electronic control module (ECM) consists of most of the system's sensors, which eliminates a lot of unnecessary wiring and connections. The TPS, manifold absolute pressure (MAP) sensor, and Intake Air

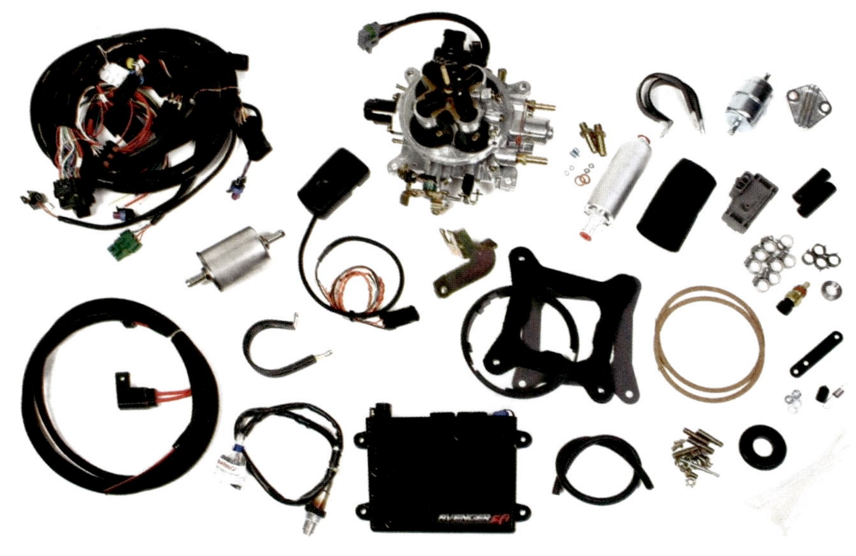

Holley's Avenger EFI is an easy bolt-on system designed to fit the standard square flange of either a single- or dual-plane manifold and it installs in a matter of hours. Avenger EFI is an engine management system you may tune yourself. It is also self-tuning based on your driving patterns and engine conditions. Holley provides nearly everything you need to get going.

The F.A.S.T. EZ-EFI throttle body fuel injection system is one of the nicest I have seen because it is compact and very simple in its execution. You can install it in a matter of hours with the Setup Wizard. You can even go with a dual 4V package for up to 1,200 hp.

Temperature (IAT) sensor are all configured inside this high-tech throttle body. The MSD Atomic EFI system is self-calibrating and adapts to your driving habits and engine/vehicle configuration.

Holley Performance Products

Holley offers the Cleveland enthusiast a variety of systems for Holley 4150/4160 flange manifolds. The Avenger EFI throttle body engine management system is a bolt, plug, and go system you can install in a weekend. Once installed, you don't have to do much because this is a self-tuning system with hand-held tuner for fine-tuning purposes. No laptop is required for tuning.

Fuel Air Spark Technology

Fuel Air Spark Technology (F.A.S.T.) offers the enthusiast throttle body fuel injection with easy tuning and without a laptop. EZ-EFI is a self-contained, self-tuning electronic fuel injection system you can install yourself in a matter of hours. Because it has been proven widely successful with thousands of installations, there aren't the functional issues there used to be with aftermarket fuel injection systems. EZ-EFI bolts right onto any 4150/4160 Holley square flange. The only modification required is the wide-band, oxygen-sensor bung at the exhaust pipe. EZ-EFI is good for up to 650 hp.

Nitrous Oxide

The first thing to remember with nitrous oxide is that it makes fuel burn faster. This means you must be mindful of what it can do, both productively and counterproductively. All that instantaneous power comes for a reason. As a result, extraordinary attention to detail must be paid on the road to power.

Using nitrous oxide generates greater amounts of power from the air/fuel charge you introduce to the combustion chambers. Think of nitrous as a very simple gas composed of two nitrogen atoms attached to one oxygen atom. Chemists know it as N_2O.

Nitrous oxide, or "squeeze," is popular today for those looking for quick and easy power (50 to 150 hp) on demand. And it makes boatloads of power at the touch of a button. But nitrous can be very harmful to an engine that isn't properly prepared and tuned. Nitrous severely damages pistons, rings, and bearings if not properly executed. It can and does hammer rod bearings, resulting in severe wear. It is also hard on main bearings due to the severe loads. And no matter what the nitrous crowd tells you about "laughing gas," nitrous shortens engine life. So don't be drawn into believing it's a magic horsepower pill without consequences. If you use nitrous oxide, be prepared for shorter engine life. Contrary to what you may believe about nitrous oxide, it is not a poisonous gas nor is it harmful to the atmosphere. This doesn't mean you should breathe it, however. Because nitrous oxide is an asphyxiant, it can suffocate you if inhaled in heavy quantities. It would have a similar effect as inhaling carbon dioxide: oxygen deprivation.

The Science of Nitrous Oxide

Nitrous oxide is available in three basic grades: commercial, medical, and high-purity. Commercial-grade nitrous oxide is what you use in your engine for performance gains. The medical grade is commonly known as laughing gas used by dentists and surgeons. It has to be very pure for human consumption. You must be licensed as a medical professional to get it. High-purity is also a medical grade nitrous oxide that is extremely pure, and priced and controlled accordingly.

Commercial-grade nitrous oxide is marketed as Nytrous+ and sold by the Puritan-Bennett Corporation. You can find it all across the country. It is a mix of 99.9 percent nitrous oxide and .01 percent sulfur dioxide. Puritan-Bennett adds the sulfur dioxide to give it a gas odor just as you experience with natural gas.

When you buy nitrous oxide, it is pumped into a storage tank that you provide the supplier. You need an appropriate tank capable of holding at least 1,800 pounds per square inch (psi). To be safe, your tank(s) must have a visible certification date within the past five years.

In nature, nitrous oxide is a gas. Inside a pressurized tank, nitrous oxide is in liquid form. When it leaves the tank, it's very cold, similar to refrigerants and propane. The use of nitrous oxide to make power is nothing new. During World War II, it was used to help aircraft engines make power. Nitrous oxide stored under pressure must be anchored securely. I stress safety because a carelessly handled nitrous oxide bottle with nearly 1,000 psi of pressure behaves like a bomb if the bottle fails. It can explode, maiming or even killing you. To get the nitrous needed for performance use on demand, the gas is metered from the bottle via electrical solenoids that are fired when you press the button. Nitrous oxide should be administered on demand at a time when it is safe to do so. Too much nitrous oxide and not enough fuel can destroy an engine in nanoseconds. For one thing, nitrous oxide should never be administered to the intake ports unless the throttle is wide open. Set up properly, the throttle should close a nitrous oxide solenoid switch when in the wide-open position. Closing the switch activates the nitrous oxide solenoid, releasing the nitrous oxide into the intake manifold.

Nitrous oxide gets into the intake ports a number of ways, depending on how the engine is set up. Carbureted engines get their nitrous oxide diet through a fogger plate located beneath the carburetor. If you pin the butterflies, the nitrous oxide "fogs" the intake plenum, assisting the air/fuel mixture en route to the chambers.

Carbureted engines may also use nozzles at each intake port to administer the nitrous oxide. The nice part about this design is being able to tune each cylinder bore based on the individual needs of each cylinder. The center ports typically receive more fuel and air than the perimeter ports. The outers tend to run leaner than the centers, which is critical when you are running nitrous oxide.

Port fuel-injected engines also use nozzles off a common tube manifold to administer nitrous oxide at each port. Like its carbureted counterpart, the port-injected nitrous oxide arrangement can be port-tuned for better performance. This is especially true when you think of your V-8 engine as eight separate engines operating on a common crankshaft. One popular misconception is that you get power from the nitrous oxide itself; this isn't true. Nitrous oxide works hand-in-hand with the air/fuel mix to make power in each cylinder bore. Nitrous oxide brings out the best in the fuel. Not only is the nitrous oxide mist cold (good for thermal expansion), it is also loaded with oxygen, which gives the igniting air/fuel mix a bad attitude. It makes the air/fuel mix burn faster, which creates a powerful thermal expansion experience in each combustion chamber.

Be careful with nitrous oxide in how you feed it to your engine. Perhaps this isn't the best parallel, but using nitrous oxide can be thought of in the same way as you would use cocaine, crystal meth, or nicotine. The more powerful the experience, the more you want. So you keep feeding your engine more nitrous oxide in your quest for power until it fails under the stress. You must recognize your engine's limits before even getting started on a nitrous oxide diet.

Engine Tuning

Administering nitrous oxide to the combustion chambers should not be done with reckless abandon. Too much of it burns pistons. You have to think of nitrous oxide and your air/fuel mixture just as you would oxygen and acetylene. When you're using oxygen and acetylene to weld or cut steel, you use lots of oxygen to blaze a path through the steel. It's the same inside your engine when you use too much nitrous oxide: You burn right through the piston like a cutting torch. And aluminum pistons aren't as forgiving. They melt at 1,300 degrees F.

When tuning a small-block Ford to run on nitrous oxide, air/fuel mixture and spark timing must be just right or you face certain destruction. So how do you get there? First, you have to control fuel delivery to where it jibes with the flow of nitrous oxide. Too much nitrous oxide and not enough fuel overheats the chamber and melts the pistons. This means controling fuel and nitrous oxide flow to a finite point so you get the most power possible without engine damage. This takes practice.

Light-Off

The key to getting the most power from nitrous oxide is getting spark timing, fuel delivery, and peak cylinder pressure going at the same time. Ideally, the air/fuel/nitrous mixture lights when you have peak cylinder pressure, making the most of the incoming charge. When everything is working well together, you get a smooth, firm light-off that nets a lot of power. Things go wrong when the light-off resembles an explosion, exerting a shockwave on the top of the piston. This is the spark knock you hear as a multiple "rapping" under acceleration.

When fuel, air, and nitrous ignite violently, why don't you net more power from the explosion? The answer is simple. When an engine is running smoothly, you get that "quick-fire" discussed earlier in this chapter. A smooth light-off applies pressure to the piston dome, forcing it downward in the cylinder bore, turning the crank and completing the power stroke. Detonation is what occurs when you get a spontaneous light-off, especially from two points in the chamber. The two waves of power collide, causing spark knock or pinging under acceleration. The problem with this kind of light-off is violent combustion spikes that don't really yield much power.

Fuel System

So how do you safely make the most of nitrous oxide? First address the fuel system because you need to have enough fuel to meet the demands of nitrous oxide. Without enough fuel, the engine gets toasted. Another issue is fuel octane rating. What octane rating do you expect to use? Next is ignition timing. Where does yours need to be? And finally, what is your engine's compression ratio? Too much compression with nitrous causes destructive detonation where damage happens in a nanosecond. Getting each of these elements dialed in is crucial to productive performance.

Compression

Compression has to be thought of two ways: static and dynamic. Static compression is the swept volume above the piston, with the piston at BDC, versus the clearance volume left when the piston is at TDC. If you have 100 cc of volume with the piston at BDC and 10 cc left with the piston at TDC, then you have a static compression ratio of 10.0:1, 100 to 10 cc.

Dynamic compression is the kind of compression that happens with pistons, valves, and gasses in motion through the engine. Dynamic compression comes from huffing lungfuls of air through the engine during operation. With the engine running, more volume pumps through the cylinders and chambers than when simply hand-cranking the engine. This actually increases the compression ratio, which means dynamic compression is higher than static compression.

So what does all of this mean for your engine? It means you need to consider the dynamic compression ratio as your engine's actual compression figure when you're planning nitrous oxide.

Nitrous-burning engines need different camshafts than those that are naturally aspirated or supercharged. Dynamic compression ratio is affected by camshaft profile. A camshaft profile with a short duration yields greater dynamic compression. When you lengthen the duration, dynamic compression is lost. On the exhaust side, duration is a very important component with nitrous. Because the air/fuel/nitrous charge coming in expands with fury during ignition, it needs a way to escape when the exhaust valve opens. You need a longer exhaust valve duration with nitrous for good scavenging and thorough extraction of power, which means nitrous cams must be ground differently.

While you're thinking about exhaust valve duration, you must also consider overlap. Less overlap, more dynamic compression. More overlap, less dynamic compression. Overlap is the process in the power cycle where the exhaust valve is closing and the intake valve is opening. The incoming charge helps scavenge the outgoing hot gases through the overlap process. This means the exhaust valve needs to open earlier in the cycle and stay open longer for adequate scavenging. Fuel octane plays into the power process because you need to understand when and how the fuel ignites. The higher the fuel octane rating, the more slowly it ignites and burns, which reduces the chances of detonation and pre-ignition. A higher octane rating produces a smooth, more predictable light-off in the chamber. A lower fuel octane rating produces a more unstable fuel that lights quickly and causes pinging. When you throw nitrous oxide into the equation, you can count on a quick-light that can be violent in nature. This is why a higher octane rating is so critical to a cohesive performance package.

Air/Fuel Ratio

Now let's address the all-important topic of the the air/fuel ratio. You change it by adjusting jet size in the carburetor or controlling fuel injector pulse width. Jet size and pulse width both determine how much fuel enters the chamber.

If your tuning effort involves a carburetor, you have to get jet sizing down to where your engine can live on nitrous oxide. Jetting needs to be richer to compensate for the abundance of nitrous and higher combustion temperatures. As a rule, carbureted engines live happily with an air/fuel ratio of 12.5:1 to 13.0:1. This is where you have just the right amount of air and fuel to make power. Going too lean can cause engine damage and lost power. Too rich and power can be lost as well.

When you're working with fuel-injected engines, you can control fuel mixture by reprogramming the ECM or changing injector size. With nitrous, you typically increase injector size and fine tune from there. Too large is better than too small. Factory fuel injection systems run a fuel manifold pressure of 30 to 45 psi. If you're running nitrous oxide, you need a lot more fuel pressure to get the job done safely. Around 80 psi is considered the norm for nitrous oxide and electronic fuel injection. This is when you need to step up to high-pressure hoses and fittings.

There is a formula that helps you prepare a fuel system for nitrous operation. The air/fuel ratio in a naturally aspirated engine should be between 12.5:1 and 13.0:1. This is a range where engines are happiest and make the most power. Things change dramatically when nitrous oxide is introduced to the air/fuel mixture. More fuel is needed to both make power and prevent engine damage.

Most nitrous experts suggest a nitrous/fuel ratio of 5.0:1 as a starting point for engine tuning. Starting here means going decidedly rich, but it's the safest approach. Begin at 5.0:1 and steer your tuning toward 6.0:1 for optimum results. If your power goal is, for example, 500 hp on nitrous oxide, you need 37.94 gallons per hour, or .63 gallons per minute, to run happily on nitrous oxide. Obviously, you're not going to stay on nitrous oxide for an hour, but it gives you a good idea of how much fuel you need.

Ignition Timing

Ignition timing is the next big hurdle because it can kill an engine as quickly as a lean fuel mixture or too much compression when you're running nitrous. You want the spark to occur in advance of peak cylinder pressure because it takes time for the air/fuel/nitrous mixture to ignite. Under normal circumstances, without nitrous, you want full spark advance around 36 to 38 degrees

BTDC. Exactly where the spark occurs depends on how the engine is equipped and how it performs at full spark advance at 3,500 rpm. Because every engine is different, full advance is going to vary from engine to engine.

Total spark advance and its effect on an engine is determined by taking the engine to 3,500 rpm with vacuum advance connected. It's a good idea to goose the throttle and watch your timing mark just to make sure it isn't going any further than 36 to 38 degrees total. In other words: engine at 3,500 rpm, watch mark, and goose throttle. Watch the mark; if it moves any further, you haven't reached total advanced timing.

The acid test is to load the engine either in a car or on the dyno. With a load at wide-open throttle, you should see crisp acceleration without spark knock. If there is spark knock, retard timing 1 degree and try it again. There is also fuel mixture to consider, which may be too lean.

When you throw nitrous oxide into the equation, you have an air/fuel/nitrous mixture that is going to ignite more rapidly than the conventional air/fuel mix. The pros suggest retarding the ignition timing to approximately 12 degrees BTDC with the throttle open because the air/fuel/nitrous mixture ignites much more quickly. With the full spark advance at 36 to 41 degrees BTDC, you would waste the engine in short order. Retard timing to 12 degrees BTDC total timing and go from there. Twelve degrees BTDC at 3,500 rpm needs to be your baseline, then slowly advance ignition timing from there. Test it out at wide-open throttle under a load, beginning at 12 degrees BTDC, then advance from there 1 degree at a time.

Atomization

There are other points to consider when running nitrous. To be effective, fuel has to atomize (vaporize) properly. This means the fuel has to "mist" as it enters the intake manifold and, ultimately, the combustion chamber. The problem here is, nitrous comes out of the fogger or nozzle at a frigid –100 degrees F. This makes it very difficult to atomize the fuel effectively. At that temperature fuel tends to exist as large droplets, rather than the mist you need for good ignition and combustion.

Nitrous oxide system manufacturers have dealt effectively with the issue of fuel atomization by designing systems that allow the gasoline to atomize with the nitrous oxide fog or mist. The finer you can get the mist, the more power you're going to make.

Supercharging and Turbocharging

Supercharging, like nitrous oxide injection, was conceived to extract as much power as possible from a given displacement. Unlike nitrous oxide, supercharging is more involved, yet easier to tune and manage. Easier to tune because you know you're getting into trouble before getting there. Knowing you're in trouble comes from the sound of detonation. Superchargers and turbochargers don't come on as strongly and quickly as nitrous. For the most part, they cannot damage the engine as quickly as nitrous, because you can come off the power in time to prevent engine damage. There is also a safety device, called a wastegate, designed to prevent overboost with superchargers and turbochargers. With nitrous oxide, damage, and certain engine death, are instantaneous if you deliver too much of it without enough fuel, or with too much ignition timing.

Anytime you raise your engine's stress level with nitrous oxide, supercharging, or turbocharging, you should remember the importance of cylinder sealing. Opt for only the best competition head gaskets. Be prepared to spend more than $100 for a set. If you're going to blow a ton of squeeze or boost into the chambers, think seriously about O-ringing the block for adequate cylinder sealing.

Supercharging and turbocharging both accomplish the same objective. They each force air into the cylinders to make the most of a combustion power cycle. They mechanically increase cylinder pressure, which, given enough fuel, makes more power. Superchargers are driven by the engine's crankshaft. Turbochargers are driven by exhaust gas pressure. The compressor of both moves the air you're feeding into the intake manifold.

Superchargers give engine nearly immediate power. With an increase in RPM, the compressor turns faster, forcing more air pressure into the intake manifold, which gives more power. Overpressure is prevented by fitting the supercharger with a waste-gate, which vents excessive pressure.

Turbochargers take a certain amount of time to give you induction pressure when you step on the gas. This is called turbo lag. Because it takes the turbocharger time to spool up during acceleration, there is a certain amount of lag before you get the boost or pressure, and the resulting power. Turbochargers have a wastegate, which also bleeds excessive boost pressure, which prevents engine damage.

The greatest challenge facing the Cleveland enthusiast is supercharger kit availability. A thorough check of the Internet reveals very few, if any supercharger kits for the Cleveland engine family. If you want a supercharger, you have to fabricate most of it yourself. The same can be said for turbocharging where you need to fabricate and collect most of the system yourself. Another issue is compression, which needs to be around 8.0:1 if you want to run a lot of boost. This means a Cleveland needs to be built specifically for supercharging or turbocharging.

Types of Superchargers

The basic types of superchargers are: centrifugal, rotary, axial flow, Roots (two-lobe and three-lobe), vane type, and Lysholm screw. The most common type seen on small- and middle-block Fords are centrifugal and Roots lobe types.

The type of supercharger you should choose and why is hard to answer because everyone has different expectations and needs. Which supercharger you choose is going to depend on your needs. You choose the Roots blower for different purposes than you choose a centrifugal huffer.

Roots Blower: The Roots lobe-type supercharger has served many purposes during its service lifetime. The most common Roots supercharger duty has been to feed hungry, Detroit two-stroke diesel engines. You've undoubtedly heard the term "6-71 blower" in hot rodding circles. Detroit two-stroke diesel engines, once manufactured by General Motors, were named based on displacement, number of cylinders, and cylinder arrangement. The Detroit 6V-71, for example, is a V-6, with 71 ci of displacement per cylinder. A Detroit 8V-92 is a V-8, with 92 ci per cylinder. The Detroit 6-71 is an inline six, with 71 ci per cylinder. So when you see a huge 6-71 blower atop a well-fed small-block Ford, it's a blower originally designed for huge heavy-duty Detroit diesels that power semi-trucks.

The thing that makes a Roots blower quite effective is its positive-displacement design, which a Detroit two-stroke diesel engine needs for proper ingestion of air and scavenging of exhaust gases. This kind of positive-displacement design creates plenty of cylinder pressure when and where it counts in a high-performance V-8 engine.

When I speak of positive displacement in a Roots blower, this is because its very design doesn't allow much, if any, air to escape en route to the chambers. Roots blowers have two- and three-lobe rotor designs where rotors interlock to ensure consistent airflow, under pressure, into the engine.

Ford has been using the Roots design on factory production engines for many years, beginning with the 1989 3.8L Essex V-6 Thunderbird SC. Today, it is used atop the 5.4L SOHC V-8 engine in the Lightning and Harley-Davidson F-150 trucks, just to name two variations. This reliable, highly successful supercharger works quite well on a small-block Ford.

Centrifugal Style: A more common type of supercharger is the centrifugal type you see and hear at a lot of Ford events on newer 5.0L and 4.6L Mustangs. It's that familiar whistle associated mostly with the Vortech and Paxton superchargers. Instead of the interlocking rotors used in the Roots positive-displacement supercharger, centrifugal superchargers employ a fan that draws air into its center and pushes it outward into a duct where it enters the intake manifold.

Simply, centrifugal force is the energy of a spinning object that tends to throw the object (or parts of the object) outward. In this case, air is the object you sling outward from the spinning fan (compressor). The compressor takes the air in through its center and blows it outward with the whirling blades (or fins) that thrust it outward into the shell and into the intake tube. Not only does the compressor move the air outward from its center, it also squeezes the air in the shell, feeding it to the intake tube.

Turbochargers are like a centrifugal supercharger because they work much the same way. Instead of being belt-driven, they're driven by a turbine that is propelled by hot exhaust gases. As you accelerate, hot exhaust gases drive the turbocharger's single stage turbine, which drives the centrifugal compressor.

IGNITION

Ignition systems have a tricky job to do. They must be pinpoint accurate with potent spark timing to ensure a lighted mixture and power. It's easy to light the air/fuel mixture at low RPM. It gets tricky at high RPM where conditions change dramatically. When you first learn about how engines work, the discussion is confined to four simple cycles: intake, compression/ignition, power stroke, and exhaust. However, it is more complicated than that. It is the finite timing of these events that determines how reliably your Cleveland runs and makes power.

This becomes even more complex when you consider cam profile, combustion chamber size and shape, valve size and shape, and dynamic and static compression ratio. Confusion sets in when you have seemingly identical engines, yet ignition timing doesn't offer the same reaction or power. That's because no two engines are exactly the same. There are just enough variables for each engine to mandate its own tuning agenda.

Quick Fire

Although it is generally thought that the air/fuel mix "explodes" in a combustion chamber, it does not. Fuel and air ignite in a quick fire, which is a light-off across the piston dome that begins with a spark. In fact, the ignition of air/fuel always begins at the ignition source, whether it's a spark plug or a red-hot piece of carbon. As the air/fuel mix ignites, it flashes and expands across the chamber at a rate of about 700 feet per second where thermal expansion acts on the piston, rod, and crank. Thermal expansion is the energy driving the piston downward, where linear action becomes rotary motion and torque.

Because fuel and air ignite in a quick fire, you need to allow time for the thermal reaction to happen. Contrary to popular belief, the spark plug doesn't fire when the piston reaches TDC; rather, it fires BTDC. It fires BTDC because fuel needs time to ignite and go to work. This all happens in a nanosecond, even at idle. At high RPM, it happens in a fraction of a nanosecond and must happen earlier in the compression/ignition cycle. Under optimum conditions, you get a smooth light-off and a generous outpouring of power.

Ignition Timing

Adjusting ignition timing must be performed with a timing light with an accurate harmonic balancer. Be sure your harmonic balancer has its timing marks

The standard Autolite/Motorcraft single-point distributor looks like this. If you're going to stay with points, always use Motorcraft vented contacts with phenolic pivot and rubbing block, which wear the longest. Use plenty of distributor lube on the cam and rubbing block.

The basic Autolite/Motorcraft ignition system consists of single breaker points and a condenser inside a dual-advance distributor. What makes it "dual advance" is a vacuum advance and a mechanical centrifugal advance. The vacuum advance is operated off throttled vacuum advancing the spark when you step on the gas. As revs increase, vacuum advance smoothly hands off to the centrifugal advance, though both work continuously.

Beginning in 1968, Ford went to a dual-advance/retard unit on some engines to retard spark under deceleration and advance spark under acceleration. This was known as "improved combustion (IMCO). The advance/retard unit isn't in full operation until the engine reaches operating temperature. This happens through a thermal vacuum switch (valve) at the thermostat housing, which opens to allow vacuum to reach the retard side. The retard port is closest to the distributor housing. Retarding spark under deceleration reduces tailpipe emissions.

properly indexed. You'd be surprised how many times you get it wrong using a worn-out balancer or one improperly indexed from the factory. Even a new harmonic balancer must be checked for proper indexing. I've seen them as much as 11 degrees off, which causes a lot of confusion.

Once you have established the balancer is properly indexed, you must find true TDC at cylinder number-1, which is midway in the crank rollover point for the crank journal (12 o'clock). Install and index the distributor at cylinder number-1. This is called static timing, and where you begin tuning.

Be ready to set ignition timing right off the bat with the engine at 2,500 to 3,500 rpm. With the vacuum advance connected at 3,500 rpm, where is your ignition timing? Igniton timing should be checked two ways at 2,500 to 3,500 rpm: vacuum advance connected and disconnected. Total ignition timing with

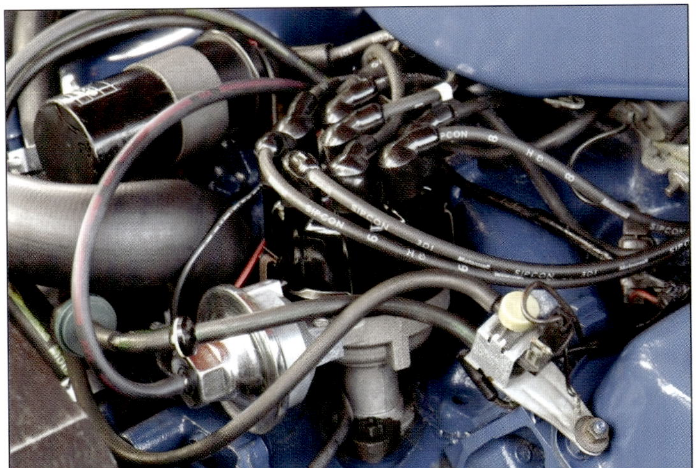

By 1973, distributor vacuum control became more complicated, with some applications having an advance/retard unit and some having only an advance unit. Unless you're restoring to stock, this should never be of concern.

Ford factory vacuum advance units have a spring and series of shims designed to control rate of advance. The more shims (washers) you add, the slower the rate of advance. When you remove shims, there's less spring pressure, which speeds up rate of advance.

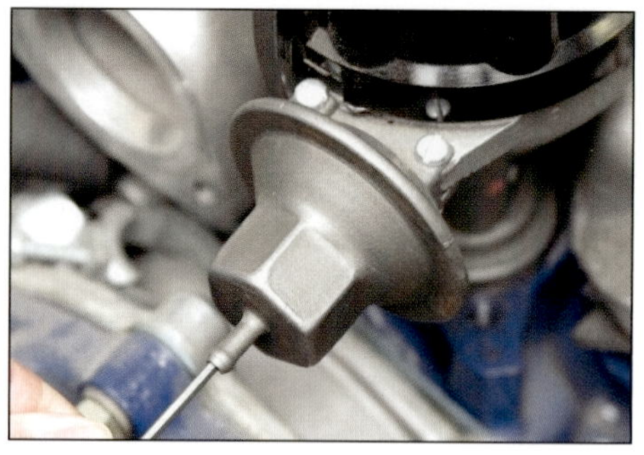

Aftermarket vacuum advance units are adjusted by inserting an Allen wrench and slowing rate of advance by turning clockwise (increasing spring pressure), or increasing rate of advance (decreasing spring pressure) by turning counter-clockwise.

vacuum advance connected should be no more than 36 degrees BTDC. At idle, it should be 6 to 12 degrees BTDC.

When dialing in total timing, begin conservatively at 30 to 34 degrees BTDC and observe operation. Push it as far as 36 to 38 degrees BTDC, but no higher. Under hard acceleration or loaded on a dyno, listen for spark knock. If you have spark knock, retard ignition timing 1 degree at a time and try again.

When you're checking ignition timing, you want to know total ignition timing (advance), and the rate of advance when the throttle is opened. When you goose the throttle, timing mark movement should roll with throttle movement. You want spark advance to roll quickly with RPM increase and throttle movement. If you don't have a vacuum advance, spark advance should increase in linear fashion with RPM—more slowly. Ultimately, at 2,500 to 3,500 rpm, total timing should never be more than 36 degrees BTDC. Of course you can push it to 38 or even 40 degrees BTDC, but it is risky even if you don't get spark knock.

Conditions change when it is hot and you're roaring around a road course at wide-open throttle, which is when you can get pinging (spark knock) and not be able to hear it. That is when the damage is done. This is why you want to start out conservatively with ignition timing and change it 1 degree at a time.

Spark Knock

You may know it as spark knock, but it's basically the same as detonation, pinging, and pre-ignition. Spark knock happens when you have early-ignition timing, a red-hot piece of carbon or ragged edge, overheating, a fuel octane rating that's too low, compression that's too high, a cam profile harboring too much cylinder pressure or working compression, or the ambient air being too hot. The rattling or knocking is abnormal combustion resulting in a strong shock wave across the piston dome, which acts on the piston pin and skirts causing a metallic sound under hard acceleration.

Dual-point ignitions were conceived to handle high-RPM operation by increasing dwell time. This allows the ignition coil to achieve greater saturation and a stronger discharge. However, the main reason for dual-point ignition is to get stability at high RPM. Go with Motorcraft ignition points, which have the best track record based on breaker arm tension and rubbing block durability. Many aftermarket ignition points have too much tension and they wear faster.

To eliminate spark knock during tuning, you must first establish why there is spark knock. What do you have for fuel octane? Have you confirmed compression ratio? Do you have carboned-up chambers? What is the known cam profile? Is the ambient temperature extraordinarily hot?

Begin your spark knock troubleshooting with a fuel octane rating based on the fuel you have in the tank. Total spark timing should be no more than 36 to 38 degrees at 3,500 rpm. You may know the static compression ratio, but you also have to know the dynamic compression (working compression).

Breaker-Point Ignition

Point-triggered (breaker-point) ignition is a simple on/off switch that opens and closes the primary ignition circuit to charge the coil and reduce a brief discharge of high-energy current to fire a spark plug. It can be debated who invented the breaker high-energy discharge ignition system, but who cares? What you're interested in knowing is how it works and how to make it better.

When you turn on the ignition switch, power travels to the primary ignition circuit to energize the coil and breaker points. Current travels through resistance wire in a Ford to the primary circuit. If points are closed, current flow across the contact points tends to burn the contacts. As current flows through the primary side of the ignition coil, it creates a strong magnetic field, which in turn induces a huge surge of current on the secondary side to the distributor. The condenser is there to take up the surge of high-energy electricity, which would otherwise arc violently across the open point gap. This action would quickly burn and pit the contacts. The condenser also allows the ignition system to build an electrical momentum to a steady 20,000 to 30,000 volts to the secondary side to fire the spark plugs.

The average garage mechanic tells you an engine can run without the condenser. However, engines generally don't run very well without condensers because the condenser acts as an electrical cushion—a shock absorber for high-energy electricity. Without it, electricity returns to ground, arcing across the points, and being of little value to operation.

Dwell Time

Ignition points are a rotary cam-actuated switch that operates in time with your Cleveland's firing order. This switch turns electricity on and off through the ignition coil. Dwell time is the amount of time in distributor shaft rotation degrees that points are closed. Each time the points open, a spark plug fires.

With a dual-point distributor, dwell time is increased to build more coil saturation and get a more potent spark. You also eliminate the limitations of a single set of ignition points, which are point bounce and incomplete coil collapse especially at high RPM. Key to improved performance is increased dwell time and a stronger spark. When you widen the point gap, you increase dwell time.

Electronic Ignition

The main reason automakers went to electronic ignition in the 1970s wasn't so much for performance, but reducing emissions because every misfire is unburned hydrocarbons and increased emissions. If you listen to new cars and trucks today, they don't misfire. That comes from a potent high-energy spark and the precision of electronic fuel injection.

Despite a point-triggered ignition's time-proven ability to fire spark plugs with precision accuracy, it has shortcomings. As you increase engine speed, there's less dwell time to build adequate current, which reduces spark potency. This causes misfire at high RPM because you need a spark powerful enough to overcome high cylinder pressures. At high RPM, points tend to bounce and flutter, also causing misfire. These shortcomings prompted creation of other types of ignition systems, such as transistorized ignition, triggered electronic ignition (Hall Effect), and capacitive-discharge ignition.

Transistorized Ignition

Ford was among the first to use transistorized ignition in the early 1960s. And later, Duraspark in 1975. Chrysler was the first US automaker to go with electronic ignition in 1974. Somewhere in there was General Motors' first shot at magnetic-triggered electronic ignition, then HEI (high energy ignition) in the late 1970s. HEI was a great idea because it eliminated the external ignition coil.

Triggered Electronic Ignition System

There have also been light-triggered electronic ignition systems with shutter-wheel triggers and light-emitting diodes (LEDs), such as Mallory's Unilite ignition in the 1970s. Light-triggered ignitions have performed very well and with great reliability. Most electronic ignition systems since the 1970s have been Hall Effect (magnetic-trigger) systems, which are the most reliable. In fact, even in this age of coil-on-plug, fuel injected engine control systems, Hall Effect is still used in the crank trigger role.

Capacitive-Discharge Ignition

Combining electronic ignition with capacitive discharge allows an inductive type of ignition system to build tremendous amounts of electricity for the secondary side to fire spark plugs. These systems pack a wallop and discharge huge amounts of electricity for each spark plug firing. In fact, these systems are designed to handle up to 12,000 rpm, which most Clevelands never see.

The key to performance and cleaner emissions is a potent spark. How you get that potent spark depends on your support system and what you use for spark

Pertronix Ignitor series electronic ignition retrofit kits are the 30-minute solution to all of the problems associated with point-triggered ignition systems. Simply remove your points and condenser, bypass the factory resistor wire (which unplugs near the ignition switch), and install the Ignitor. Set the air gap, make sure you have the ground link, and you're good to go.

Ford's Duraspark II electronic ignition offers the greatest reliability of any electronic ignition system. It is good well into high RPM and enjoys widespread parts availability. Aside from rotor and cap replacement once in a great while, Duraspark II is maintenance-free. You can mount the ignition amplifier anywhere using a Painless Performance Duraspark wiring harness.

This is a ballast resistor, which is common with Chrysler ignitions, but can be used with any ignition system requiring resistance in the power lead. When you purchase and install an aftermarket ignition, read the manufacturer's instructions carefully. Some require a resistor and some do not. Be sure to use the exact resistance required by the manufacturer.

Remember, if you're going with a roller cam of any kind, replace your distributor's iron drive gear with a steel gear. Brass drive gears work well, but they don't last. (Comp Cams offers a composite distributor drive gear that wears quite well.) Keep in mind there are two distributor shaft sizes: .530 and .467 inch.

It's important to have distributor shaft endplay within Ford specs to eliminate any chance of extreme wear. You can make your own "go/no-go" gauge (such as this one created by Marvin McAfee of MCE Engines) to make the job of checking easier. Shaft endplay should be .024 to .035 inch. Be sure to measure distributor drive gear to block gap. Gap shown here is .012 inch. This allows room for endplay, thermal expansion, and oil wedge.

Ignition wires should be spaced apart to prevent crossfire. Crossfire happens more often than you think, including with new ignition wires and with a high-energy ignition system. Crossfire can do serious engine damage especially if it happens at high RPM.

When installing ignition wires, use a dielectric compound and make sure terminals are seated completely in the distributor cap and on spark plugs. Arcing damages terminals and only makes the situation worse.

Street engines get a vacuum advance; racing applications do not. For street and strip, go with a vacuum-advance ignition for better fuel economy and low-end torque.

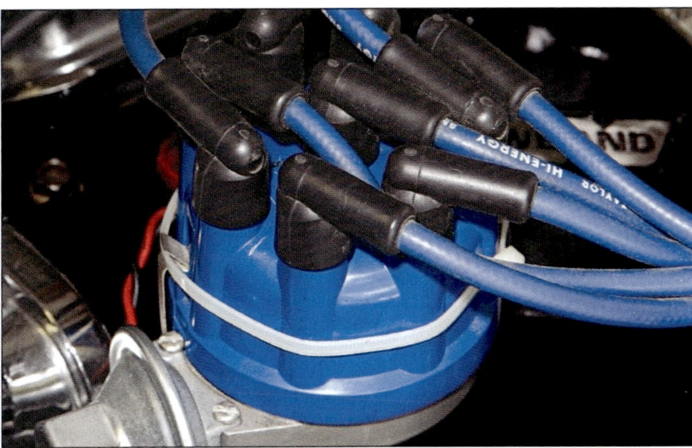
A simple failsafe modification to keep the distributor cap secure at high RPM is to use a zip tie. Although this might be viewed as overkill, it sure beats losing the cap at seven grand.

enhancement. MSD Ignition, as one example, has a variety of ignition enhancement systems—most of which are based on capacitive discharge. The MSD 6A ignition enhancers are based on this principle, and they do an outstanding job of keeping the fire lit at high RPM. One MSD enhancer, the 6 BTM (Boost Timing Master) allows you to control spark timing if you're running a supercharger or nitrous, which helps keep you out of trouble when things get hot and your foot is in it.

Ignition Coils

Most factory Ford ignition coils from the early 1970s make approximately 20,000 to 30,000 volts. This makes them inadequate for high-performance use. Stock ignition coils work fine for normal driving at low- to mid-range RPM. However, when you start spinning a Cleveland beyond 6,000 rpm at wide-open throttle, a factory coil cannot keep up. It continues to fire spark plugs, but not at the intensity they need to light the mixture. This is a combination of dwell/saturation time and spark potency.

At high RPM under great cylinder pressures, a weak spark gets snuffed out, hindering its ability to light the mixture. If you add supercharging or nitrous, it quickly becomes overwhelming. This is why you want a powerful ignition coil coupled with an ignition enhancer such as a capacitive or multi-spark discharge. You want the most spark your ignition system can pack, even with a street engine.

Distributor Sources

Unfortunately, there's not much good to say about Ford distributors because they're just not up to the job of high-RPM use. The Autolite/Motorcraft distributor family consists of distributors with bronze bushings, with some having only one bushing and others having two. Because oil distribution is so poor, bushings and shafts wear out quickly causing side play (wobble) and point bounce at high RPM. (This problem also exists with Duraspark distributors). So unless you're building a stealthy stocker, avoid using factory distributors.

Because the 335-series Cleveland engine family uses the same distributor as the 385-series 429/460 engines, there are a lot of aftermarket ignitions to choose from. Choice boils down to street or race or a combination of both. Street engines should be equipped with distributors that have a vacuum advance, which operates on throttled vacuums offering initial spark advance during startup and acceleration. Although vacuum advance helps fuel economy and acceleration, it also works hand in hand with the centrifugal advance any time you open the throttle as RPM increase.

MSD Ignition

There's a reason why you see the MSD name out there more than any other in racing—and that's because so much research and development go into its products. And talk about racetrack time? MSD products are tested in tough, grueling environments where they're subjected to the worse conditions imaginable.

Mechanical and vacuum advance must work together seamlessly. Each is tuned separately, yet ultimately together as RPM increases.

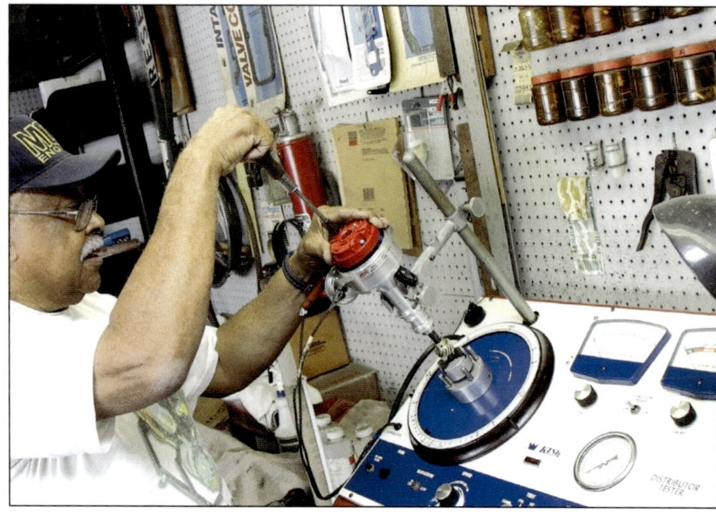

An MSD billet distributor gets the once over on a distributor machine. Most of the time, distributors are fine right out of the box.

There are three basic MSD units: billet, billet with a vacuum advance, and programmable E-Curve. At press time, the E-Curve is available only for 289/302/351W engines, but as MSD continues to develop its product line, the E-Curve also should be available for 351C/351M/400/429/460 engines.

MSD's E-Curve electronic programmable distributor enables you to dial in all timing elements based on how your engine will be used without changing weights or springs because it all happens electronically. You can adjust total timing, rev limit, rate of advance, and more with this distributor using a small, flat-blade screwdriver.

Outside of the E-Curve, choosing and tuning an MSD distributor is easy. For the street, you want the MSD #8477 Pro-Billet distributor with a vacuum advance. This is a high-performance street distributor engineered and manufactured for ease of use with an easy to access and adjust mechanical advance and a vacuum advance you can adjust with a simple Allen wrench. Mechanical advance is based on Delco distributors of long ago, which were easy to tune because the advance was right under the rotor. It's a matter of changing spring tension and and/or bushings. This distributor is C.A.R.B. approved.

Two MSD distributors are designed for racing, #8577 and #8569. The #8569 crank trigger distributor fits low in the block if you're running a tunnel ram or blower. It must be used with MSD's ignition control. The #8577 billet distributor is mechanical advance only and designed for high-revving applications. You can tune it with ease using the provided advanced springs and bushings.

Mallory Ignition

Mallory still has the same level of reliability and performance it has long had through Unilite technology. The Mallory Unilite #4756701 dual-advance distributor with mechanical and vacuum advance is primarily for street use.

The Mallory #3756701 is a mechanical advance (only) unit with Unilite for pinpoint accuracy. What makes this a great distributor is reliability and its maintenance-free disposition. Aside from the occasional cap and rotor replacement or

MSD distributors have a tunable mechanical advance so you can swap springs and bushings to get total timing dialed in. You want the mechanical advance to smoothly follow engine RPM as it increases. MCE Engines uses a good, old-fashioned distributor machine to curve distributors making adjustments to both mechanical and vacuum.

MSD's E-Curve ignition is foolproof tuning at its best. Available for small-block Fords only at press time, I suspect MSD will expand the E-Curve line to include Cleveland and 385-series engines eventually. E-Curve has been successfully tested on the dyno. It replaces vacuum and mechanical advance with precision electronic accuracy.

Choose a distributor for what your engine will do most of the time. The Mallory Unilite #4756701 dual-advance distributor with mechanical and vacuum advance is primarily for street use.

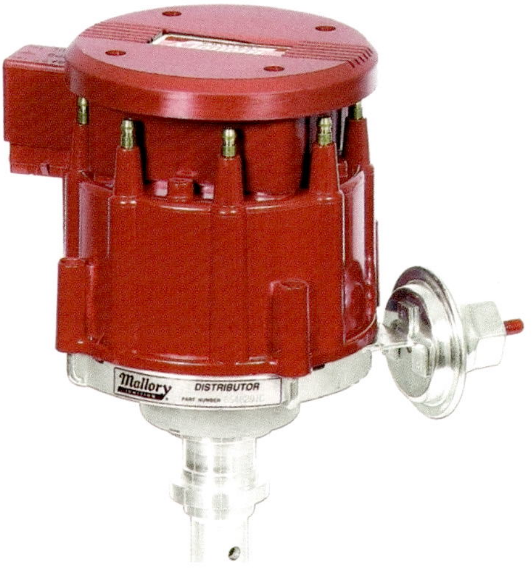

The Mallory #8556701C HEI distributor is a GM-style HEI coil-in-cap unit that is all self-contained. All you have to do is provide coil power.

The Mallory #3756701 is a mechanical advance (only) unit incorporating the time-proven Unilite for pinpoint precision. This is primarily a racing distributor, though it can be used for street.

cleaning the optics, it requires no attention. This is the distributor you want for high-RPM use.

The Mallory #8556701C HEI distributor is a coil-in-cap unit that is all self-contained. Fit may be tricky with the Mallory HEI depending on your Cleveland's induction system. This distributor can be converted for racing with an advance lockout. And if you choose to tune your Mallory HEI, both mechanical and vacuum advances are programmable and easy to access.

Performance Distributors

Performance Distributors (in Memphis, Tennessee) enjoys a great reputation for building affordable high-quality ignition systems for Ford applications. Founded by the late Kelly Davis, Performance Distributors is still a family owned and operated business. When you get on the phone with these folks, it's like chatting with an old friend. There's nothing you can't ask them.

Performance Distributors offers two basic types of electronic ignition systems for Clevelands. Both give you factory-style reliability and easy-to-get parts.

For a stock appearance in your Cleveland project, Performance Distributors offers its time-proven #32720 Duraspark ignition. This is a custom-calibrated piece curved for your application. That's why Performance Distributors wants to know all about your engine when it takes your order. Performance Distributors blueprints every distributor with a full-length bronze bushing, new hard parts, and precision calibration for a seamless advance as RPM increase. Each Duraspark distributor is capable of 10,000 rpm, though I suggest not going there. Please specify flat-tappet or roller camshaft with your order.

Your other choice is the revolutionary #32820 Davis Unified Igniton (D.U.I.), which is based on GM's HEI system with a self-contained ignition coil in cap. If you want a clean appearance without clutter, the D.U.I. system is your best choice.

The racing D.U.I. system (#328211 with vacuum advance and #328212 without vacuum advance) can handle up to 9,000 rpm. Because it delivers a greater dwell angle, it delivers a hotter spark enabling you to widen spark plug gaps to .050 to .055 inch. Because these distributors are already curved to your custom application, all you have to do is install and go.

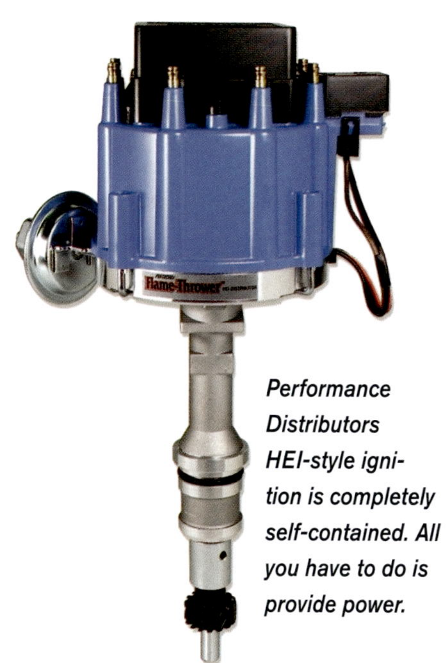

Performance Distributors HEI-style ignition is completely self-contained. All you have to do is provide power.

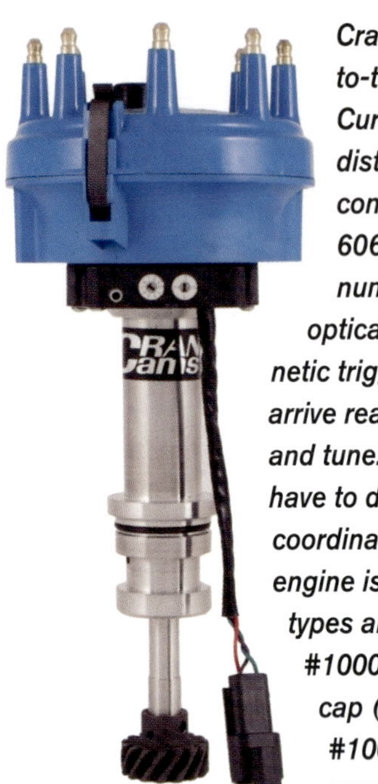

Crane's easy-to-tune Pro-Curve line of distributors are constructed of 6061-T6 aluminum with both optical and magnetic triggers. They arrive ready to install and tune. All you have to do is dial in coordinates once the engine is fired. Two types are available: #1000-1604 large cap (shown) and #1000-1605 small cap.

Crane's line of ignition enhancers include the #6000-6040 Fireball Hi-6 multi-spark capacitive discharge that can withstand up to 14.0:1 compression. The Hi-6 is fully tunable with two rotary switches you can adjust with a small, flat-blade screwdriver. These adjustments include a rev limiter. The Hi-6 works with nearly any kind of ignition, including Crane's own Pro-Curve distributors.

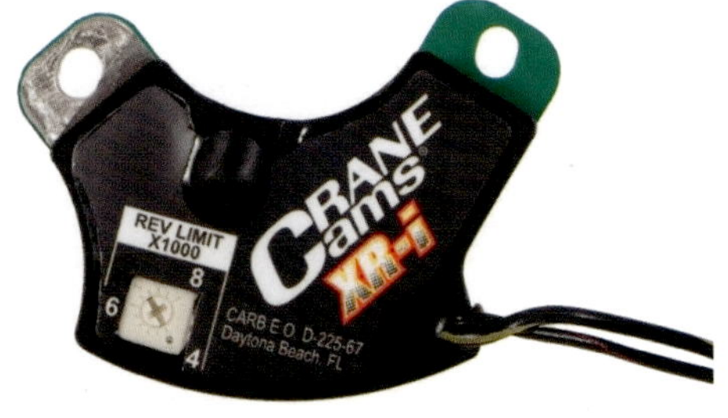

Crane offers this easy-to-install XR-i drop-in electronic ignition (#750-1700) for Autolite/Motorcraft distributors. It can be installed in 30 minutes and can rev up to 8,000 rpm. Chances are your street Cleveland isn't going to see 8,000.

Crane

When you think of Crane, you think of cams and valvetrain systems; you don't think of ignition systems. Yet a closer look at the company's offerings reveals Pro-Curve Billet distributors for 351C, 351M, and 400-ci engines. These maintenance-free, easy-to-curve distributors make light work out of a distributor installation. Made of 6061-T6 billet aluminum, Crane Pro-Curves can be tuned without removing the distributor cap. There are 27 advance curves you can play with to get the optimum power band you're looking for. Crane Pro-Curve distributors are optically triggered with a magnetic pulse output.

Magnetos

Chances are slim you're going to stuff a magneto into your Cleveland, but let's talk about it, just in case. Magnetos have been used extensively in racing because they confidently make high-energy current. In fact, magnetos were the norm before electronic ignition came into extensive use. What makes a magneto different is its self-contained design. It generates its own electricity. It also stands up to extreme vibration, heat, and other elements. Use of a magneto these days makes little sense unless you're a nostalgia buff who wants and likes the look or you do a lot of sprint, short-track, or extreme off-road racing.

Ignition Wires

Secondary ignition wires have come a long way since those original equipment Autolite/Motorcraft types installed on Cleveland engines at the factory. Back then, ignition wires consisted mostly of carbon- or copper-core conductors, which broke down rather quickly, shorting to ground or crossfiring. In either case, misfire was the result. In the years since, ignition leads have improved dramatically offering foolproof performance with minimal or no misfire.

MSD Ignition wires stand up to extreme heat and get electricity to its destination without a hitch. Because you can get MSD ignition wires in black as well as red, they render a more stock appearance. MSD wires have an 8.5-mm outer extrusion that stands up to heat. Inside this jacket is extra-heavy glass braid, then a high dielectric insulator. Next, a helically wrapped copper-alloy conductor. Inside of that is a ferro-magnetically impregnated core to get current to spark plugs at autobahn speed. It isn't only about the spark plug leads you choose, but how you route and locate them. Ignition wires should be routed parallel where possible, at least 1/4 inch apart to minimize the risk of crossfire, which is when a spark plug receives current intended for another; it can destroy an engine at high RPM. You also want to keep wires at least 1/4 to 1/2 inch from metal surfaces to prevent arcing to ground and misfire.

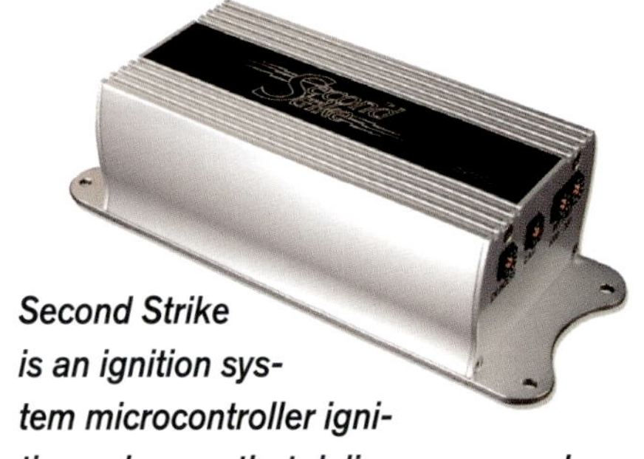

Second Strike is an ignition system microcontroller ignition enhancer that delivers a second, more potent spark within a nanosecond of the first firing to offer more complete combustion and virtually no chance of misfire. This is a Pertronix capacitive discharge system that's very effective with inductive-type ignition systems such as Ford's Duraspark.

MSD's 6A/6AL capacitive discharge keeps the fire lit well into high-RPM ranges, which is vital if you're running nitrous or supercharging.

Because high-energy electricity is very unpredictable in nature, it travels unexpected paths at times and for reasons you don't always understand. You can have the most ironclad ignition system and experience stray current, crossfire, and a blown engine. Sometimes, current travels across exhaust gases or even coolant in a water jacket causing crossfire or misfire—even more than one spark plug firing at the same time reducing the effectiveness of the one that was supposed to fire. Go with the best ignition parts you can buy and set them up with the precision of an aircraft electrical system.

Distributor Caps

Never buy cheap distributor caps and rotors. Go with the best insulation and brass terminals possible, from well-known companies (such as MSD, Accel, and Mallory) or original equipment. Although the factory gets a lot of bad press over its original equipment, that's nonsense. Original equipment caps were developed from millions of dollars in resources, which makes it acceptable for Autolite/Motorcraft distributors.

Use the Duraspark distributor cap with terminals spaced more widely apart. Make sure you have a vented cap to help keep ionized air levels to a minimum inside. Also take note of how much air gap there is between the rotor tip and terminal. Measure the distance between the rotor's center and tip. Then measure from the cap's center to the terminal. Too much gap and you run the risk of crossfire inside the cap. Once your Cleveland has been in operation, watch for carbon tracking inside the cap, which is typically caused by misfire. However, it also adds to the problem of misfire.

Spark Plugs

Spark plugs have become a very complicated subject in recent years because there are so many different types, not to mention marketing angles. The best advice I can offer is to stick with what has worked for generations, the humble cross-electrode spark plug. Platinum-tip spark plugs work best with high-energy ignition systems because they last. Outside of that feature, I suggest you stick with simple resistor or non-resistor spark plugs.

Your greatest concern when choosing a spark plug is heat range. How quickly does your spark plug get rid of heat? If a spark plug's heat range is high, it doesn't get rid of heat quickly, which can cause pinging (spark knock). And even if there's no spark knock, the firing tip can run hotter than it should causing premature failure. Heat range depends on how long the insulator is, which determines how quickly heat transfers to the head. Ideally, your spark plug's heat range keeps combustion temperatures somewhere around 800 to 1,500 degrees F.

Your best indication of heat range depends on reading spark plug insulator color after a wide-open throttle blast and shutdown. You want to see tan to light tan. Sooty black indicates you're running too cold and rich. Snow white means you are too lean and the heat range is too high. Small dots of aluminum on the insulator indicate bigger troubles, such as piston damage.

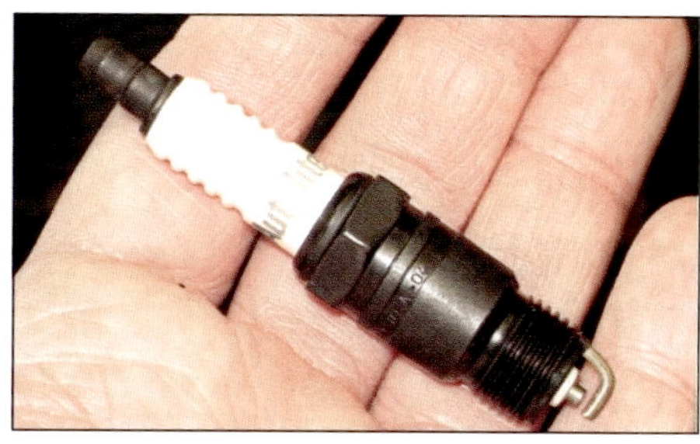

If you're running a high-energy ignition system, go with Autolite or Motorcraft platinum-tip spark plugs. Otherwise, use resistor or non-resistor conventional Autolite or Motorcraft spark plugs. High-energy ignitions need a larger gap in the .040- to .055-inch range. Index your spark plugs by marking them externally and getting the firing tip fully exposed to the chamber.

Heat range is also determined by cam profile and how much cylinder pressure is made as a result. Cylinder pressure is a product of dynamic or working compression, which affects spark-plug heat-range selection.

Another issue to consider is how far the center electrode extends into the combustion chamber. Does it clear the piston? This can be checked when you are measuring valve-to-piston clearances during mock-up. This logic falls in line with heat-range selection. The longer the center electrode, the greater the risk of piston contact. If your heads are already installed, this is something you do carefully by slowly hand-cranking the engine and feeling for resistance, then, pulling the spark plug and checking for contact.

Another thing to consider is spark plug indexing. Though some say this doesn't matter, others live by it. Thread the spark plugs where the ground electrode doesn't block the spark exposing it fully to the air/fuel mix. Do this by marking each spark plug with a Sharpie at the ground electrode prior to installation. You may have to index several plugs until the ground electrode is away from the chamber.

CHAPTER 9

Exhaust

Your Cleveland's exhaust system affects performance as much as any other part of the engine. Designing an exhaust system, beginning at the header flanges, requires a lot of thought about expected horsepower, torque, displacement, and usage. Most factory exhaust systems don't offer sufficient scavenging because they are so restrictive. They tend to be too small, which has more to do with cabin noise levels and the economics of mass production than it does performance.

With restriction comes excessive backpressure and the contamination of fresh air/fuel charges and poor performance depending upon cam profile and RPM range expected. As RPM increases, this phenomenon worsens because spent gases tend to back up into the chamber. The more backwash you have on intake stroke from spent gases, the more contaminated your engine's chambers become at high RPM, which causes serious performance issues from a tainted air/fuel mix. Contaminants take up precious space that could be better utilized by fresh air and fuel mass.

Ford Powertrain Applications (FPA) manufactures perfect-fit production headers for many types of Ford V-8s including the Cleveland. Although this is an FE big-block with FPA long-tube headers, it demonstrates the great fit of these headers in the tightest of configurations. They roll in nice and tight against the block, eliminating clearance problems.

Header Selection

You might be inclined to ask what you stand to gain from headers versus factory iron-exhaust manifolds or short-tube versus long-tube headers. You stand to gain at least 20 to 30 hp and comparable torque from long-tube headers than you would iron manifolds. Much depends on how you choose and size headers. Headers allow hot gases to roar from ports into the exhaust system more quickly than with exhaust manifolds. Because most exhaust manifolds are designed with space considerations more in mind than gas flow, you find rough cast iron inhibits flow terribly. This is why any kind of header (shorty or long tube) offers better flow than a rough cast-iron manifold. Rough cast surfaces create turbulence and restriction.

The first consideration in designing your Cleveland's exhaust system is proper pipe diameter from flange to tailpipe. Begin planning with primary tubes right off the header flanges. Then look at secondary tubes and collectors down under.

Custom header fabrication enables you to get a stepped or equal-length design configured for a difficult application. Although having custom headers made costs more, it isn't that much more and you can get exactly what you want.

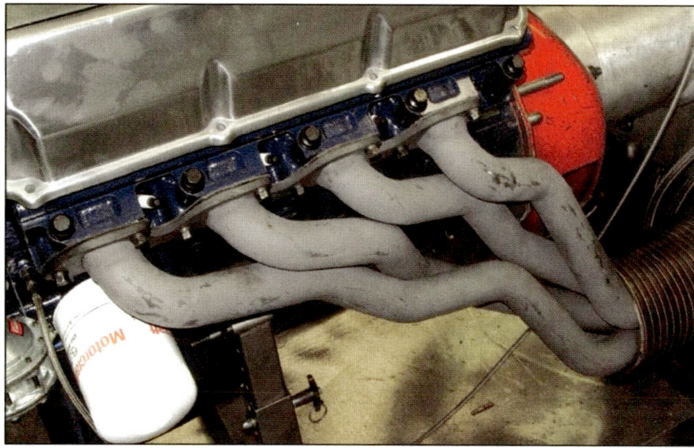

Header primary tube size and length determine where your Cleveland's torque peak falls. Primary tube size needs to stay conservative if you are seeking good low- to mid-range torque in a street engine. You also want length in the interest of torque. For more horsepower on the high end, use larger primary tubes.

Primary tube size and length are determined by where you want your torque curve. In other words, where do you want peak torque? The smaller the primary tubes, the better low- to mid-range torque.

Too small for the amount of power and things get too hot; plus you lose horsepower on the high end. Too large and you lose low- to mid-range torque. Primary tube length moves the torque and horsepower curves up or down depending on length. In other words, you either broaden or narrow the power band (torque curve) based on primary tube length. You also move the torque peak up or down depending upon primary tube length.

Primary tube diameter and length are important considerations, which can make it tricky to choose the right header for your application. With the knowledge of how primary tube size and length affect torque peak and below torque peak, you're ready to make an educated header purchase decision.

Calculating Primary Tube Size

Calculating primary tube size and length is a complex formula because there are so many variables to engine power and function: heads, induction, cam profile, and compression. Often, you buy headers right off the shelf with no real idea of what you're selecting. Header pipe sizing and length boil down to what you want your engine to do. You get caught up in the philosophy that larger is better, but only with displacement and all-out racing. Street engines do not need large header pipe sizing. On the street, you want torque because that's what you use most of the time. Low- to mid-range torque is achieved when you keep primary and secondary header tube sizing conservative. And when you are racing, you need strict calculations to determine proper pipe sizing and length.

Headers exist to reduce exhaust restriction and improve scavenging. You want exhaust gases to exit the combustion chamber more aggressively, yet hold enough back pressure to help torque. And this depends largely on valve overlap. In other words, you want enough of a low-pressure wave during valve overlap to help draw out hot gases (scavenging). This is known as pressure wave tuning. According to Phillip H. Smith and John C. Morrison who have studied this phenomenon, when the exhaust valve opens

These ceramic-coated, Hooker long-tube, Super Comps (PN 6211-1HKR) for the Mustang and Cougar 351 Cleveland are designed to accomplish two things: torque and horsepower. Primary tubes are 2 inches by 34 inches with a 3½-inch collector. If this has too much, try 1¾ inches by 30 inches (PN 6119-1HKR). Header selection depends on how much displacement you've shoehorned into your Cleveland and the type of power desired.

This is Hooker's Super Comp in black (PN 6125HKR) for the 400 and 351M with 1¾-inch primaries at 31 inches with 3-inch collectors. If you intend to blow more than 400 ci through these scavengers, you need 2-inch primaries and a 3½-inch collector. The 400 block can handle nearly 460 ci, which calls for larger primaries especially if you're going for horsepower.

and hot gases exit at high pressure, a pressure wave is formed that moves through the header primary tube at 1,400 feet per second. Exhaust gases exit the exhaust port at 300 feet per second.

The challenge is to manage this extreme difference in gas speed and gain control of the pressure wave, which roars down the exhaust pipe and reverses quickly back up the pipe to meet an open exhaust valve. If the pressure wave reaches the exhaust port during valve overlap (where intake and exhaust valves are just off their seats), it draws out the exhaust gas and draws in the intake charge. This has a forced-induction effect because the pressure wave draws fresh air and fuel in quickly.

There are two things to consider here: primary pipe diameter and length right off the header to head flange. Both determine when and how horsepower and torque are made. Primary pipe length moves the power band up or down depending upon length.

Smaller primary tubes don't flow as generously as larger primaries. However, they do offer greater velocity, which enhances torque at low- and mid-range RPM. For street and weekend strip driving, you want velocity, which gets you traffic-light torque and good power for the freeway. Primary tubes need to go larger when when you're going for higher RPM ranges and horsepower. If you're going to operate your 351C in the 1,500- to 3,500-rpm range, header tube size needs to be 1½ to 1⅝ inches. If your Cleveland is in excess of 400 ci (either as a 351M/400 raised-deck or 351C block), primary tube size needs to be on the order of 1⅝ to 1⅞ inches. If you're going for high rpm, then, you're looking at 1⅞ to 2 inches.

Secondary Tubes and Collectors

Secondary tubes and collectors have a similar effect on torque peak. It boils down to secondary tube length coupled with size. Once you have established length, you can then sort out size. This can get quite involved, but here it is in a nutshell: Collectors and H/X pipes mean something to torque production, but not as much when it comes to horsepower. Drag racers, for example, don't worry about collector length much because it has little effect on horsepower, which is where drag racers live. However, if torque is important to you, collector size and length become very important. Short or long?

It has been proven time and time again shorty headers aren't as beneficial to power as are long-tube headers. Long-tube headers make a difference in high-end horsepower with little effect on torque. Torque is affected more by primary tube length and size as said earlier. The choice depends on what you want your headers to do and how you intend to use the vehicle. Street cruisers can get by with shorty headers. Weekend and full-time racers want long-tubes.

Equal-Length, Step and Tri-Y Headers

Equal-length headers make fit a greater challenge especially with a Cleveland. However, they do serve a purpose depending upon how you intend to use them. Equal-length headers are more effective with an open exhaust system at high RPM, but make no difference through mufflers on the street. So unless you intend to spin your Cleveland high through an open exhaust, equal-lengths make no sense whatsoever.

Step headers, such as equal-lengths, are for high-RPM/open-exhaust systems. The step header begins with small primary tubes at the flange, getting progressively larger as you move toward the collector. The idea behind step headers is to create a broader, flatter torque curve. Despite claims about step header design, it doesn't make enough of a difference in performance to warrant its cost and hassle. In theory, the step header is an interesting idea. In practice, there's little to be gained from using them.

Tri-Y headers are more common with small-block Fords and FE big-blocks than Clevelands. However, the Tri-Y does exist for Clevelands and here's why: The Tri-Y design funnels hot exhaust pulses from four primary pipes into two, then into one collector. This approach creates a broader torque curve primarily for racing where you need grunt coming out of a turn into the straights. In other words, Tri-Ys provide better low- to mid-range torque. This happens by pairing cylinders that fire farthest apart to create a pulsing momentum with improved scavenging. This momentum creates velocity and, depending upon cam profile, draws out hot gases while hauling in fresh air and fuel. The Tri-Y approach doesn't always work for all engines because its effectiveness is determined by firing order.

Exhaust System

As much as we've complained about noise ordinances in the years since "back in the day," people are finding noise just isn't cool anymore. Open headers may free up horsepower, but torque and your hearing suffer as a consequence. Racers are learning there's torque hidden in those silencers. Companies such as Flowmaster, Magnaflow, Hooker, and others are discovering more horsepower and torque through advanced muffler design and pipe-sizing technology. Fortunately, the aftermarket offers a huge variety of complete exhaust systems for all kinds of vintage Fords, which makes selection and installation easier. Not all off-the-shelf systems are a great fit. In fact, you probably need the expertise of a good exhaust shop to install just about any system because nearly all of them require some kind of tweaking to achieve proper fit.

Summit Racing Equipment's website offers excellent advice on how to design an exhaust system. It suggests first knowing what size pipe to choose once you get past the header collectors. Summit also advises knowing the difference between a crush bend and a mandrel bend, which affects exhaust flow, before you buy an exhaust system. Crush bending causes flow restriction along the way. Mandrel bending provides a smooth journey and it looks better. Always go with an H-pipe or X-pipe dual-exhaust system (balance tube) for improved scavenging and better sound. Without a balance tube, performance suffers and you wind up with an exhaust system that sounds like a popgun at the tailpipes.

National Parts Depot offers the most extensive line-up of exhaust systems for vintage Fords in the industry. You may combine these systems with a wide variety of aftermarket mufflers depending upon pipe size desired. Which Flowmaster muffler you choose for your Cleveland project depends on desired performance and noise levels. Remember, noise isn't cool anymore; mellow and throaty are.

FPA long-tube headers are a true Tri-Y design with four-into-two-into one cleanly alongside the block and bellhousing with a ball/socket collector.

The FPA ball/socket collector design eliminates header gaskets and the pesky nature of three-bolt disconnection. Installation is simple and easily performed by any reputable exhaust shop. Jet Hot did the ceramic coating on this FPA header. And remember, if you're going to dyno your Cleveland, wait to have the ceramic coating done until after dyno testing. Extreme heat fogs the coating.

This is an FPA header collector prior to Jet Hot coating. What makes the FPA header a good value is cost, craftsmanship, and fit. You may order them in the raw and clean them up, then have them Jet Hot coated. You may also use a high-temperature exhaust paint with a tolerance of up to 1,700 degrees F. Pop for the ceramic coating; it will last the life of the header.

Right sizing includes the exhaust system having a balance tube between sides. Pipe size is everything to torque mostly. If you go too large, you lose torque. Go too small and you lose horsepower.

Pipe sizing must be consistent throughout. If you have 2¼ or 2½ inchers, it must be this size from header collector to tailpipe. Flowmaster mufflers are among the best in the industry. They deliver great throat. If you go with Delta Flow 40 or 50 Flowmasters, that resonance is gone, accompanied by cabin quiet.

Aluminized or Stainless

Another item you don't think about enough is material. Stainless or aluminized steel? Because exhaust systems are more a work of art these days as well as functional, additional thought has to be given to material and aesthetics. Aluminized exhaust systems are more affordable; however, they are more susceptible to corrosion as time passes especially if you live where humidity is high. If appearance is important to you, you can ceramic coat headers and pipes. However, it is very expensive. The beauty of ceramic coating is color choice including a natural metal finish if you desire. Ceramic coatings such as Jet Hot can withstand temperatures up to 1,700 degrees F. If you're going to dyno test your Cleveland, remember ceramic coating doesn't like the extreme heat of a dyno pull. It fogs badly.

Factory mufflers offer quiet, but quiet comes at a price—impeded scavenging. You want backpressure, but not too much. Much depends on cam profile as well as pipe size and muffler baffling.

Though you rarely hear about this subject, it is important. Exhaust system seams need to be welded, which gets rid of noise issues. It also keeps backpressure consistent.

One of the largest exhaust system challenges is header flange and gasket security. The key to gasket security is header bolts that stay tight. Stage 8 (PN 8912) locking header fasteners are tightened and locked so it is impossible for them to become loose.

Equal-length shorty headers offer improvement with an open exhaust at high RPM, but have never really been proven effective for the street in terms of horsepower gain. Go with a more conventional header for the street.

For all the hype over step headers, there's no real evidence they improve power significantly for the cost and the complex nature of their manufacture.

Exhaust Pipe Sizing

The chart below came from www.exhaustvideos.com.

Based on the calculations, you should never need more than 3.00 inches of pipe diameter for a 600-hp Cleveland. And remember, when you go too large, you lose torque. The best path to pipe selection is common sense. You don't need 3-inch pipes with a 350 hp engine. You can get away with 2¼- to 2½-inch-diameter pipes with a 400 hp Cleveland. Keep in mind how much space large pipes consume. It is very difficult to fit 2½- to 3-inch pipes underneath a Mustang or Torino.

The folks at www.exhaustvideos.com base their calculations on raw facts. They suggest your engine needs to flow 1.5 cfm through the intake per one engine horsepower. The exhaust system needs to flow 2.5 cfm per one engine horsepower because hot gases consume more space than cool incoming air.

Pipe Diameter (inches)	Pipe Area (square inches)	Total Estimated CFM	Maximum Horsepower Per Pipe	Maximum Horsepower for Dual Exhaust
1.50	1.48	171	78	155
1.75	2.07	239	108	217
2.00	2.76	318	144	289
2.25	3.55	408	185	371
2.50	4.43	509	232	463
2.75	5.41	622	283	566
3.00	6.49	747	339	679
3.25	7.67	882	401	802
3.50	8.59	1029	468	935

Note: Mandrel bending adds 3 to 5 percent improvement to these flow numbers.

If your budget allows, stainless steel is the best choice for an exhaust system because it will last the life of a restoration. Although stainless is corrosion resistant, it is not corrosion proof. It can rust in pinpoint locations if not cared for.

Not much attention is paid to exhaust tips, but they do affect performance to some degree. You want exhaust tips that are not restrictive, such as small quad-tips or those louvered first-generation Mustang trumpet tips. Both are quite restrictive though they're at the end of the system. GT trumpets have never been much on sound quality nor are original rolled-tip quad tips.

CHAPTER 10

Break-In and Tuning

There are about as many approaches to engine break-in and tuning as there are engine tuners. Yet you can't change the basic fundamentals of engine physics and the way power is made. Once you have an assembled engine ready for operation, you are then married to its blueprint.

Getting Started

When you fire your Cleveland for the first time, you get a rush of excitement and anticipation because all of your hard work either proves or disproves itself with the roar of combustion. Don't get so caught up in the experience, however, that you forget what you're supposed to be doing.

Preparation is everything before firing your Cleveland. You want all moving parts soaking wet with lubrication, which is why you want to prime the oiling system first to get bearings and cylinder walls wet. This is performed by driving the oil pump shaft counterclockwise with a high-torque, 1/2-inch-drive drill made for endurance. During the priming process, spin the starter (spark plugs removed) to get the cylinder walls wet with oil. There is a lot of blue/white smoke when it fires; however, all is good and wet with less risk of damage to dry surfaces. Fire your engine with straight SAE 30 weight conventional engine oil and then do the first oil change at 500 to 1,000 miles including filter. Never use synthetic engine oil for break-in.

Begin your dyno test and tune on the rich side with conservative ignition timing in the 32- to 34-degree BTDC total timing range and adjust from there. Do you have too much carburetor or not enough? Carburetor sizing depends on displacement and what you want the engine to do. A 351C needs little more than 750 cfm if you're going aggressive. When you add displacement and power, carburetor size demand goes up.

Mix in a bottle of ASL Camguard to soften the break-in process because it does the good work of a zinc additive (only better), reducing wear and tear. At the minimum, you want a zinc additive to minimize wear, especially with a flat-tappet cam.

Ignition timing should be somewhere around 6 to 12 degrees BTDC at idle and total timing at 3,500 rpm at 34 to 36 degrees BTDC. This keeps things safe and minimizes the risk of detonation. You want the air/fuel mixture on the fat (rich) side to prevent detonation and a lean meltdown. You can always go leaner with time and testing. Oil pressure should be around 40 to 60 psi or 10 pounds per 1,000 rpm. At 5,000 rpm, you want a solid 50 pounds minimum.

With piston number-1 at true TDC, set and time the distributor. All Ford small-block V-8s are frustrating when it comes to getting the distributor to seat fully. As the distributor begins to seat, bump the starter and it should drop into place. Check rotor indexing.

Dual-point ignitions are designed to provide for a more complete coil saturation and a more potent spark at high RPM. Unless you are obsessed with originality, points of any kind make little sense. If you must go with points, you want high-quality ignition points with a phenolic rubbing block and vented contacts for cooler operation.

Just because the harmonic balancer indicates TDC doesn't mean you've found true TDC. Even a new balancer is suspect because the outer ring isn't always completely accurate. I've seen new balancers as much as 10 degrees in error. This is why you check for true TDC going in.

Tuning includes curving the distributor, which includes dialing in the rate of centrifugal advance. Autolite/Motorcraft distributors have both centrifugal (mechanical) and vacuum advance. Centrifugal advance gets tuned primarily in a distributor machine though it can be tuned during break-in. Here, "10L" indicates the advance limit. One side may be "10L" and the other "15L" for a total of 25 degrees maximum not including vacuum advance.

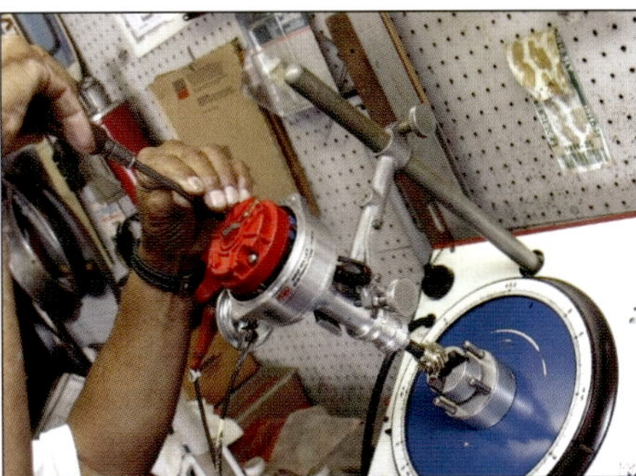

Like the rest of the engine, every distributor should be blueprinted and curved prior to installation based on how the engine will be used. Retune and curve again once installed and the engine has been fired because curving is based on what you believe the engine will do.

Ford distributors are fitted with three basic types of tunable vacuum advance units. Factory advance units (one shown here) are adjustable by adding or subtracting shims to control spring pressure. Add shims and you slow the rate of advance; subtract shims and you speed it up. Aftermarket advance units are adjusted via an Allen screw through the vacuum port. Clockwise to slow advance or counterclockwise to speed it up.

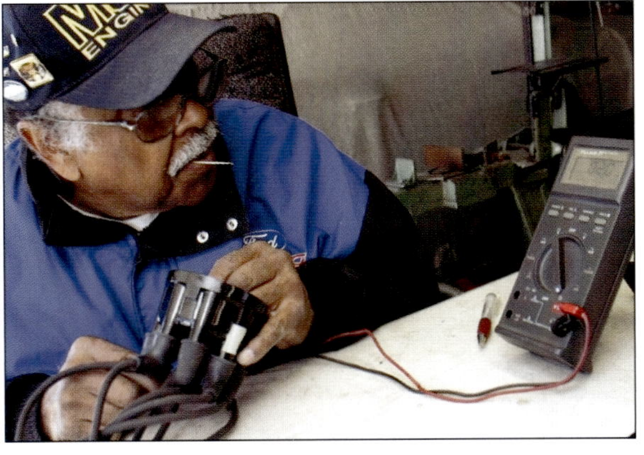

Detailed troubleshooting is critical, beginning with the simplest items. A misfire, for example, begins with a thorough check of the ignition system with a multimeter.

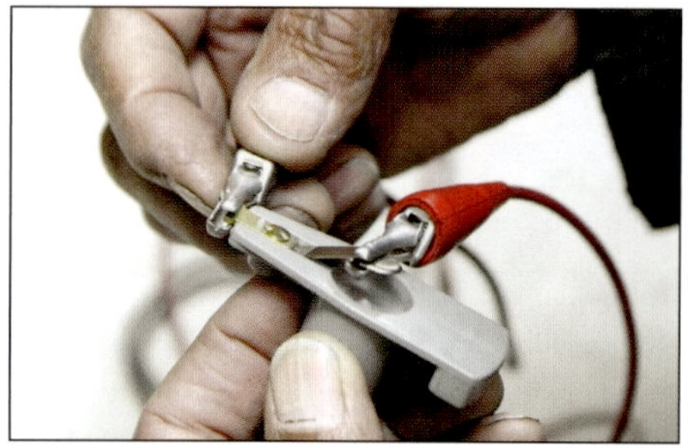

Even a new distributor rotor isn't always ready to install. If it doesn't conduct electricity or intermittently conducts electricity, it is ineffective. Rotors and distributor caps must always be checked for continuity (resistance) with an ohmmeter.

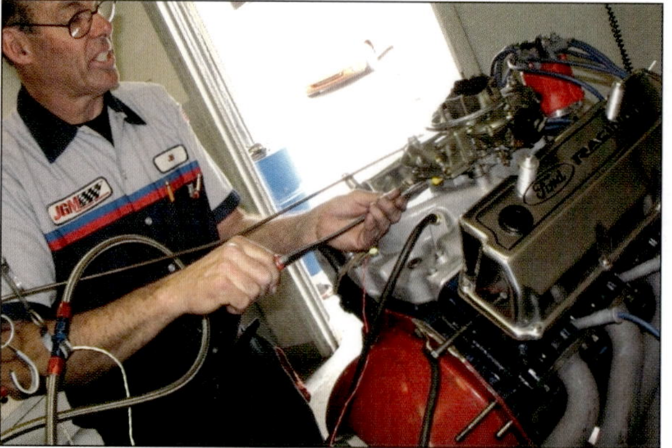

There is a tremendous amount of set-up time before an engine is fired on the dyno. Jim Grubbs of JGM Performance Engineering does his homework before a dyno session: determining proper carburetor jetting, ignition timing, and header configuration. Once the engine is fired, he performs a minimum 30-minute warmup at 2,500 rpm for ring seating and work-hardening cam lobes (flat tappet only). He uses a zinc-additive engine oil to get started.

Marvin explains he's had his share of open circuit spark plugs right out of the box. He suggests the use of Autolite spark plugs. Platinum-tip spark plugs last longer, but don't make the spark any more potent.

This 400 has been built and tuned for low- to mid-range torque with stock bore and stroke with a lot of thought put into heads, manifold, and camshaft. These are Aussie 302C heads with super-small wedge chambers for good quench on top of KB2344 forged pistons. It has been tuned for pulling power with 30 degrees BTDC total timing at 5,500 rpm. The result is 390 hp and 454 ft-lbs of torque.

Jim Grubbs of JGM Performance Engineering readies a 351C for dyno tuning with SAE 30 weight Chevron Delo 400, which is a heavy-duty lubricant designed for diesel and gasoline alike. It allows rings and bearings to seat while maintaining a good oil wedge.

Use a dual-throttle spring setup in the interest of safety. You can go side by side like this or a spring within a spring. This redundancy can save your neck if a spring fails.

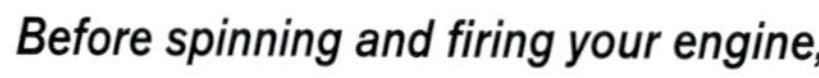

Before spinning and firing your engine, give the oil pump a good workout, which pumps oil throughout the engine to all moving parts. You need a 1/2-inch-drive electric or pneumatic drill with reverse rotation. Run the drill for at least one minute and observe both oil flow and pressure.

Use an anti-collapse spring in the lower radiator hose. Though some hose manufacturers suggest the anti-collapse spring was for factory fill use only, this is not true. The anti-collapse spring keeps the lower hose from collapsing at high RPM.

There are a number of schools of thought on automotive coolants. Water is the most effective heat-transfer liquid. However, because water causes corrosion, you must use a corrosion inhibitor. One engine builder here in Los Angeles suggests 100-percent antifreeze for zero corrosion though it is not as effective as a heat-transfer medium. Evans non-aqueous coolant (no water) is the best approach because it never has to be replaced. The downside for Evans coolant is its cost at approximately $70 a gallon.

Break-In

Begin engine tuning with proper break-in. Regardless of what type of cam you have (roller or flat-tappet), the rules of proper break-in apply to every type of engine because you want to seat rings and bearings with a proper run-in. When the engine fires, confirm oil pressure and take it immediately to 2,500 rpm and let it run at that speed for at least 30 minutes. The best scenario is to fire the engine on a dyno with an experienced dyno operator and run it in under a load after it has been running at 2,500 rpm for 30 minutes. For good piston ring seating, you want a load at 2,500 to 3,000 rpm. Loading with throttle builds cylinder pressure. Cylinder pressure allows rings to expand and seat into cylinder walls once the oil is at operating temperature.

If you have dyno access, you can break-in an engine with proper tuning and operation so all you have to do is install it in the car. Dyno time begins with that good warmup at 2,500 rpm for 30 minutes to get the oil hot (minimum 140 degrees F).

The first pull you make is called a jet check. To perform a jet check, load the engine and go wide-open throttle for 15 seconds at 4,500 rpm and immediately shut down. Pull all eight spark plugs and inspect them. All the basic rules of spark plug reading apply here: tan/beige, you're good; sooty black, rich; snow white, lean. If you see tiny dots of aluminum on the insulator, you are dangerously lean. When you are lean, go up several jet sizes bordering on rich, then come back in small steps and observe spark plug color. Spark plug insulator color is the best barometer of engine health and spirit.

Resist the desire to push ignition timing too far ahead. Start out in the 34- to 36-BTDC range and watch your power curve. No matter what anyone tells you, no more than 36 to 38 BTDC above 3,500 rpm. Testing under the controlled

Once you have burped all the air from your Cleveland's cooling system, use a 12- to 15-pound pressure cap. The greater the pressure, the higher your coolant's boiling point. Always have a coolant recovery system on board.

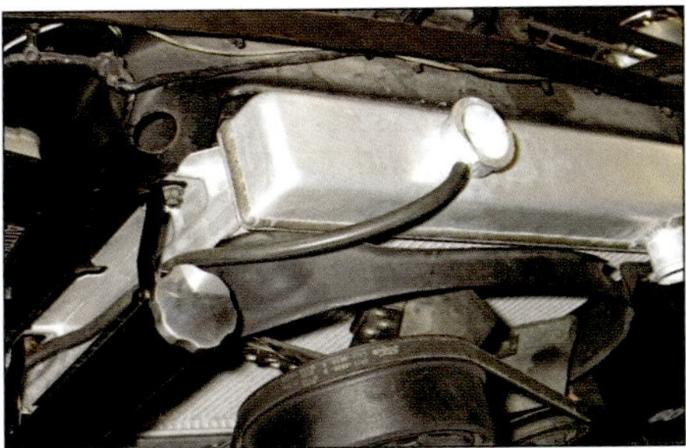

Fan selection and positioning is important. I suggest the use of a fan shroud and either a thermostatic clutch fan or lightweight flex fan. The fan should be positioned halfway into the shroud for optimum airflow. Also keep proper pulley ratio in mind. You don't want a fan/water pump that turns too fast.

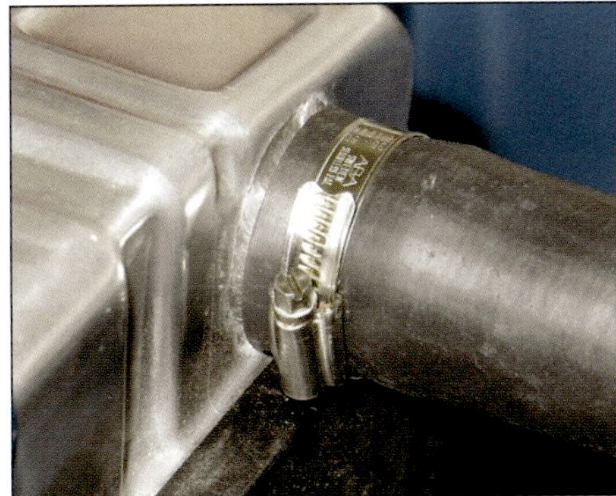

Engine builders all have different approaches to cooling system security. Use a heavy-duty stainless worm gear clamp on all cooling system hoses. MCE Engines suggests the use of two clamps side-by-side.

conditions of a dyno room is one thing; on the road with 92-octane fuel in a hot engine compartment under varying conditions is another thing entirely. Pin the throttle and trash your new dyno-tested engine in short order because you're too lean or ignition timing is too far ahead. Be conservative and keep it in one piece.

Redline Cooling manufactures the best radiators I've ever seen with great cooling capacity and outstanding quality. This 24-inch version for the Mustang/Cougar is fitted with SPAL electric fans, which keep your Cleveland cool in the hottest of conditions.

All fresh engines and radiators must have a cooling system filter to keep iron particles and other debris out of the radiator. Install one in the upper radiator hose and watch it capture debris that can clog your radiator.

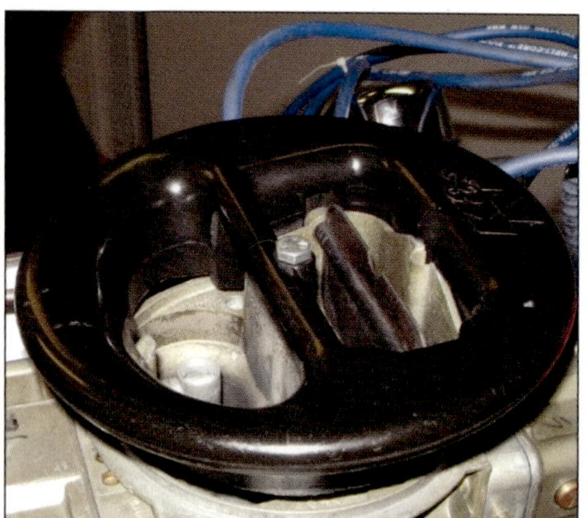

Regardless of what type of coolant you use, top it off with a water-retention product (such as Hy-Per Lube or Water Wetter), which reduces and eliminates surface tension. The absence of surface tension allows coolant to transfer even more heat as it flows because there's more contact area.

There are at least two approaches to valve adjustment. With a mechanical camshaft, valve lash is .022-inch cold for both intake and exhaust at the cam lobe's heel (valve closed). With hydraulic lifters and a bolt-fulcrum setup, valve lash is adjusted with different pushrod lengths. If you have gone to a stud and adjustable rocker (shown), slowly tighten the adjustment until there's no up and down play at the pushrod, then tighten 1/4 to 3/4 turn. There are variables depending upon what you want the valvetrain to do. Never go beyond 1/2 turn.

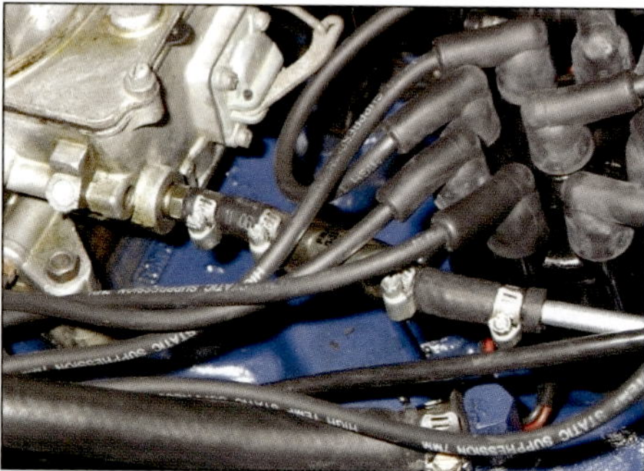

Although Ford put fuel filters at the carburetor, you should place the fuel filter away from a hot engine to prevent vapor lock. For safety hard line your fuel system between pump and carburetor. If you must use hose, use high-pressure, fuel injection or braided hose. And one more thing: A 351C should never have less than 3/8-inch-diameter fuel line. When displacement goes above 400 ci with 500 hp, you need 7/16 inch. You must have the same size line from tank to carburetor.

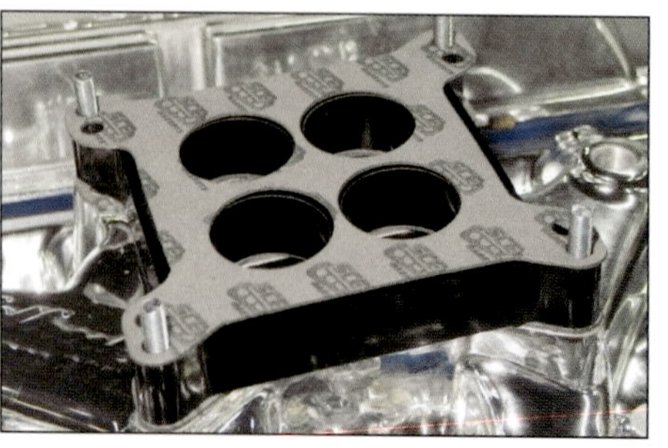

K&N's Stub Stack may look like one of those gimmicks from infomercial television. However, this easy modification is dyno proven and I've seen it with my own eyes. It improves both horsepower and torque by streamlining airflow at the air horn.

There's a lot of debate about whether or not carburetor spacers work. They do improve torque and afford you a certain amount of horsepower. There comes a point width-wise (beyond 1 inch) where a carb spacer becomes too wide and ineffective. Around 1 inch seems optimum for most applications as long as it can clear the hood.

If you want the best numbers possible on the dyno, always go with a velocity stack, which affords you cooler ambient air (depending on outside air temperature) and streamlined airflow. It also measures airflow.

A good idea is a jet check for your first dyno pull, which is wide-open throttle at 4,500 rpm under load for 15 seconds. This gets spark plugs to their true fuel mixture color. Tan is perfect; sooty black is too rich; snow white is too lean. You want a light tan. Particles of aluminum on the insulator mean danger–you are way too lean.

Exhaust System

Header tube size is yet another very important component to dyno testing. Too small and you drive exhaust gas temperature skyward and lose power. Too large and you lose torque, which is the lesser of two evils. Exhaust pipe sizing is just as critical as header tube sizing and for the same reason. Pipes that are too large might feed the ego because they sound throaty. However, you lose torque. Pipes too small cause higher backpressure, stifle power, and raise exhaust gas

Accelerator pump shot determines throttle response right off idle. If you have a stumble or lag, check spring tension, cam, and nozzles. You want a good healthy pump shot as throttle comes off idle.

temperatures. Header primary and secondary tube size depends upon exhaust port size and power expected.

Not all of us have the luxury or the cash for a dyno session, which typically costs $600 to $1,000 per day. This is where you give your fresh engine a workout with a little roadwork. You want to approach engine break-in much as you would on a dyno with proper ring and bearing seating and settling in.

On the road, load the engine as you would on a dyno. Once the engine is at operating temperature, get vehicle speed where engine RPM is around 2,000 to 3,000, in final drive (not overdrive). Run the engine through a series of acceleration tests while remaining within the legal speed limit, which helps ring and bearing seating. Lean on the throttle hard and slowly back off. Listen for detonation (spark knock) under acceleration. After doing this approximately five times, return to base and check engine vitals: coolant condition, oil level/condition, ignition timing, and a spark plug reading. Conduct a valve adjustment as necessary.

The break-in process is about getting piston rings and cylinder walls to mate

Every Cleveland engine build needs to begin its new life with ASL CamGuard, which provides additional protection because zinc is gone from most engine oils today. Engine assembly lube of any kind should already be on those moving parts prior to fire-up.

perfectly. The same can be said for bearings and journals. And if you are running a flat-tappet camshaft, break-in work hardens cam lobes and lifter mating surfaces. One more thing: Ceramic-coated headers don't like the extreme heat of a dyno pull. This is why it's a good idea to dyno test using bare steel or painted headers to prevent damaging the ceramic coating.

After the Break-In

Once break-in is safely out of the way, what's next? For the first 500 miles, keep your driving aggressiveness conservative. Continue those bursts of power for ring and bearing seating, but don't overdo it. At 500 to 1,000 miles, change oil using conventional SAE 10W30. If you're going to run it hard, use 10W40. At 1,000 to 2,000 miles, change oil to synthetic 10W30 or 10W40 including filter.

At 1,500 miles, check the basics: spark plug reading on all eight cylinders, examine coolant and thermostat function, inspect oil for color and content. Check underneath for leaks around the pan, timing cover, rear main seal, and freeze plugs.

Power Builds

So far, I've discussed how to build a powerful Cleveland engine. Now, I'm going to introduce you to builders who understand how to get power and reliability from Ford's legendary 335 engine family. Building a durable Cleveland boils down to physics, technique, and selecting the right combination of parts.

400 Horsepower

It isn't hard to get 400 hp from a 351C. All you need is the right combination of parts, including CNC-ported, factory, iron-head castings from Powerheads and a budget stroker kit, and get ready for great street power. Here are two examples: one from MCE Engines and one from TMeyer, Inc.

Marvin begins with a freshly machined D2AE-CA four-bolt main block. Nice thing about this block is its 4.030-inch bore that needs only a fine honing for good ring seating. There is no ridge and there was still a crosshatch pattern. That's red GE Glyptol coating in the lifter valley for improved oil return flow and iron sealing.

Marvin looks to Eagle for his inspiration with this 393-ci stroker kit (#16800030) with a 3.850-inch stroke and 4.030-inch bore, which is affordable and offers the mechanical advantage of stroke. With a cast-steel crank, beefy 6.000-inch I-beam rods, and forged Mahle pistons, there's all kinds of power (torque) to be made here. Though Marvin is content with 410 hp, you can push this kit closer to 500 and still be safe.

MCE Engines

Marvin McAfee of MCE Engines welcomed me into his Los Angeles shop where he was working on a customer's 351C-4V engine. The customer, located 1,500 miles away, wanted 400 hp and comparable torque from his 351C.

When Marvin received this engine, it was worse for wear and suffered from poor building technique. It was worn out before its time. Poor valvetrain geometry had damaged fresh Comp Cams Magnum roller rockers. Fouled spark plugs indicated cylinder-sealing issues.

Marvin decided this Cleveland needed a complete teardown along with the full complement of machine work and the right combination of parts to achieve more than 400 street horsepower. When Marvin tore this engine down, he found 4.030-inch bores with minimal wear and taper.

Another affordable pathway to power is an aggressive hydraulic roller cam from Comp Cams (#SK32-431-8). When you reduce friction, you free up power. And when you allow a more aggressive ramp, you make more power. This Comp hydraulic roller is good for 2,000 to 5,500 rpm, with .566-inch valve lift, 224 degrees of duration at .050 inch, and 110-degree lobe centers. It has good idle and aggressive amounts of torque with a broad torque curve.

One of the cheapest ways to bolster your Cleveland's bottom end is ARP main studs. A stud girdle delivers even more strength when power numbers court 500 and beyond. Never bottom out these studs, but instead leave about 1/8 to 1/4 inch between stud and bottom.

You can free up more power with a Torrington bearing timing sprocket, which reduces friction. Every place you reduce friction, you release power lost to friction.

Install and torque main caps one at a time and check rotation. You should be able to turn the crank with one hand and it should roll over smoothly. If you can't, clearances are too tight.

MCE 351C-4V Street

351C block, D2AE-CA four-bolt main block

351C-4V heads, Boss 302 C8AE head castings

Powerheads CNC port work and Manley 2.19/1.71-inch valves

Comp Cams kit (#SK32-431-8) with Ultra Pro Magnum (#1630-1) 1.7:1 roller rockers and one-piece pushrods

Comp Cams valvesprings (#924-16)

Comp Cams dual-roller timing set (#2121) with needle bearing insert (reduced friction)

Pioneer fuel pump eccentric (#P10-PF113/114)

Eagle nodular iron 3.850-inch stroker kit (#16800030) with 6.000-inch 5140 steel I-beam rods, SRP 4.030-inch forged pistons, file-to-fit rings, Clevite 77 bearings, and 393-ci displacement

Edelbrock LB dual-plane intake manifold (#2665)

Holley Street Avenger 770-cfm carburetor (#HLY-0-8077)

MSD Pro Billet distributor (#8350) with Blaster coil

Powermaster 65-amp alternator (#17076 1G)

MCE 393C on the Dyno

Horsepower	410 at 5,500 rpm
Torque	436 at 4,000 rpm

Powerheads did a nice CNC port job for MCE Engines on these Boss 302 heads, which have been modified to work on a 351C. Cooling passages have been plugged and modified for the Cleveland. With good port and bowl work, you can expect 340 cfm from these intake ports and roughly 190 cfm from exhaust. This masterful CNC port work includes 2.190/1.710-inch stainless valves.

Assisting Edelbrock's Performer manifold and an aggressive Comp Cams hydraulic roller is Holley's new Street Avenger (#HLY-0-8077) at 770 cfm at wide-open throttle. Whenever you conduct a dyno test, first perform a jet check to confirm air/fuel ratio. Spark plug color determines course of action.

Valve timing events and degreeing a new cam are everything to power. Closely examine valve timing events with a degree wheel to determine cam specs and what to do about timing. When you advance valve timing, you improve low- to mid-range torque. When you retard valve timing, you increase horsepower and lose torque. Sometimes, you do little more than move the power band.

Marvin's racing and aviation backgrounds make him more cautious than most builders. This doesn't net power, but safety wiring bolt heads keeps things safe.

This is Edelbrock's Performer 351C-4V dual-plane manifold for the 4V head. The Performer 351C-4V gives you good low- to mid-range torque coupled with high-end power to 6,500 rpm.

This completed 393C stroker is ready for the dyno. With an MSD billet distributor with vacuum advance properly curved for the power expected, Marvin expects 410/436 HP/TQ. The beauty of Marvin's street engines is a broad torque curve that begins to come on strong at 2,200 rpm handing off to horsepower at 5,200.

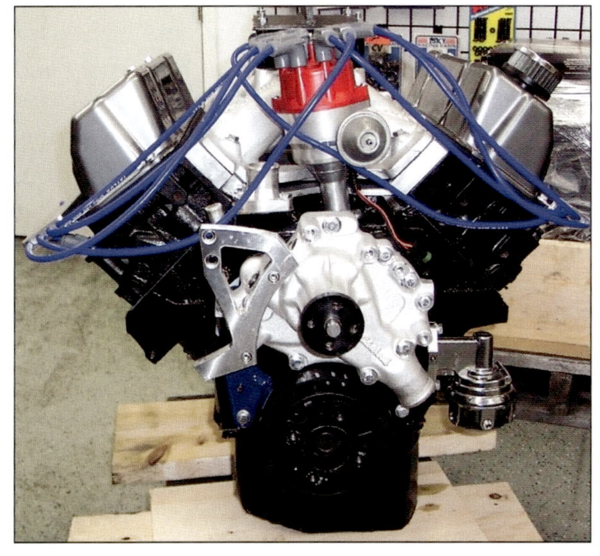

Tim Meyer's tall-deck 400 made 396 hp and 449 ft-lbs of torque on its best pull using a single-plane manifold and a 700-cfm Holley carburetor at 32-degrees BTDC total. This is a great street engine for a Ford pick-up or classic sport utility because it pulls. If you want more torque, go with a dual-plane manifold with long runners.

TMeyer, Inc.

Tim Meyer of TMeyer, Inc., in rural Minnesota is a recognized and respected engine builder who has built a lot of 351C and 400 engines for clients around the country. Though the 400 gets a lot of criticism for being an underpowered smog slug, it remains a 351C with increased deck height and larger main journals; a small-block with the personality of a big-block.

If you strip the 400 of factory design shortcomings, it is an engine long on potential because you get big-block power without the weight penalty. The 385-series 460, as one example, weighs at least 100 pounds more than a 400.

When Tim took on this 400, he knew what it needed to make more power. The 400's cylinder heads are open-chamber 351C-2V castings, which suffer from the absence of quench and are prone to detonation. This is why Tim went with Australian 302C closed-chamber wedge heads with 57- to 60-cc chambers on top of the 400. Good quench for the money amid a nice, small, wedge chamber.

With the 400, Tim has an opportunity to get 1 hp per cubic inch or roughly 400 hp from a 400 along with approximately 450 ft-lbs of torque. This comes from topping the 400 with cylinder heads that make the most of bore and stroke along with a good cam and an induction system. And he gets it done with 9.8:1 compression and 87-octane pump gas. This happens with Tim's own custom KB #2344 forged pistons (30-cc reverse dome) for a 400 with Aussie 302C cylinder heads and a stock 400 bottom end.

TMeyer 400, Pull 1

Tim began his 400 dyno thrash with a Weiand Action Plus (#8010), an Edelbrock 600-cfm carburetor, and the D.U.I. ignition system from Performance Distributors. Here's what happened on the first pull in Tim Meyer's own words, "So far the engine has had a 25-minute break-in. We have started with the Weiand Action Plus dual-plane intake. After 25 minutes with 10W40 weight oil with oil temperature at 225 degrees F and water temperature at 200 degrees F, we were able to idle at 900-rpm and maintain 40 to 50 pounds of oil pressure." The first pull net 365 hp and 425 ft-lbs of torque with total ignition timing at 25 degrees BTDC. There's room for improvement.

TMeyer 400, Pull 2

"Best news yet: Exhaust gas temperatures are about 1,200 degrees F. Most low-compression engines have a higher exhaust temperature around 1,400 to 1,500 degrees F," Tim comments. "This time, we went to 5,500 rpm and bumped the timing to 30 degrees BTDC total. We've developed a misfire at 5,500 rpm. As a result, we're installing another set of advance springs after trying different distributor parts. Despite the misfire, we've gained power: 370 hp and 430 ft-lbs of torque." Tim adds he has changed the oil to 10W30, with pressure dropping at hot idle to 40 pounds. A compression check shows an average of 170 psi.

TMeyer 400, Pull 3

"Final pull with the Weiand manifold. We've changed to an MSD billet distributor with vacuum advance and a Holley 650-cfm carburetor with the Weiand Action Plus," Tim comments. "We bumped the timing to 36 degrees BTDC and it did ping under load." Tim retarded total timing to 32 degrees BTDC to get 384 hp and 450 ft-lbs of torque. With the Weiand Action Plus dual-plane manifold, you can see the TMeyer 400 is about torque, not horsepower, which makes this 400 in current trim perfect for a Bronco or F-Series truck. The dual-plane induction system is happiest between 2,500 and 5,500 rpm.

TMeyer 400, Pull 4

Next, Tim tried a Holley single-plane manifold and 650-cfm Holley carburetor just to see what happens to the power curve: 390 hp and 451 ft-lbs of torque. Total ignition timing is 30.5 degrees BTDC.

TMeyer 400, Pull 5

Next, Tim went with an Edelbrock 750-cfm carburetor for a drop in horsepower and torque (perhaps too much carburetor): 380 hp and 437 ft-lbs of torque. Disappointing numbers with a carb swap and the same 30.5 degrees of total timing.

TMeyer 400, Pull 6

Tim installs a 700-cfm Holley to achieve 396 hp and 449 ft-lbs of torque. The power message here seems to be the velocity you get with a smaller carburetor. With velocity comes torque.

TMeyer 400, Pull 7

On Pull 7 Tim decided to go with the Edelbrock Performer 400 dual-plane manifold and a 600-cfm Holley, probably not enough carburetor because horsepower is down at 387, with torque improved at 458 ft-lbs, which proves the velocity theory. It is all in what you want from your Cleveland. If you want high-end horsepower, increase carburetor size conservatively in 50- to 100-cfm increments. If you want stump-pulling torque, go smaller in the 600- to 650-cfm range. Single-plane manifolds make sense for high-RPM use or when you increase displacement. They don't perform well down low. Dual-plane manifolds such as the Edelbrock Performer and Performer RPM series make the most sense for drivers, tow vehicles, and haulers.

TMeyer 400, Pull 8

Back to the Weiand Action Plus dual-plane manifold and 650-cfm Holley for the best results of this dyno session: 393 hp and 458 ft-lbs of torque. Tim kept timing conservative at 30.5 degrees BTDC, which I think could have been pushed a bit higher along with fatter jetting. With Ford's 4.000-inch bore/4.000-inch stroke combination and conservative tuning, you can achieve 400 hp and 450 torque numbers along with durability.

500 Horsepower

There are two Cleveland engine builds for you here: one from Trick Flow Specialties and another from *Hot Rod* magazine contributor Jeff Huneycutt of www.horsepowermonster.com. Each of these builds shows what can be done with both the 351C and 400 given budget and savvy engine-building technique.

Trick Flow Specialties

Trick Flow recognized the dilemma facing Ford buffs saddled with rather pathetic factory iron heads in North America. The 351C-4V heads have great 62- to 64-cc wedge chambers with outstanding quench characteristics, yet have huge ports that deliver at high RPM, but suffer at low speed. The 351C-2V head has right-sized ports designed for low- to mid-range torque and even good high-end power. However, they're ineffective for the kind of power you want to make.

Trick Flow introduced its new PowerPort Cleveland head designed specifically for the 351C, 351M, and 400 with right-sized intake and exhaust ports based on Ford's 351C-2V. These are ports that give this engine what it needs: velocity at low speed for all kinds of torque. And when it's time to pin the throttle, you get torque that segues into horsepower at 6,000. Wedge chambers offer the kind of quench Ford chambers never had.

When Trick Flow engineers set out to design these heads, they wanted everything Ford heads didn't have: exhaust ports raised .100 inch for better scavenging, cooling passages designed for both the Cleveland and Windsor small-blocks, better oil return flow, and right-sized intake ports somewhere between 2V and 4V for the perfect balance of low-RPM torque and high-RPM horsepower. Trick Flow decided to build a great street/strip 351C stroker (383 ci) with 3.750 inches of stroke and 4.030-inch bores.

Engine builder Ron Greczanick was enlisted by Trick Flow to build this Cleveland with more than 500 hp. Truly remarkable is the power this engine makes

Trick Flow's 383C gets mechanical advantage from stroke. This is the Probe forged piston (#14213-030) with 16-cc reverse dome and Eagle Specialties 4340 H-beam 6.000-inch rod.

Trick Flow 383C

Trick Flow PowerPort 190 cylinder heads (#TFS-51600004-M62)
Probe 4340 steel crankshaft (#10012)
Eagle Specialties ESP H-beam 6.000-inch rods
Probe SRS forged pistons (#14213-030) with 16-cc reverse dome
Probe Piston Rings (#315-0036-030)
Clevite H-series main and rod bearings
Dura Bond cam bearings
Comp Cam hydraulic roller lifters
Crane .630-inch-lift hydraulic-roller camshaft
Trick Flow chromemoly 8.000-inch pushrods
Trick Flow 1.73:1 roller rockers
Milodon stock replacement steel oil pan
Milodon pick-up
Melling standard pressure/high volume oil pump
ARP oil pump shaft
ATI Super Damper
Edelbrock Performer RPM Air Gap manifold
MSD billet distributor with bronze gear
Autolite copper-core spark plugs
Mezeire electric water pump
Ford Racing cast valve covers
ARP fasteners throughout
Fel-Pro gaskets throughout
Sealed Power engine plug kit
Dupli-Color Ford Blue paint

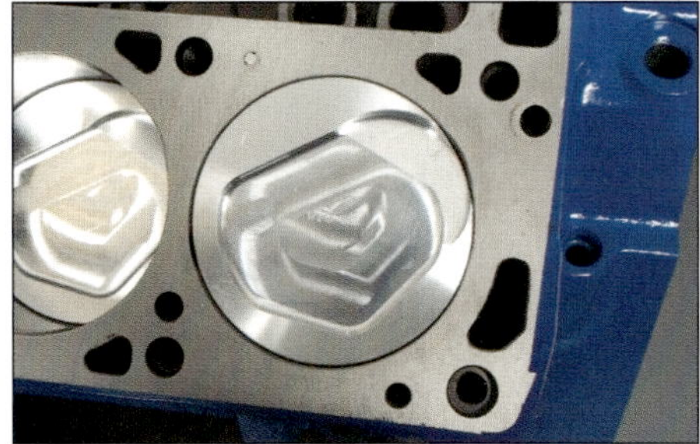

In the bore, the Probe reverse dome (dish) looks like this. The dish enables you to control compression by size. The larger the dish or reverse dome, the lower the compression.

Confirm and dial in valve timing by using a degree wheel and dial indicator to confirm actual cam dynamics versus what's on the cam card. Valve timing is advanced or retarded as necessary depending upon where you want peak power.

Trick Flow went with a .650-inch-lift Crane hydraulic roller cam with small base circle to clear stroker rod bolts. With a 3.500-inch stroke, a large base circle camshaft clears.

Permatex's The Right Stuff is used in critical leakage areas such as cooling passages to keep oil and coolant where they belong. Although there are many different types of sealer, The Right Stuff is used with great success by lots of engine builders.

This is the ATI Super Damper from Summit Racing, which keeps vibration and crank rebound under control at high RPM. The ATI Super Damper differs from a stock balancer because it is to SFI specification and fine-tunes crank dampening.

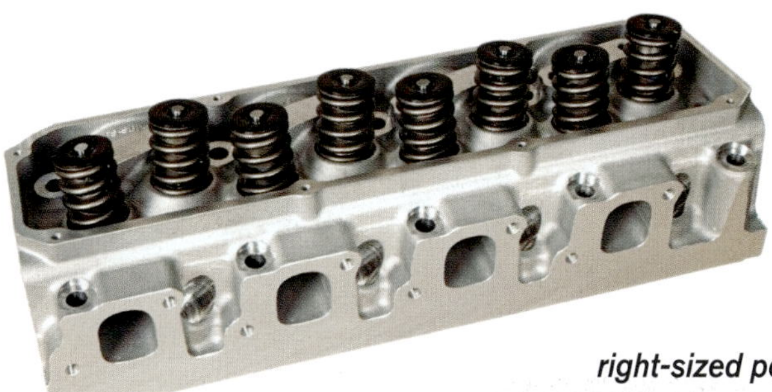

Trick Flow has chosen the PowerPort 190 cylinder head with 190-cc intake volume, 2.080-inch intake, and 1.600-inch exhaust valves. These right-sized ports and valve offer a nice balance of torque and horsepower for the street.

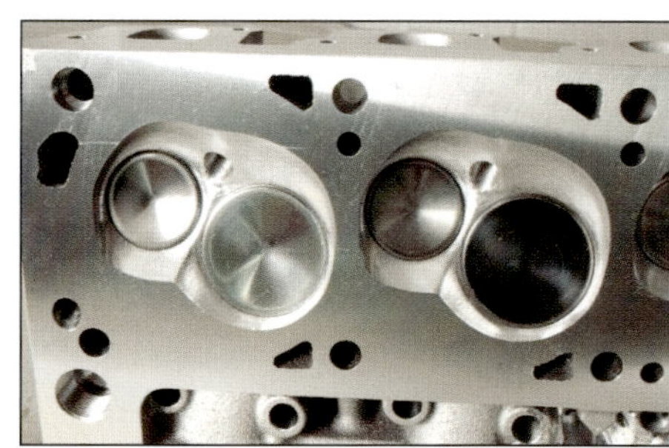

High-swirl, 62-cc chambers mix it up along with good quench. Valve sizing is generous with minimal shrouding. Quench comes from abundant surface area around Trick Flow's high-swirl chamber.

Trick Flow has studded the Cleveland block for improved cylinder head stability. The downside to head studs with a Cleveland is head removal once engine is in the car. This is why bolts are better for vintage Mustang, Cougar, Fairlane, Torino, and other intermediates.

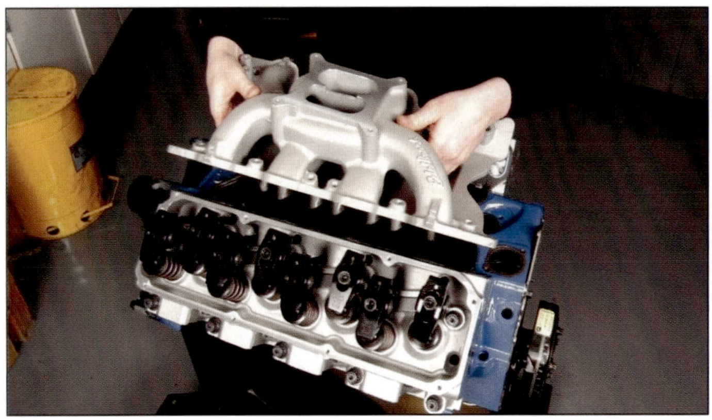

Although Trick Flow offers a deep-breathing, single-plane manifold for the 351C, it was more interested in torque numbers, which is why it decided on the Edelbrock Performer RPM Air Gap manifold. Dual-plane manifolds have long runners for better low- and mid-range torque. The Air Gap feature allows cooler runners.

On the Trick Flow dyno, this 383C stroker makes 524 hp and 480 ft-lbs of torque. This means plenty of good mid-range torque handing off to horsepower at high RPM.

on pump gas and 9.65:1 compression:524 hp at 6,000 rpm and 480 ft-lbs of torque at 4,500 rpm on the Super Flow 902.

Horsepower Monster 400

Engine builder and tech writer Jeff Huneycutt calls this one "The Mutt" as it appeared in *Hot Rod* magazine. The Mutt, a Ford 400, made more than 500 hp and 565 ft-lbs of torque. Jeff says engine building is all about compromise. To get one thing, you often have to give up another. Although the 400 gets a lot of flack for being a gutless smog mill, it falls under this description only in factory form with dished pistons and those awful 351C-2V open chamber heads. Give this engine a fighting chance with good cylinder heads, induction, and flat-top pistons and you have real power you can use.

The 400 with the factory's 4.000 x 4.000-inch bore and stroke along with a 10.297-inch deck height makes boatloads of power if you top it with good cylinder heads and stuff it with the right pistons. With healthy cylinder heads and more than 9.0:1 compression, the 400 becomes an animal with the kind of torque you need and want from 400 ci. If you stroke it to 4.200 inches with a 4.040-inch overbore, you get 431 ci of displacement.

Jeff got there by taking a stock 400 cast crank and grinding the rod journals down to 2.100 inches to increase stroke to 4.200 inches. He did not do this with a stroker kit. He looked to the Chevy small-block parts bin for 6.300-inch connecting rods that had to be machined

The Huneycutt 400, which has a 10.497-inch deck height, is set up to be decked .027 inch to get a piston deck clearance of .030 inch. Because .027 inch is being taken off the deck, a mock-up is needed to determine intake manifold fitment.

Dynamic balancing involves a lot of thought due to the amassing of custom pieces such as 6.300-inch Chevy rods, 4.040-inch Chrysler 340 pistons, and a Ford 400 crank with offset-ground 2.100-inch rod journals. Counterweights have been machined down .495 inch to clear KB pistons. What this means in terms of balance is using a 164-tooth and balancer for a 5.0L High Output with 50-ounce offset balance. The balancer has to be machined to get the pulley aligned with the water pump and accessories.

Crankshaft endplay is checked. Allowable endplay is .004 to .010 inch. Because Huneycutt and his team are going for more than 500 horsepower, endplay will be pushed closer to the .010-inch mark.

Valve-to-piston clearances are checked in the mock-up phase. Team Huneycutt had to notch the 340 pistons with an Isky cutting tool to achieve sufficient clearance.

With a 2.100-inch offset-ground 400 crank, 6.300-inch Chevy H-beam rods, and 4.040-inch Chrysler 340 pistons, displacement rises to 431 ci. The pistons have been notched for intake valve clearance.

Edelbrock Cleveland heads with the Yates-style combustion chamber are much more advanced than stock 351C or 400 head chambers, with better quench while retaining the poly-angle valve design that makes the Cleveland head legendary.

The nice thing about the Edelbrock Cleveland head is right-sized intake ports that give you generous flow and real velocity, which translates to torque. And torque is what you want from a 400.

More mock-up work with the Crane Energizer roller rockers to again check valve to piston clearances. Valve lift is .609 inch, which tightens up clearances significantly.

Edelbrock Performer RPM 351C-2V heads shave a bunch of weight off the 400. Power gains come from 190-cc flow intakes and 75-cc exhaust along with 60-cc chambers. Spring pressure out of the box was not enough for the cam profile at 130 pounds on seat and 340 pounds open. Huneycutt went with Comp Cams #929-16 springs, which offer 150 pounds on seat and 420 open.

Horsepower Monster 400

400 cast crank, rod journals ground to 2.100 inches to get 4.250-inch stroke
Advance Auto Parts harmonic balancer (#15950147)
Advance Auto Parts flexplate (#2922510)
Chevy 6.300-inch H-beam connecting rods machined to 400 journals
KB chrysler 340 hypereutectic 4.040-inch pistons (#KB243), reliefs cut deeper to clear valves, 15-cc reverse dome
Isky piston notching tool valve reliefs, (#PNT-216)
Sealed Power piston rings (#E251K40)
Sealed Power main bearings (#5078M1)
Clevite rod bearings (#CB-1227-P)
Sealed Power cam bearings (#1403M)
Crane hydraulic roller camshaft (#52HR00032)
Ford Racing roller lifters (#M-6500-R302)
CV products pushrods 8.750 x 5/16 inch
Crane energizer rocker arms (#13744-16)
Fel-Pro gaskets throughout
Edelbrock valve covers (#4461)
Edelbrock performer Cleveland cylinder heads (#61629)
Edelbrock performer 400 manifold (#2171)
Holley street avenger 870 cfm (#80870)
Mr. Gasket 2-inch carburetor spacer (#6007)
Milodon oil pan (#30927)
Milodon pick-up (#18355)
Melling oil pump (#M84A)
Clevite oil pump shaft (#6011431)
Carter fuel pump (#M6978)
ARP fasteners throughout
Sealed Power timing set (#KT3498SA2)
MSD distributor (#8580)
MSD ignition wires (#31390)
MSD ignition coil (#8202)
Autolite spark plugs (#3924)
Dynomax headers (#WLK-85064)

Under the gun, Huneycutt's Mutt 400 (431 ci) makes 504.8 hp at 5,500 rpm and 565.0 ft-lbs of torque at 4,300 rpm with an 870-cfm Holley Street Avenger, Edelbrock 2171 manifold, and Crane hydraulic roller (#52HR00032).

Although the Ford 400 has long been the performance pig no one has ever wanted, look at what you can do with this engine for around $7,000. The message here is real torque at 565 ft-lbs for your Ford F-series, Bronco, or full-size sedan.

at the big end to fit the Ford 400 crank. He found that pistons for the Chrysler/Plymouth/Dodge 340-ci LA small-block from KB Pistons worked, thanks to 1.840-inch compression height, but called for a 4.040-inch bore.

Valve reliefs had to be cut to clear the valves. Decking the block .027 inch achieved a deck clearance of .030 inch. Because the Chrysler small-block pistons had larger pins (.9842 inch), the small ends had to be reamed to .9240 inch. The crank had to be machined to remove .495 inch from the highest point on the 400 crank's counterweights, which left Jeff without enough weight. Because the 400 is externally balanced (like most small-block Fords), Jeff went to the parts shelf for a 50-ounce, 164-tooth flywheel and harmonic balancer for a late-model 5.0L engine instead of the stock 400 flexplate and balancer. The only snag was pulley alignment; easily remedied with a fan spacer.

Jeff decided to go with a hydraulic roller cam from Crane with 234 degrees of duration at .050-inch lift on both valves with lobe lift at .352 inch coupled with 1.71:1 rockers for .598-inch valve lift. Edelbrock Cleveland heads can withstand .600-inch lift thanks to 1.900-inch installed spring height.

600 Horsepower

When I proposed building a 351C for this book, Jim Grubbs of JGM Performance Engineering hauled out a fresh D2AE-CA four-bolt main block and boldly suggested 600 hp at 7,500 rpm.

That's when I contacted Alan Davis at Eagle Specialties for a 4340 steel crank, H-beam rods, and Mahle forged and coated pistons to fill the block. Eagle stepped up with a 4.000-inch stroke 4340 crank, 6.000-inch H-beams, and custom Mahle pistons.

JGM Performance Engineering

Jim has been a Ford enthusiast all of his life and has been in the engine building business for thirty years. He likes to experiment with Ford engines, primarily the 385-series big-blocks and older FEs.

In planning this 600-hp Cleveland stroker, Jim said he wanted to try Trick Flow's new PowerPort Cleveland CNC 225, a CNC-ported aluminum casting with 225-cc intake ports, 60-cc chambers, 2.080/1.600-inch intake/exhaust valves, 340-cfm intake, 240-cfm exhaust, and capable of more than 600 hp. "That's the head I want for this project," Jim commented—and no wonder.

TFS begins with a strong idea of what it wants in a cylinder head and induction system, then its engineers use 3D and computer aided design (CAD) to design and flow test the idea. Thanks to modern technology, once TFS has a real-world prototype part, it is quickly pressed into testing and operation: on the flow bench for continued port and chamber work;

Comp Cams #32-000-9 Custom Grind

Lobe	*Duration (degrees at .050 inch)*	*Lobe Lift (inch)*	*Valve Lift (inch) at 1.70:1*
3207 Intake	260	.440	.748
1660 Exhaust	275	.420	.714

Trick Flow PowerPort Cleveland CNC 225

	JGM Flow Bench		*Trick Flow Bench*	
Valve Lift (inch)	*Intake (cfm)*	*Exhaust (cfm)*	*Intake (cfm)*	*Exhaust (cfm)*
.100	84.2	55.4	68.0	55.0
.200	134.7	106.2	146.0	115.0
.300	201.6	151.8	223.0	162.0
.400	255.6	180.9	282.0	204.0
.500	289.4	200.5	313.0	231.0
.600	309.6	211.1	336.0	240.0
.700	317.2	216.8	339.0	244.0
.800	327.1	218.8		

Note: JGM Performance Engineering used clay as an entry, short exhaust tube.

JGM Performance Engineering begins with a D2AE-CA four-bolt main block bored and honed to 4.030 inches with cylinders notched to clear an Eagle 4.000-inch-stroke 4340 steel crank with H-beam rods and forged Mahle pistons.

For good oil control and friction reduction, hone lifter bores to a nice crosshatch and check for size. JGM hones lifter bores on every engine it builds.

Mains are fitted with ARP studs for rigidity and security. Consider the use of a main stud girdle, which provides abundant support, when you're going for this much power.

Check and hone line bore to a consistent crosshatch for good main bearing retention and crush. Rare is the block you'd have to line bore.

Match hone bores to each Mahle piston to achieve adequate piston to wall clearances. The objective is to get good sealing with the least amount of friction possible.

This is an Eagle 4340 steel stroker kit with 4.000 inches of stroke on tap, 6.000-inch H-beam rods, and 4.030-inch Mahle-coated pistons with just enough of a dome to give 13.0:1 compression.

This is a custom Comp Cams mechanical roller (#32-000-9) with .440/420-inch lobe lift and 260/275-degree duration at .050 inch.

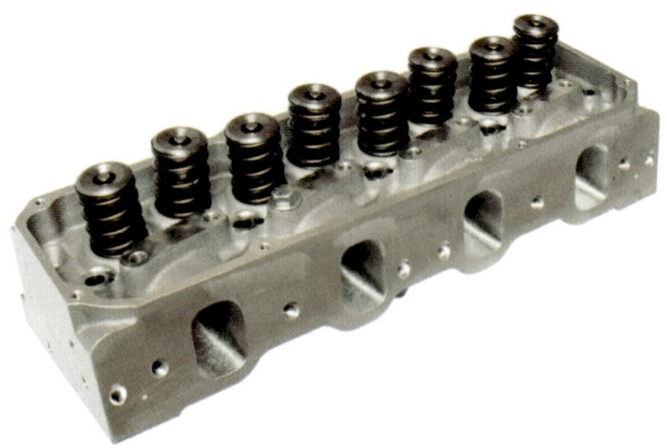

The Cleveland cylinder head marketplace went from no choices to abundant choices. JGM Performance Engineering chose the Trick Flow CNC 225 Cleveland head for its right-sized 225-cc intake ports and 2.080/1.600-inch valves.

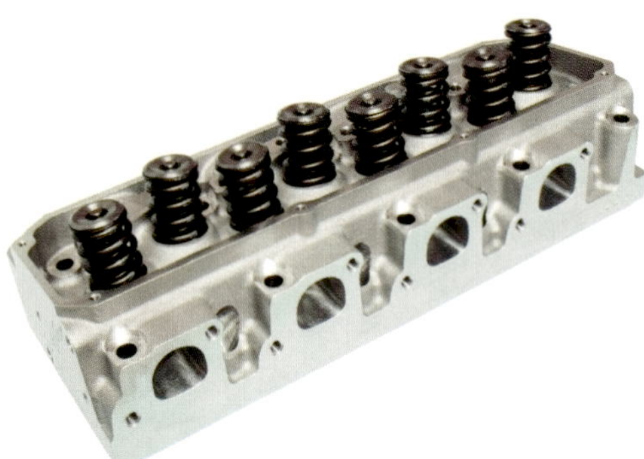

On the exhaust side, the CNC 225 head enjoys a great exit with minimal restriction with a smooth floor. Valve size is conservative at 1.600 inches because it helps torque.

Trick Flow's CNC 225 Cleveland has poly-angle valves like the factory head with a choice of either 1.460- or 1.530-inch spring heights. Viton fluoroelastomer valve seals offer good oil control and excellent sealing.

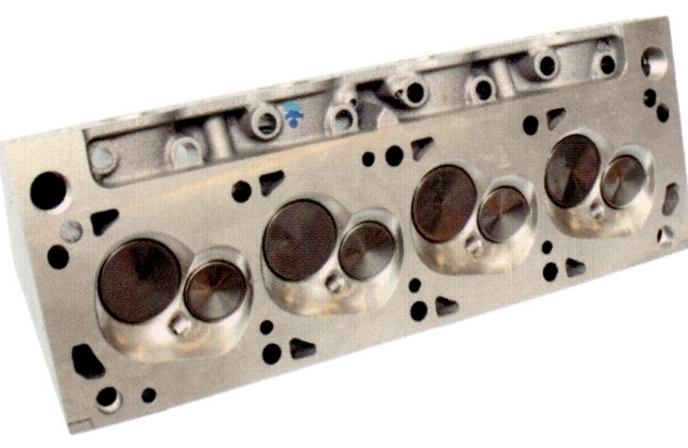

High-swirl 60-to 62-cc chambers with 2.080/1.600-inch valves and hardened seats are CNC machined with excellent quench that eliminates detonation tendencies. These heads are also designed to fit 289/302/351W.

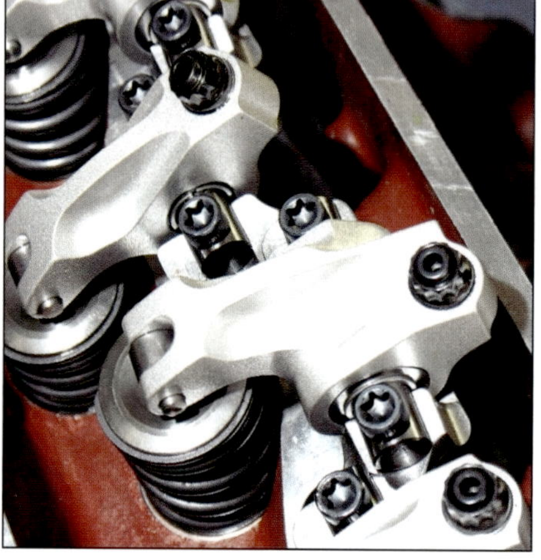

Jesel Pro Series Mohawk Beam shaft-mounted rocker arms are made from a custom-blended aluminum alloy that is shotpeened for strength.

This is a single-plane Trick Flow TFS-5160111-C intake manifold, which is a perfect match for the CNC 225 heads. As with most manifolds, some port matching is required if you want things spot on.

Holley's new 950-cfm HP aluminum carburetor offers the flow and fuel delivery the JGM Cleveland needs to make more than 600 hp.

then to the engine dynamometer lab to see how it performs; and finally to the racetrack for real-world experience and final tweaking.

When Jim Grubbs specified this head, he had also done his homework learning everything he could about the TFS PowerPort Cleveland CNC 225. And when our 225s arrived from TFS, they were everything Trick Flow said they would be. Jim immediately disassembled the heads and flow bench tested them to see numbers.

JGM/Trick Flow PowerPort

- **D2AE-CA** four-bolt main block
- **Eagle** 4340 steel crankshaft (#14702)
- **Eagle** 6.000-inch H-beam rods (#CRS-6000-BS)
- **Mahle** 4032 custom forged pistons (custom dish/reverse dome)
- **Fel-Pro** gaskets
- **Comp Cams** custom-grind mechanical roller(#32-000-9), 3207/1660 intake/exhaust on 108-degree lobe centers
- **Comp Cams** roller tappets (#840-16)
- **Comp Cams** .080-inch-wall pushrods
- **Jesel Pro Series** shaft-mounted rocker arms
- **Trick Flow** PowerPort Cleveland CNC 225 cylinder heads
- **Trick Flow** single-plane intake manifold
- **Trick Flow** cast-aluminum valve covers
- **Melling** high-volume oil pump
- **ARP** oil pump shaft
- **Canton** drag race pan and windage tray

More Than 600 Horsepower

Making 600 hp has never been easy for even the most savvy of engine builders. You must possess a good understanding of cylinder head flow, cam specifications, valve timing events, compression, and a host of other variables. When Jim Grubbs plans an engine, he takes all of these variables into consideration. It is often the little things that add up to make a big difference in power.

400 Proof Positive

Enthusiasts know Richard Holdener for his extensive dyno experience. Richard was kind enough to share his knowledge with me for this book, and prove what you can do with Ford's low-respect 400.

Richard cuts to the chase with Ford's 400 in *Muscle Mustangs & Fast Fords* magazine, "Let's face it, 400M Ford owners get no respect. Sure, mention the word Cleveland and watch everyone's eyes light up, but the fire dies right out when you try to include the Modified/Midland family in the discussion. This seems odd since the two engines share so many components. In fact, it can be argued that the 400M engines are nothing more than a tall-deck, stroker Cleveland. Think about it, that is all that separates

The Dyno Room

RPM	*Horse-power*	*Torque (ft-lbs)*	*BSFC*
2,000	102	268	.502
2,500	147	309	.452
3,000	199	348	.441
3,500	248	372	.438
4,000	344	452	.426
4,500	457	533	.423
5,000	544	571	.430
5,500	594	567	.441
6,000	647	566	.458
6,500	673	544	.463
7,000	675	507	.483
7,500	664	465	.498

Richard Holdener began with a stock rebuild 400. Rods have been cleaned up and shotpeened for strength and fitted with ARP bolts. Crank has received specialize preparation consisting of journal machining and polishing along with dynamic balancing. Those are forged flat-top pistons in the bores. (Photo Courtesy Richard Holdener)

Forged flat-top pistons a few thousandths in the bore offer 9.5:1 compression with 75-cc chambers. This 400 makes 568 hp at 9.5:1 compression. With higher compression on the order of 10.5:1 and higher, it could make in excess of 600 hp. (Photo Courtesy Richard Holdener)

Richard opted for stamped-steel, no-adjust rockers with a flat-tappet hydraulic cam to get 265 hp and 412 ft-lbs of torque. The 412 pounds of torque demonstrates what the Ford 400 was born for: producing real torque. (Photo Courtesy Richard Holdener)

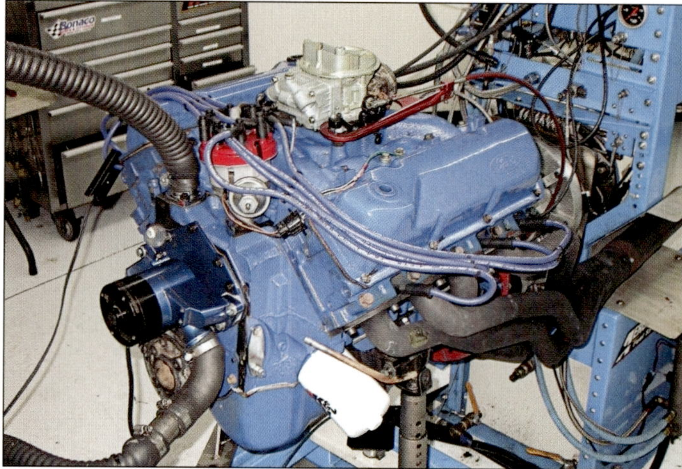

Here's the 400 as tested in stock trim with the only exception being a 500-cfm Holley 2-barrel carburetor. Factory carburetion is considerably smaller. (Photo Courtesy Richard Holdener)

the legendary 351 Cleveland from its torque-oriented 400M."

He's right. The 400, often called the 400M, is a raised-deck 351C with all the same attributes of the legendary Cleveland. Why does the 400 garner so much disrespect when it is no more than a stroked Cleveland?

Much of this disrespect comes from the 400's neutered factory personality with 351C-2V open-chamber heads and decidedly low compression ratio along with the stifling nature of Motorcraft 2150 carburetion. The same can be said for the 351M, 351 ci in a 400 block, which never made any sense to begin with. The 351M and 400 weren't intended to be performance engines, but instead high-torque workhorses. Ford put them in full-size cars and trucks.

"If any motor could take advantage of the benefits of a 4-barrel carb, it was the comparatively larger 400. In fact, it can be argued that a proper 4-barrel induction system would not only improve towing power, but might improve mileage as well, providing a spread-bore carb design was employed to allow cruising on the smaller primaries," Richard comments.

"We rebuilt a stock 400 yanked from the engine bay of a 1976 F250. The engine was in running condition, but we found a couple of bent pushrods and other evidence of abuse so we took Demon Engines up on their offer to perform the necessary rebuild. Working with L&R Automotive [a machine shop] and Probe Racing, the guys from Demon Engines were able to transform the tired 400M into a healthy stocker. In fact, the engine was treated to a piston upgrade in the form of a set of forged flat-top pistons from Probe Racing. The .030-over forged slugs were originally designed for a 351 Cleveland application, but fit perfectly in the freshly machined bores on our 400 block."

To the Dyno

Richard demonstrates what can be done with the 400's most basic foundation: 4.030-inch bores with a 4.000-inch stroke topped with stock 2V open-chamber heads and 2-barrel induction. Richard's first pull using a 500-cfm Holley 2-barrel and a flat-tappet hydraulic cam delivers 265 hp at 4,100 rpm and 412 ft-lbs of torque at 2,900 rpm. These are numbers illustrating this engine was born to make torque.

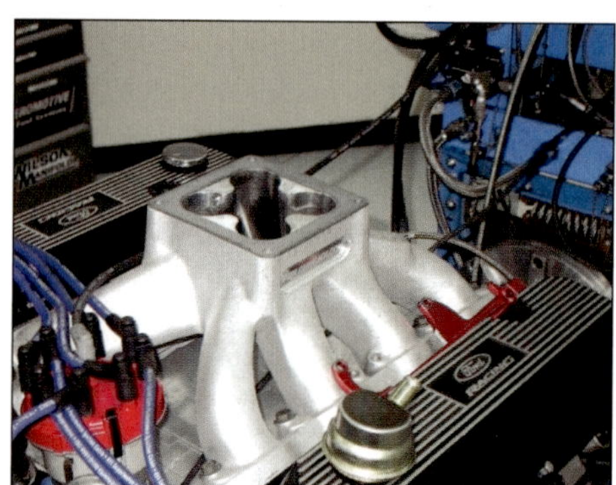

With the CHI single-plane, super high- rise and a Holley 1,000-cfm Dominator, Holdener's Ford 400, power went to well over 500. (Photo Courtesy Richard Holdener)

Weiand Action Plus 400

"After confirming the baseline numbers, we replaced the stock 2-barrel induction with the Weiand Action Plus intake and 750-cfm Holley carb. Since Westech had it jetted and ready to rock, we ran their Holley 750-cfm HP Street carb, but know that this combination would work equally well with something as small (and inexpensive) as a 600-cfm vacuum secondary Holley. Equipped with the Weiand/750-cfm Holley combination, the peak numbers jumped to 301 hp at 4,100 rpm and 429 ft-lbs of torque," Richard tells *Muscle Mustangs* readers. This test shows you can wake up the 400

How you cam an engine determines its personality. Richard went with the stock flat-tappet hydraulic cam as a baseline. When he stepped up to a Crower mechanical roller, power increased significantly. And when he looked to Cam Research for an even hotter mechanical roller with an aggressive induction system, numbers went well over 500. This exercise demonstrates the benefits of cam selection and induction upgrades. Richard more than doubled torque and horsepower with heads, induction, and cam selection. (Photo Courtesy Richard Holdener)

Once a hotter Crower mechanical roller cam was installed, testing continued with an Edelbrock Performer RPM Air Gap with spacers. Power shot up to nearly 500 and grew more intense from there. (Photo Courtesy Richard Holdener)

with a better induction system. And just imagine what you could do to this engine with closed-chamber 351C-4V heads and 4-barrel induction.

Building In More Power

Once Richard demonstrated what was possible from a 400's bones, he decided to kick it up a few notches with a hotter roller cam, heads, and more. "While solid rollers are usually reserved for race engines, we first chose a street roller from Crower Cams. With slightly milder ramp rates than a race roller, the street roller was much more parts friendly and would require less maintenance over the long haul. The roller profile allowed us to have much more aggressive ramp rates than a flat-tappet grind. What this meant was that we could have our power with less duration [measured at .050-inch]. Basically the solid street roller allowed us to make more power with less cam. The Crower street roller offered a .570/.572-inch valve-lift split, a 234/244 duration split [at .050-inch], and a 110-degree lobe separation angle. Crower also supplied the matching solid roller lifters to work with the cam."

Richard cautions, "It is certainly possible to exceed the 500-hp mark using a solid or even hydraulic flat-tappet cam, but you'd have to run a minimum of 10 to 15 degrees more duration than the roller to make equivalent power. Making sure we maximized the cam profile was a set of 1.73-ratio aluminum roller rockers from Comp Cams. Naturally the factory stamped-steel rockers [non-adjustable on the 400-2V heads] were not adequate for our needs, nor would they work, as Pro Comp heads were set up to accept rocker studs and guide plates."

Needless to say, Richard had big plans for the 400 that transcended stock 351C-2V heads, and this is where the 400 comes alive. Keep in mind this is a stock 400 bottom end with 4.000-inch stroke and 4.030-inch bores. Compression ratio is 9.5:1. Rods have been shotpeened and cleaned up using ARP bolts. It has also been dynamic balanced for smoothness. This is where you develop deep faith in the 400's bottom end.

"These large combustion chambers required a flat-top piston to produce a reasonable compression ratio (near 9.0:1). All of the later open-chamber 2V and 4V heads have a reputation for detonation. Open-chamber heads (including those on the 400) were designed to lower compression ratio, but the lack of a proper quench area actually makes them more sensitive to detonation. Thus the static compression ratio should be kept lower when running factory open-chamber heads compared to the more desirable closed-chamber or quench heads. We cured this situation with the installation of a set of aluminum Cleveland heads from Pro Comp," Richard comments.

Richard goes on to say, "The Pro Comp heads featured all of the positive aspects of the Cleveland family, poly-angle valve configuration, including the large 2.19/1.71-inch stainless-steel

Pro Comp's 351C Cleveland ported cylinder head (#PC3062) has a 74- to 75-cc high-swirl chamber, 2.190/1.710-inch valve combination, and excellent quench for good anti-knock qualities. Flow is 342.7-cfm intake and 238.2-cfm exhaust at .800-inch lift. These heads are completely assembled. (Photo Courtesy Richard Holdener)

valve combination. You might be wondering why we chose a set of aluminum heads for our low-buck build, but the Pro Comp aluminum heads can be had for about the cost of a set of used factory 4V heads. In addition to the low cost, the Pro Comp heads also offered a significant weight reduction, dramatic improvements in airflow, and additional detonation control."

The nice thing about the Pro Comp heads is their cost coupled with pretty respectible engineering nuances—and for what it would cost you to buy a set of closed-chamber iron 4V heads, port work, and a valve job. With Pro Comp aluminum heads, you shed unnecessary weight and get good heat transfer, which enables you to run more compression and more timing.

Richard continues, "Impressive right out of the box, our Pro Comp Cleveland heads were given a once-over by Bryce Mulvey of Dr. J's. Bryce worked his magic on the heads by applying not only a precision valve job, but further improving the flow potential. As received, the unfinished Pro Comp Heads flowed 325 cfm on the intake and 228 cfm on the exhaust.

"After Bryce completed the porting and valve job, the flow numbers jumped to 348 cfm on the intake and 252 cfm on the exhaust [all measurements taken at .800-inch lift at 28 inches]. Since airflow equals power, proper porting can unleash some serious ponies. What the additional airflow does is allow you to reach a given power level with milder cam timing. Thus you have a powerful engine combination without the usual idle quality and drivability issues associated with wilder cam timing."

Check out the flow numbers for a complete rundown on the porting provided by Dr. J's and note the significant improvements in low- and mid-lift flow:

Flow Comparison

Lift (inch)	*Pro Comp (intake/ exhaust)*	*Dr. J's (intake/ exhaust)*
.050	31/22	40/28
.100	66/46	78/58
.200	127/95	149/99
.300	183/129	217/135
.400	225/161	273/169
.500	263/182	318/209
.600	291/207	335/231
.700	314/219	343/247
.800	325/228	351/253

Once the Pro Comp heads were in place, Richard had a challenge. "There are a few different aftermarket manifolds available for the 400M, but both the Edelbrock Performer and Weiand Action Plus manifolds were designed for milder applications equipped with the factory 351C-2V heads. Given the success in Engine Masters Challenge competitions with legendary builder John Kaase, the boys from CHI decided to design and cast a high-performance, single-plane, intake designed specifically for use with their aluminum Cleveland heads on the tall-deck 400 engine.

"Lucky for us, the port configuration on the intake was close enough to the Pro Comp heads to allow us minor port matching to facilitate use of the CHI 400M intake on our test engine. The CHI 400M intake came to us on loan from the Cleveland experts at MPG." MPG also provided adaptor plates that allow use of a 351C manifold on top of a 400, which increases induction options.

Swapping Up...

When Richard did the Pro Comp head swap, combustion chamber size went from 79 to 75 cc, increasing compression.

These heads are fitted with Comp Cams 1.73:1 roller rockers and some port work. Power is amazing considering there is a stock 400 bottom end. The 400's bottom end withstands this kind of punishment and proves it can take more. (Photo Courtesy Richard Holdener)

Carburetion with the Edelbrock Performer RPM Air Gap was this Holley HP 750 cfm, which brought about dramatic increases in power. (Photo Courtesy Richard Holdener)

Richard went with a more aggressive Crower mechanical roller cam with 1.73:1 Comp Cams roller rockers. A Holley HP 750-cfm carburetor with easy-to-swap Percy's Adjust-a-Jets went on top. With Pro Comp heads, Edelbrock Performer RPM Air Gap, Holley HP 750, Crower mechanical roller, Comp Cams 1.73:1 roller rockers, flat-top pistons, and a stock bottom end, Richard and Westech were rewarded with 489 hp and 502 ft-lbs of torque from easy weekend upgrades and with an engine all finished at 5,900 rpm.

Although most might be content with these numbers, Richard believed there was more to be found through good old-fashioned intake and carburetor swaps. "Though we suspected a dual-plane intake was the best choice for a street engine, we wanted to see how well the CHI single-plane intake performed on the 400M. Off came the RPM Air Gap and aluminum spacers plates and on went the CHI intake. The CHI intake required use of the lower valley cover plate employed with the spacer plates, but the intake swap was very straightforward. The CHI intake on loan from MPG was equipped with a 4500 carb flange, so we installed a two-circuit Holley 1150 Dominator carburetor, a tad overkill on this application. The huge carb looked pretty menacing on the aluminum-headed 400M."

Richard went ahead with the pull anyway, netting 529 hp and 506 ft-lbs of torque. Torque didn't change much but horsepower increased by a whopping 40 hp.

We learn from Richard's experience proper induction is everything so an engine makes power. A dual-plane manifold is more conducive to street use because you get good mid-range torque. A single-plane manifold isn't much on torque, but optimum if you are seeking horsepower in a drag racer.

Cam Swap to Close the Gap

Knowing there was more power to be made from Ford's no-respect 400, Richard called Cam Research and ordered a more aggressive mechanical roller cam. The Cam Research profile increased both the lift and duration figures compared to the Street Roller cam from Crower. The Cam Research cam offered .726-inch lift and dual-pattern duration figures of 250/254 degrees at .050 inch. The cam also featured a tight lobe separation angle of 106 degrees.

"Looking just at the specifications, you might be tempted to dismiss the cam as excessive, but just check out the power gains and you'll realize that there is much more to the cam grind than simple lift and duration figures. While we'd expect additional power gains from the increased duration, what really surprised us was that the Cam Research profile improved the power output everywhere, from 3,000 all the way to 6,500 rpm."

Richard decided to play with the numbers a bit, first going back to the Air Gap dual-plane and the hotter Cam Research bumpstick. He netted 519 hp and 519 ft-lbs of torque with a 750-cfm Holley HP. He lost horsepower but gained torque thanks to the dual-plane Air Gap.

When Richard increased carb size to 1,000 cfm, numbers went to 525 hp and 528 ft-lbs of torque.

And when Richard shelved the Air Gap and went to the CHI single-plane drive-through manifold with the 1,000-cfm Holley Dominator, the numbers were staggering at 568 hp and 542 ft-lbs of torque.

With a steel crank, more stroke, and H-beam rods, this 400 could easier go over 600 hp with comparable torque.

Never count Ford's 400 out because it can do so much more.

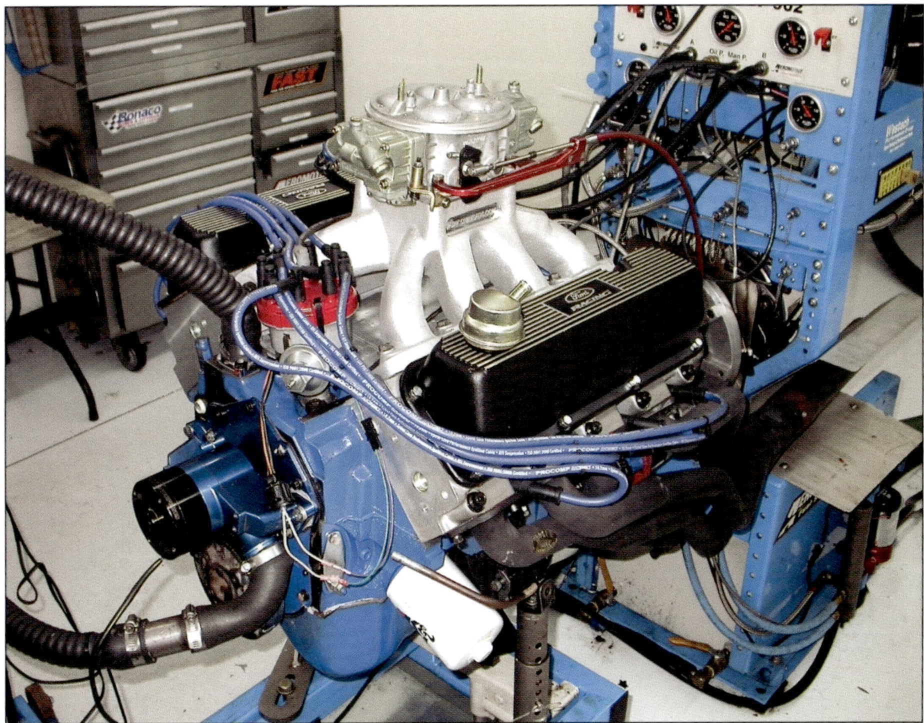

With the CHI manifold and 1,000-cfm Holley Dominator, the only thing left was a hotter cam from Cam Research, which got Richard to 568 hp. This proves the kind of power a 400 can make with good cylinder heads, induction, and a hot cam. (Photo Courtesy Richard Holdener)

Source Guide

Advance Auto Parts
877-238-2623
www.advanceautoparts.com

Air Flow Dynamics
61 408 705 942
www.airflowdynamics.com.au

Air Flow Research
661-257-8124
www.airflowresearch.com

ATI Performance Products
877-298-5039
www.atiracing.com

Automotive Racing Products
800-826-3045
www.arp-bolts.com

Cam Research Corporation
303-762-0022
www.camresearchcorp.com

Comp Cams
800-999-0853
www.compcams.com

Crane Cams
866-388-5120
www.cranecams.com

Cylinder Head Innovations
011-61-3-9464-7658
www.chiheads.com.au

Demon Carburetion
270-901-3346
www.demoncarbs.com

Denny's Auto Machine
301-582-2848
www.dennysauto
machineinc.com

Eagle Specialty Products, Inc.
662-796-7373
wwww.eaglerod.com

Edelbrock Corporation
310-781-2222
www.edelbrock.com

Fluidampr
716-592-1000
www.fluidampr.com

Fuel Air Spark Technology
901-260-3278
www.fuelairspark.com

Holley Performance Products
270-782-2900
www.holley.com

Horsepower Monster
www.horsepower
monster.com

Jesel
732-901-1800
www.jesel.com

JGM Performance
Engineering
661-257-0101

Jon Kaase Racing Engines
770-307-0241
www.jonkaaseracing
engines.com

Mahle/Clevite
www.mahle.com

Mallory Ignition
216-688-8300
www.mallory-ignition.com

MCE Engines
323-731-0462

McKeown Motorsport
Engineering, Inc.
301-932-9292
www.mmeracing.com

Melling Engine Parts
517-787-8172
www.melling.com

Milodon
805-577-5970
www.milodon.com

MPG Head Service
303-762-8196
www.mpgheads.com

MSD Ignition
915-857-5200
www.msdignition.com

Mustangs Plus
800-999-4289
www.mustangsplus.com

National Parts Depot
www.npdlink.com

Performane Distributors
901-396-5782
www.Performane
Distributors.com

Pioneer Automotive
Industries, LLC
601-483-5211
www.pioneerautoind.com

Powerheads Performance
Engineering
951-678-7035
www.powerheads.com

Powermaster Performance
Company
909-794-1600
www.powermaster
performance.com

Pro Comp USA
800-776-0767
www.procompusa.com

Proform
586-774-2500
www.proformparts.com

Redline, Inc.
800-733-2277
www.redlineweber.com

Scat Enterprises
310-370-5501
www.scatenterprises.com

Scott Cook Motorsports
011-61-0408664-160
www.scmengine
developments.com

Summit Racing Equipment
800-230-3030
www.summitracing.com

The Mustang Ranch
888-657-7669
www.themustangranch.com

TMeyer Inc. Precision
Automotive Machining
507-238-4141
www.tmeyerinc.com

Trans Am Racing
310-612-7560

Trick Flow Specialties
888-841-6556
www.trickflow.com

United Engine & Machine
Company
KB Pistons/Silv-O-Lite/Icon
Forged Racing Pistons
800/648-7970
www.kb-silvolite.com

Weiand Company
www.weiand.com